El Salvador's Civil War

El Salvador's Civil War

A Study of Revolution

Hugh Byrne

LYNNE
RIENNER
PUBLISHERS

BOULDER
LONDON

Published in the United States of America by
Lynne Rienner Publishers, Inc.
1800 30th Street, Boulder, Colorado 80301
www.rienner.com

and in the United Kingdom by
Lynne Rienner Publishers, Inc.
3 Henrietta Street, Covent Garden, London WC2E 8LU

Library of Congress Cataloging-in-Publication Data
Byrne, Hugh.
    El Salvador's civil war : a study of revolution / by Hugh Byrne.
       p.   cm.
    Includes bibliographical references (p.   ) and index.
    ISBN 978-1-55587-606-7 (hc : alk. paper)
    ISBN 978-1-55587-196-0 (pb : alk. paper)
    1. El Salvador—History—1979–1992.   2. Insurgency—El Salvador—
History.   3. Counterinsurgency—El Salvador—History.   I. Title.
F1488.3.B95   1996
972.8405'3—dc20
                                                              96-14147
                                                              CIP

British Cataloguing in Publication Data
A Cataloguing in Publication record for this book
is available from the British Library.

Printed and bound in the United States of America

    The paper used in this publication meets the requirements
∞ of the American National Standard for Permanence of
    Paper for Printed Library Materials Z39.48-1992.

To the people of El Salvador . . .
that these generations of
struggle and sacrifice
may bear fruit

Contents

Preface

My interest in El Salvador began in spring 1980 while I was a graduate student in political science at UCLA. At that time thousands of Salvadoran refugees were arriving in southern California with stories of mass organizing and death-squad violence, while front-page stories told of the killing of Archbishop Romero and the attack on mourners at his funeral. I became deeply involved in organizing work on El Salvador, and since I was not ready to write a dissertation immediately after finishing my Ph.D. exams, I put academic pursuits on a back burner and began to work as a full-time organizer on Central America.

For the next several years I was actively involved in the contentious struggles of the Reagan (and later, Bush) era—on human rights in El Salvador, aid to the contras, and general U.S. policy toward Central America—and spent the years from 1987 to 1991 in Washington, D.C., as political director of the Committee in Solidarity with the People of El Salvador. This work taught me more than I could ever have learned in an academic setting about revolution, social change, and the role of strategy within them. I saw firsthand the importance of strategy in our own work—how it made a real difference to our goal of changing U.S. policy in El Salvador whether we put our energy and resources into building a national demonstration in Washington, or generated community pressure on key members of Congress to change their votes on aid to El Salvador, or organized a national media campaign to increase public awareness of the policy. I also came to better understand the role played by the strategies of the U.S. government and its Salvadoran allies, on one side, and the FMLN insurgents and their supporters, on the other, in how the conflict progressed and the way it was ultimately resolved.

I came to appreciate, too, the role of will and belief in processes of social change—how building the belief that you can succeed, even against great odds, and generating the will to make it happen can become a material force in the equation of social change. But I saw the downside, as well—the tendency to confuse beliefs about the rightness of one's cause and the levels of support for it with objective analysis. So, at times, on both sides of the divide in the Salvadoran conflict, there was a good deal of wishful thinking and triumphalism. There is, I think, an inevitable tension in organizing for change (or against it) between the positive spin that is put on a given situation to mobilize, motivate, and get people to make sacrifices for a vision, and the actual conditions that may be much more sobering, much less inspiring. I believe it is possible to find the point where "truth" and successful mobilization meet, even in difficult circumstances, but in this area wishful thinking too often replaces objective analysis, with predictable consequences.

Following the signing of the peace accords to end El Salvador's civil war, in January 1992, I was fortunate to be able to resume my academic work, and I felt I had something to say. It was with a deeper understanding of strategy, and questions about the relationship between the subjective and objective within processes of change, that I shifted my approach to the Salvadoran conflict. The discipline of a Ph.D. dissertation provided the conditions to undertake an impartial analysis of the role of strategy in El Salvador's civil war. My objective was to understand as fully as possible the social, political, economic, and human dynamics that gave rise to a revolutionary conflict and a long civil war—a process that continued to engage me after many years of involvement. This book, which I hope retains the rigor of the original study while being more reader friendly, is the next stage in this learning process.

The history of El Salvador in the last twenty-five years and of U.S. involvement there (particularly since 1979) is a rich one. There are lessons to be learned on all sides—about revolutions and counterrevolutions, political and military strategies, peasant organizing, strategies of alliance, the effectiveness of large-scale repression, the impact of U.S. involvement, and the way a bitter conflict can end through political negotiations, among many others. It is a pity that too rarely are lessons drawn before the policy and media spotlight shifts to another country or region and a high-level committee is formed to reinvent the wheel. I wrote this book in part to clarify my own understanding of these years. I reached two main conclusions: that strategy is an important dimension of processes of social change that is too often overlooked and underestimated; and that a strategic framework is extremely helpful for understanding El Salvador's prolonged conflict. I hope that I have made this argument clearly and that this book makes some contribution to an understanding of what happened and is happening in El Salvador, the role of the United States and other external actors, and the larger social processes of which El Salvador's struggle forms a part.

In the years since the war ended, reflecting on its enormous human costs and those of other conflicts, I have come to believe that all war is a war against ourselves; it is an illusion that we are separate from each other. While affirming the justice of the grievances that led to the war, the depth of oppression, and the courage and self-sacrifice of so many participants, I have come to see strategies of violence as leading to strategies of counterviolence, which escalate in a spiral of polarization and conflict from which escape becomes ever more difficult. That the weight of moral responsibility is not equally shared does not alter this dynamic. It is a great tribute to the participants in El Salvador's long conflict, as well as a hope for the future and an example for those involved in similar struggles, that an exit was found that did not necessitate the destruction of one or the other side but provided the conditions for peaceful political competition.

Although I am responsible for any errors, omissions, or weaknesses in this book, many people were helpful at different stages of the project:

Mike Lofchie, my doctoral committee chair at UCLA, has been wonderfully supportive for many years. Barbara Geddes forced me to sharpen my argument. The late E. Bradford Burns asked me to state my argument in fifty words; I think I can now. Along with thousands of students and colleagues, I will miss his honesty, commitment, and love of Latin America and its people.

Colleagues and friends with whom I worked for many years—Angela Sanbrano, Michael Lent, Cristina Cowger, Mike Zielinski, and many others—helped me appreciate the importance of strategy and organizing.

Cynthia McClintock shared my belief in the argument expressed here and helped convince others of its merit.

George Vickers, Cindy Arnson, Kate Doyle, and Peter Kornbluh, colleagues on a related project, helped sharpen my understanding, particularly on death squads and U.S. policy.

A large number of minor and major actors in El Salvador have helped clarify important areas for me. These include members of the five parties that made up the FMLN during the conflict: Ana Guadalupe Martínez, Juan Ramón Medrano, Eduardo Sancho, Nidia Díaz, Miguel Saenz, Ramón Suarez, Leonel González, Facundo Guardado, Gerson Martínez, Rebeca Palacios, Milton Méndez, Salvador Samayoa, and Salvador Cortes.

General Mauricio Vargas and David Escobar Galindo provided insights into the peace process from the government side. Norma de Dowe, the Salvadoran government's secretary for national reconstruction, and René Dominguez of the Foreign Ministry, gave their assessment of the peace accords. Ana Cristina Sol, El Salvador's ambassador to the United States, and embassy staff member Grace Awat, helped facilitate meetings with government and military officials.

Sara Stowell provided hospitality in El Salvador and interviews from the countryside; Anita Colby gave feedback and insights at all stages of this effort; Jack Hammond, Bill Stanley, and Rebecca Tarver provided helpful suggestions and advice. Thanks to Lynne Rienner, Bridget Julian, Jacqueline Boyle, Michelle Welsh-Horst, Lesli Brooks, and the anonymous reviewer for Lynne Rienner Publishers for helpful suggestions.

Finally, thanks to Cricket, Emma, and Joseph for daily life and support; and my mother, late father, and family in London and Ireland who remind me where I come from.

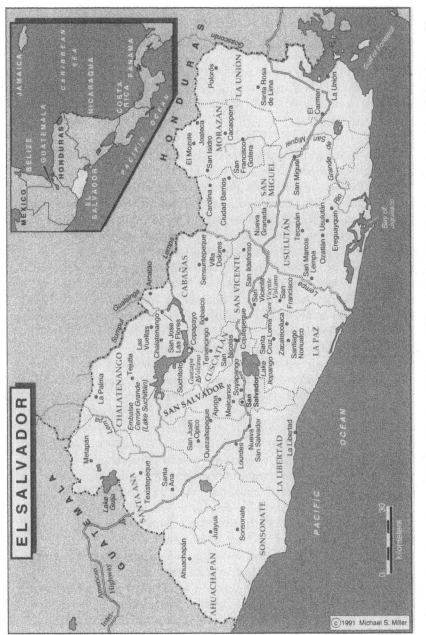

Source: Americas Watch, *El Salvador's Decade of Terror: Human Rights Since the Assassination of Archbishop Romero.* New Haven, Conn.: Yale University Press, 1991. Reprinted with permission.

1

Strategy and Revolution

Rebellions against systems and rulers perceived as unjust have taken place throughout recorded history. In the last two hundred years, particularly since the French Revolution, the phenomenon of social revolution—the rapid and fundamental transformation of socioeconomic and political structures and relations brought on, at least in part, by revolt from below—has become an object of close study and examination by historians and social scientists, as well as by political organizers and actors seeking to achieve or prevent fundamental social change. Attempts to understand the phenomenon of revolution have focused on different variables to explain revolutionary situations and outcomes. Some have focused on the cohesiveness and general health of social and political systems and the types of societies most susceptible to revolutionary change. Others have emphasized the psychological orientations of major participants and the conditions that generate changes in these orientations. Yet others have highlighted a society's social and economic structures, particularly the relationship between major social classes.

This work stresses the importance of human agency—people and the choices they make—in revolutionary processes. It is framed largely within a debate that focuses on socioeconomic and political factors as key variables in explaining revolutionary processes and outcomes. I seek to contribute to an understanding of these processes through the study of revolution and strategies of insurgency and counterinsurgency, using El Salvador's civil war as the example.

The conventional wisdom regarding revolution emphasizes the importance of certain economic conditions and relationships (particularly in the countryside) and/or political conditions and developments (e.g., the weaknesses of regimes, the role of political crises) to explain why revolutionary situations arise and their likelihood of success or failure. What is largely left out of the reckoning is the importance of key choices, or strategies, made by insurgents and incumbent regimes that can be critical to the success or failure of revolutions. Even Marxist revolutionaries who have, in practice, put much time and energy into the development of appropriate strategies have tended to underemphasize their importance, and have focused on seemingly inexorable historical processes or such factors as revolutionary will to explain their successes or failures.

This study emphasizes the role of strategy as an important and at times indispensable element in understanding revolutionary conflicts and their outcomes. Although it is not possible to create a revolutionary outcome without certain fundamental economic and political conditions, the mere presence of these conditions will not ensure a desired outcome without the development and implementation of appropriate strategies. Through an in-depth examination of El Salvador's civil war, I argue that the strategic choices made by revolutionaries and incumbent regimes are critical to a full understanding of the causes and outcomes of revolutionary conflicts.

In the past thirty years a large body of literature has developed on revolutionary and counterrevolutionary strategy. Many of these works, written during and after the Vietnam War, have focused on the most effective methods for defeating revolutionary insurgencies. A key weakness of much of this literature is its almost exclusive focus on one side in the conflict. Thus, in-depth assessments are made of the strengths and weaknesses of different approaches to counterinsurgency, while the strategies of the opposition are treated in a static fashion. Examples of this approach in the counterinsurgency literature on El Salvador include such powerful critiques of U.S. policy in that country as the so-called Four Colonels' Report[1] and Benjamin Schwarz's *American Counterinsurgency Doctrine and El Salvador*.[2] Although these approaches may point out the strategy and policy weaknesses of one side, they cannot capture the dynamic and interactive nature of a prolonged conflict such as El Salvador's any more than examining only white's moves in a chess game could provide a full picture of the game.

The attempt here will be to map out the conflict in El Salvador throughout the civil war, observing the changes over time as one side's strategy responded to changes in the other's or to domestic or international developments; assessing the effectiveness of particular strategies and the relationship between these and political outcomes; and examining the human and other costs of the choices made by each side in the conflict.

Much has been written on El Salvador's civil war and its causes. Relatively little, however, has been written from an explicitly strategic perspective that examines the dynamic interaction of the main protagonists. The end of the war and the release of a trove of internal U.S. documents provide an unprecedented opportunity to examine U.S. strategy in what was the most significant U.S. counterinsurgency effort since Vietnam. Over fifty thousand pages of documents released by U.S. agencies involved in El Salvador, internal insurgent strategy papers, and interviews with participants on both sides of the conflict provide the basis for a comprehensive study of strategies of insurgency and counterinsurgency in El Salvador's civil war. Though secrets will remain on both sides and certain issues may continue to be obscure, there is now enough information in the public domain to provide an overall assessment of strategy in this war. And though the media and U.S. policy focus have shifted away from Central America with the end of the Cold War and the resolution of the region's major conflicts, there remains much to be learned from this long, tragic, and costly war.

Social-Scientific and Historical Approaches to Revolution

There is an important element missing from current explanations of why social revolutions occur and the conditions under which they succeed or fail. Academic theorists, approaching the subject from social-scientific or historical perspectives, have emphasized socioeconomic and political factors as essential elements in generating revolutionary crises. Although these factors provide part of the explanation, they are not sufficient to account entirely for revolutionary outbreaks. What is missing is an acknowledgment of the role played by *people* in these processes, and the role of the strategies of revolutionaries and incumbent regimes in turning serious economic or political situations into revolutionary crises that threaten to overturn the existing political and economic order.[3]

Three influential approaches—by Barrington Moore, Jr., Eric R. Wolf, and Jeffery M. Paige—point to the strengths and limitations of much of the current academic analysis of revolution. For Barrington Moore in *Social Origins of Dictatorship and Democracy*,[4] the key variables in accounting for peasant revolutions "have been the absence of a commercial revolution in agriculture led by the landed upper classes and the concomitant survival of peasant social institutions into the modern era when they are subject to new stresses and strains."[5] For Eric Wolf, peasant revolution results from the extension of the capitalist market and relations worldwide that tear asunder the traditional world and relationships of the peasantry, and rebellion, under certain conditions, is a defensive reaction.[6] Jeffery Paige sees the key to understanding peasant revolution in the relationship between landowners (noncultivators) and direct producers (cultivators), with the essential element being how they gain their income (land or capital in the case of the upper class; land or wages in the case of the lower). Where the noncultivator depends on land for income and the cultivator relies on wages, the conditions are ripe for peasant revolution. "An organized working class . . . confronts an economically weak and politically rigid upper class. The result is a revolutionary war."[7]

These approaches shed valuable light on the underlying socioeconomic conditions and relationships that are conducive to revolution, but they provide very little guidance on the political and strategic factors that are essential to turning these conditions into revolutionary upheavals or outcomes.

Another important contribution to understanding peasant revolution has been generated by the debate between the proponents of "moral-economy" and "political-economy" approaches to the question, Why do peasants rebel? James C. Scott in *The Moral Economy of the Peasant*[8] argues that rebellion and revolution have their roots in the destruction of the peasants' institutional context for reducing risks and in peasant judgment that their moral economy—particularly, their right to subsistence—has been violated. Peasant rebellions are an appeal to the past and "are best seen as defensive reactions."[9] In contrast to the moral-economy approach to peasant society, Samuel Popkin in *The Rational Peasant*[10] argues for a view of peasants as individual decisionmakers who make rational choices and are motivated both by short-term needs and by medium- and long-term costs and benefits. Peasant rebellions, according to Popkin, are best seen not as a dying gasp but as collective actions by peasants to improve their situation, often to obtain rights previously denied them, and do not necessarily result from a decline in peasant welfare.[11]

These approaches provide necessary attention to the role played by rural social relations and deteriorating conditions in the countryside in generating opposition to the existing order. But what are the factors that determine whether the opposition remains isolated or threatens fundamental societal change? For Moore, Wolf, and Paige, outside agents are necessary to turn isolated revolt into revolution. As Moore states: "By themselves the peasants have never been able to accomplish a revolution."[12] And Popkin emphasizes the role of the "political entrepreneur": "someone willing to invest his own time and resources to coordinate the inputs of others in order to produce collective action or collective goods."[13] But these theorists stop short of exploring the relationship between socioeconomic relations and political processes. Ultimately these approaches must be supplemented with explanations of the largely political factors that turn grievances into effective collective action to remold society.

Two recent examinations of revolution focus effectively on the political dimension in revolutionary processes. Theda Skocpol in *States and Social Revolutions*[14] argues that social revolutions are produced by state political crises, often exacerbated by international factors, that may then be exploited by revolutionary vanguards. It is these political crises that have created the conditions under which "revolutionary leaderships and rebellious masses contributed to the accomplishment of revolutionary transformations."[15] Revolutions are not made, she argues; they come. Timothy Wickham-Crowley also adopts a structural approach to revolution in his *Guerrillas and Revolution in Latin America*[16] and argues that the key factors in the occurrence of revolutions is the combination of a guerrilla movement with sufficient peasant support and military strength confronting a weak regime. Between 1956 and 1990 revolutionaries came to power in Latin America "only when a rural-based guerrilla movement secured strong peasant support in the countryside and achieved substantial levels of military strength" and also faced "a patrimonial praetorian regime."[17]

Both Skocpol and Wickham-Crowley emphasize the role of the state and political crises in generating revolutionary situations and outcomes. But what is strikingly absent from both is an incorporation of the role of strategic choices made by revolutionaries or incumbent regimes in the development of the crisis or the ultimate outcome. The choices of either side are viewed as an outgrowth of economic or political conditions. For Skocpol in *States and Social Revolutions,* this position is explicit: Rejecting Marxist and neo-Marxist approaches that stress the subjective element, she argues that political and economic crises set the stage for the collapse of the old regime, at which point the revolutionaries are in a position to pick up the pieces and build a new order. For Wickham-Crowley, likewise, the choices made by revolutionaries are largely structurally determined by the economic or political realities rather than operating as a potentially independent variable that may contribute to revolutionary crises or outcomes.

The models presented by Skocpol and Wickham-Crowley, then, also provide only a partial picture of the key elements in revolutionary change. In ignoring the strategic dimension they present a model that is overly deterministic (economically or politically) and ultimately insufficient. The revolutions of the twentieth century argue for the inclusion not only of the indispensable economic and political elements discussed here but also the strategic choices of revolutionaries and incumbents that, in many cases, affected the outcomes of the conflicts.

Marxism and Twentieth-Century Revolutions

The history of revolutions in the twentieth century challenges the conception that social revolutions arise only from economic contradictions or from political and state crises. This history points to the need for a broader model that incorporates economic and political conditions and relations along with an assessment of the strategic choices made by revolutionaries and incumbent regimes. Some general observations can be made regarding twentieth-century revolutions.

Though Marxist revolutionaries and their successors have been singularly unsuccessful in building socialist societies that responded to the material and spiritual needs of their people, Marx's theory and Marxist revolutionaries have played a central role in consolidating discontent within largely agrarian societies and channeling it toward revolutionary action to overthrow incumbent regimes. Some of the major social revolutions of the twentieth century have been influenced or guided by Marx's analysis and model of revolution, and directed by leaders who believed that revolutionary practice was a crucial determinant in bringing about revolution.

But whereas Marxist theory and practitioners have been central to many twentieth-century revolutions, there has been a significant shift in the Marxist paradigm from a conception of working-class-led, urban-based revolution via general strike or insurrection (associated with Marx and Lenin) to peasant-based, rural revolution through guerrilla warfare waged by a revolutionary army or guerrilla force (linked in varied forms to Mao, Giap, and Guevara). This shift has resulted from the success of industrialized capitalist democracies in generating sufficient wealth and political participation to avoid serious revolutionary challenges, and from the ability of revolutionaries in largely agrarian societies to adapt the Marxist model to different situations in which existing regimes were unable to satisfy the expectations of their people.

At the same time, there has been a much greater emphasis on human agency within revolutionary processes in the twentieth century—particularly the role of organization and strategy. But whereas, in practice, strategy has played a central role in such processes, this dimension has been underemphasized in Marxist theoretical formulations, presumably because it would make revolution much more contingent and less an inevitable outcome of capitalist exploitation and the will to victory of oppressed classes.

For Marx, the historical subject of revolutionary change was the working class, the only class capable of leading the advance to socialism. The peasantry, due to its isolated and atomized position in the production process, could only play an auxiliary role.[18] The states in which Marx expected social revolutions to occur were those in which the forces of production and the class contradictions were most developed: the leading industrial societies of France, Germany, and England. The cities would be in the vanguard of revolutionary upheaval because they contained the major factories and workshops employing thousands of industrial workers. The socioeconomic contradictions inherent in capitalist society and its relations of production were, for Marx, the fundamental guarantees of the transition from capitalism to socialism because workers would be obliged to organize to transform their societies to achieve even the basic benefits of civilized life.

Lenin harnessed Marx's theory of revolution arising from the structural contradictions of capitalist society to a strategy of revolution that placed a central emphasis on both taking advantage of and helping to create favorable conditions for socialist revolution. A major contribution of Lenin was to see the need for a catalyst, the revolutionary party, that could provide leadership to the working class and give focus and direction to what might otherwise be diffuse revolts. He also saw the strategies of the revolutionary party as a critical element of a successful process. Revolutions do not just come, he argued; they must be made. But they can only be made if the objective conditions—a crisis of the regime and organized revolutionary opposition—are present, and if the right decisions are made by the revolutionary party and its leaders, particularly regarding timing and the forms by which the challenge to the regime is advanced (e.g., general strike, insurrection, guerrilla war, etc.).

The Russian Revolution involved a shift in the Marxist paradigm because it took place in a peripheral capitalist society in which the forces of production were less developed (though the working class, while small in number, did play a central role in the process). The revolution also elevated the role of the Bolshevik Party as an essential force in providing leadership and direction, and pointed to the importance of strategic choices made by revolutionaries to the outcome of the process. The Chinese and Vietnamese revolutions brought about a further shift in the Marxist model of revolution. These revolutions occurred in overwhelmingly agrarian societies. As in Russia, a revolutionary party played a central role in organizing and directing the process. But a new element in these revolutions was the major role played by a guerrilla army and prolonged insurgencies in achieving the overthrow of the incumbent regimes.

In both China and Vietnam the strategic choices of the revolutionaries appear to have been critical to the outcomes of the conflicts.[19] In each case, deep-rooted economic and political conditions laid the groundwork for revolutionary upheaval. In China the disintegration of the old (Manchu) regime and the failure to establish any strong centralized authority left a great deal of space open for new and existing social movements to attempt to gain power over the state. The economic and social crisis and its impact on the peasantry provided a social base that could potentially be mobilized. But the strategic decision to mobilize the peasantry as the main base of the revolution—following the defeat in 1927 of a working-class uprising in Shanghai—appears to have been essential to the ability of the revolutionaries to take power. Other important strategies were to build a politicized army that would challenge the Kuomintang and the Japanese occupation through guerrilla warfare while educating and mobilizing peasant support for the policies of the Communist Party. In Vietnam, once the peasantry was identified as the main social base of revolution, the strategies that contributed to the resolution of the conflict included launching deep agrarian reforms (with a differentiated approach to distinct strata of the peasantry) to win peasant support; incorporating the peasantry into a politicized, revolutionary army tightly controlled by the Communist Party; and engaging in prolonged guerrilla warfare that maximized revolutionary strengths and minimized weaknesses.

Whereas the Chinese and Vietnamese revolutions involved a significant shift from the original Marxist model of revolution, the Cuban Revolution that overthrew the Batista regime, and the Sandinista-led defeat of Somoza in Nicaragua, involved the further leap of elevating the role of a guerrilla army as the catalyst of revolution. In both Cuba and Nicaragua the strategies of the revolutionary movements also appear to have been an essential element of the revolutionary outcome.

In Cuba, a small guerrilla band, poorly armed, beginning with little institutional support and basing itself in inaccessible rural areas (though it developed important networks of support in urban areas), was able to win sufficient backing to fortify itself militarily. In a period of two years Castro's forces inflicted defeats on the armed forces that culminated in the ouster of Batista and allowed them to take power. In explaining the ability of Castro's movement to overcome a much larger military force and take power, analysts have pointed to both the weaknesses of the Cuban state and the particularities of rural social relations that made Cuba vulnerable to revolt.[20] But this vulnerability appears insufficient to explain why revolution succeeded in Cuba while stronger guerrilla movements in societies with more serious economic and political problems were defeated elsewhere in Latin America. In Cuba's case, the strategies of Castro and his insurgent army appear to have been critical to the outcome. These strategies included launching a guerrilla war in a part of the country in which the peasants were most open to challenging the regime; conducting a military campaign that demoralized and ultimately defeated Batista's army; and mobilizing broad opposition around what was essentially a democratic program to replace the dictatorship.

In the decade following the Cuban Revolution, the strategies that were successful in Cuba were generalized throughout Latin America with singular lack of success. Guerrilla armies were formed and attempted to build areas of activity (*focos*) in the countryside from which they could branch out, expand peasant support, and defeat the incumbent regime. These attempts ended in failure as peasants proved unwilling to risk supporting the guerrillas, and the isolated focos were found to be vulnerable to increasingly sophisticated counterinsurgency strategies. Such failure pointed to the inappropriateness of attempting to export effective strategies rather than basing strategic choices on a close examination of the economic, political, and other realities of a given society; this lesson was learned by revolutionaries in Nicaragua and El Salvador.[21]

In Nicaragua the success of the Sandinista revolution owed much to the particularly venal nature of the Somoza regime, which isolated the dictator from privileged sectors that ought to have formed the regime's support base and galvanized the opposition among subordinate classes that allowed the Sandinista Front to mobilize. The nature of the regime and its actions were critical to Somoza's defeat, but the strategies ultimately adopted by the Sandinistas were an essential element of the outcome. These strategies included the forming of alliances that effectively mobilized both elite and popular opposition to Somoza under the leadership of the Sandinistas; developing a democratic discourse that focused on the antidictatorial goals of the struggle against the regime; and launching a popular insurrection at a time that took advantage of the breadth and depth of public repudiation of Somoza.

In all five of these twentieth-century social revolutions, deteriorating economic conditions that impacted most severely on the peasant majority provided the basis for a revolutionary movement seeking popular support to overthrow the regime. Political factors, such as war or foreign intervention (in Russia, China, and Vietnam) or weak and vulnerable regimes (in all five countries) were also essential to the revolutionary outcome. But to turn these (favorable) conditions into a successful revolution involved the building of an organized, disciplined, politicized, and (at least in the final stage) armed opposition movement to challenge the incumbent regime. That movement then had to gain significant popular support and make choices that could take advantage of the opposition's strengths and the regime's weaknesses. None of the strategies that contributed to the overthrow of these regimes was inevitable and some flew in the face of orthodox theory. Yet the willingness of revolutionary organizers to adapt or ignore existing theory and dogma, and take innovative actions that responded to the specific conditions of their own societies, appears to have been a crucial factor in their ultimate success.

The Role of Strategy

The history of twentieth-century revolutions shows strategies of revolutionary groups and incumbent regimes to be an important but
underemphasized element in the generation of crises and the success
of revolutions. Revolutionary situations arise and revolutions succeed
or fail due in part to the ability of revolutionaries (or their opponents)
to make appropriate decisions on major questions. A more inclusive
model of the elements necessary for a successful revolution include
the following:

1. Revolutionary upheavals are precipitated by certain socioeconomic conditions or structures that, by generating poverty, discontent,
or negative changes in the conditions of subordinate classes (particularly the peasantry), lay the basis for broad-based opposition to the
regime in power. Unsatisfactory or deteriorating economic conditions,
generated by the actions of regimes or landowners, by foreign
intervention, or by a breakdown of authority, appear to have been an
essential element of the revolutions in Russia, China, Vietnam, Cuba,
and Nicaragua, as well as in Mexico (1910–1920),[22] and Bolivia
(1952).[23]

2. Certain types of narrowly based regimes, which close off the
opportunity for democratic and reformist change, thus strengthening
the possibility for the opposition to develop broad-based class alliances
between workers and peasants and the middle and upper classes, are
particularly susceptible to revolutionary challenges. The connection
between a regime's isolation from potential bases of support and its
defeat by a revolutionary opposition is seen clearly in the Cuban and
Nicaraguan cases, in the overthrow of the Shah of Iran in 1979, and in
a variety of conflicts involving decolonization.[24]

3. Broad-based popular opposition to the incumbent regime is a
necessary condition for social-revolutionary change. But without a
social force (such as a revolutionary party or guerrilla army) capable
of strengthening, coordinating, and articulating the interests of the
opposition, a revolutionary outcome is much less likely. The formation
of cross-class alliances (often aided by the unpopular actions of an isolated regime, as in the Cuban and Nicaraguan cases) appears to be an
important factor in the revolutionary overthrow of incumbent
regimes. But as can be seen in myriad popular uprisings, general
strikes, and other forms of mass opposition that failed to unseat
incumbent regimes, something beyond broad popular opposition is
also needed.

4. The outcome of a revolutionary conflict, and in some cases
whether a revolutionary situation develops, will be a product of the
strategic interaction between the regime and the opposition (and per-

haps third parties) in addition to the other factors. Structural socio-economic factors and the political conditions of the regime generate the conditions for the rise of a revolutionary opposition and the possibility that the regime will be overthrown. The competing strategies of the regime and the opposition will determine whether the situation reaches the stage of revolutionary crisis.

The examination of the origins and development of El Salvador's civil war explores all of these elements, with a major focus on the role of strategy in both the generation and the outcome of the revolutionary crisis in El Salvador in the late 1970s. A definition of strategy and some theses on its application will clarify the scope of its operation within revolutionary conflicts. In this context, strategy may be defined as the formulation and implementation of choices of major means to achieve overall objectives. From this a number of elements can be emphasized.

1. An essential element of strategy is its dynamic and interactive nature. Strategy, as it is used here, addresses situations of conflict in which two competing forces confront each other. Each move by one side creates an entirely new reality; the response from the adversary brings about yet another transformation of reality. Edward Luttwak, in *Strategy: The Logic of War and Peace,* argues that the entire realm of strategy is pervaded by a paradoxical logic of its own.[25] When analyzed in terms of military strategy, a bad road can be good precisely because it is bad and its use less likely to be anticipated by the enemy.

2. Strategic choices have crucial human costs and consequences. The decision by a regime to employ repression to defeat its opposition, and the decision by revolutionary organizers to take up arms to overthrow an incumbent regime, can cost the lives of thousands of compatriots. Mutual decisions on the part of a regime and revolutionaries to use arms to determine political outcomes can build up a cycle of violence from which it is extremely difficult to escape. Even most "successful" revolutions have perpetuated violence and repression as methods to ensure the objectives of the revolution in the face of opposition from old and new enemies.

3. Strategy assumes choices between alternative possibilities. Rarely will the major choices of revolutionaries and incumbents be foregone conclusions, predetermined by larger socioeconomic relations and conditions. In certain critical moments, such as the decision in China to focus on organizing the peasantry rather than urban workers, the choice between alternative options may be an essential factor in the revolutionary success.

4. Strategy is closely related to questions of organization. The form of organization that a revolutionary movement takes is itself a

strategic choice, with important implications for how strategies are developed and how effective they will be. One such implication is that there are likely to be alternative constituencies within a given organization or movement for particular strategies, and strategic questions will often be fault lines dividing different factions and groups within a movement. There may be competition between moderates and radicals, pragmatists and ideologues, those perceiving a need for violence and those eschewing it, or those seeing the potential for immediate victory and those seeing the need for a long-term struggle.[26]

5. Strategy involves both formulation and implementation. A strategy may be effectively formulated and theoretically sound (e.g., a strategy of launching guerrilla warfare in an underdeveloped nation with large disparities of wealth and income), but if the conditions are inappropriate (e.g., there is a long and positive history of electoral participation by subordinate classes) it is unlikely to succeed. Likewise, a well-thought-out strategy of social reforms by a threatened regime may be ineffective if it is inadequately implemented (e.g., the political or administrative mechanisms are not adequate to put it into effect).

6. Strategy concerns the major means used by the parties to the conflict to achieve their objectives. For a revolutionary movement or coalition some major strategic choices include whether to emphasize political or military activities or a combination of both to achieve power; whether to focus organizing efforts on workers, peasants, students, intellectuals, or some combination of these groups to form the core social base of the revolution; whether to focus organizing activities in urban or rural areas; and what forms of alliances to develop. For a regime seeking to defeat a revolutionary movement, some of the major strategic choices include whether to implement social, political, or economic reforms to undercut the base of the revolutionary movement; whether and how much to engage in repression to defeat the opposition; and whether to enlist outside support.

7. Strategy is closely related to objectives. In situations of revolution and counterrevolution the objectives are normally clear. In most cases a revolutionary movement is seeking to overthrow the incumbent regime to achieve control of the state and effect radical social, economic, and political changes. A regime confronting a revolutionary movement will, in most cases, have as a fundamental objective the defeat (political or military) of that opposition. Where there is lack of clarity as to the overall objectives or lack of unity in their formulation or implementation, particular strategies may be effective but the overall strategy of that party is likely to be seriously impeded.

8. Strategy operates within the context of larger socioeconomic and political realities. Will and strategic genius are not enough to

effect a successful revolutionary outcome where the material conditions (e.g., particular socioeconomic relationships or regime weaknesses) are absent. Rather, strategic choice comes to play an important role where certain conditions already exist, although it may also play a role in creating those conditions. The relationship of strategy to these more familiar structural factors needs to be defined as clearly as possible in analyses of revolutionary situations and outcomes.

9. Effective strategy can overcome a multitude of obstacles and impediments. These obstacles include imbalances in military, logistical, and human resources; inequality in the levels of international support; and unfavorable domestic or international developments.

10. Strategy is highly context specific. A given approach is not easily adaptable from one society to another unless the material conditions are fundamentally similar. This is shown clearly in the failure to apply the lessons of the successful Cuban Revolution to the rest of Latin America. *Foquismo* was a strategy (elevated to the level of theory) that was meaningful in the particular conditions of Cuba in the late 1950s but proved inappropriate to other countries in Latin America whose histories, political systems, and social relations were fundamentally different.

11. Strategy is more important than strategies. In many situations success or failure of the revolutionary enterprise will not rest on any one or two factors. A grand strategy that unifies specific strategies (e.g., political, military, diplomatic, economic, psychological) and is tied closely to the desired objectives may be more important than any single strategy.

12. Successful strategy requires unity and flexibility in overall objectives and major strategies. Where there is disunity with regard to objectives or the appropriateness of certain strategies, the effectiveness of the overall project will be seriously jeopardized. Likewise, flexibility and willingness to shift when circumstances change or when particular activities do not work can make an important contribution to strategic effectiveness and the probability of ultimate success.

Notes

1. Lt. Col. A. J. Bacevich et al., *American Military Policy in Small Wars: The Case of El Salvador* (Washington, D.C.: Pergamon-Brassey's International Defense Publishers, 1988).

2. Benjamin C. Schwarz, *American Counterinsurgency Doctrine and El Salvador: The Frustrations of Reform and the Illusions of Nation Building* (Santa Monica, Calif.: RAND, 1991).

3. Other recent works challenge the structural explanations of revolution that leave people largely out of the equation. Two books that stress the

importance of human agency in revolutions are Eric Selbin, *Modern Latin American Revolutions* (Boulder, Colo.: Westview Press, 1993), which takes a people-centered approach to revolutionary processes and focuses on the consolidation and institutionalization of revolutions after the taking of power; and Forrest D. Colburn, *The Vogue of Revolution in Poor Countries* (Princeton, N.J.: Princeton University Press, 1994), which highlights the importance of imagination and culture within an approach that strongly emphasizes human agency.

4. Barrington Moore, Jr., *Social Origins of Dictatorship and Democracy: Lord and Peasant in the Making of the Modern World* (Boston: Beacon Press, 1966).

5. Ibid., 477.

6. See Eric R. Wolf, *Peasant Wars of the Twentieth Century* (New York: Harper & Row, 1969).

7. See Jeffery M. Paige, *Agrarian Revolution: Social Movements and Export Agriculture in the Underdeveloped World* (New York: Free Press, 1975), 120.

8. James C. Scott, *The Moral Economy of the Peasant: Rebellion and Subsistence in Southeast Asia* (New Haven, Conn.: Yale University Press, 1976).

9. Ibid., 10.

10. Samuel L. Popkin, *The Rational Peasant* (Berkeley: University of California Press, 1979).

11. Ibid., 34.

12. Moore, *Social Origins*, 479.

13. Popkin, *The Rational Peasant*, 259.

14. Theda Skocpol, *States and Social Revolutions: A Comparative Analysis of France, Russia, and China* (Cambridge: Cambridge University Press, 1979).

15. Ibid., 17.

16. Timothy P. Wickham-Crowley, *Guerrillas and Revolution in Latin America: A Comparative Study of Insurgents and Regimes Since 1956* (Princeton, N.J.: Princeton University Press, 1992).

17. Ibid., 320.

18. See Marx's classic statement on the peasantry; Karl Marx, *The Eighteenth Brumaire of Louis Bonaparte*, in *Karl Marx: Surveys from Exile, Political Writings* Volume II, ed. David Fernbach (New York: Vintage Books, 1974), 238–239, where he compares peasant proprietors to a "sack of potatoes." They are "incapable of asserting their class interest in their own name. . . . They cannot represent themselves; they must be represented."

19. For a discussion of the role of strategy in the Chinese revolution, see William J. Pomeroy, ed., *Guerrilla Warfare and Marxism: A Collection of Writings from Karl Marx to the Present on Armed Struggles for Liberation and for Socialism* (New York: International Publishers, 1968); on Vietnam, see Vo Nguyen Giap, *People's War, People's Army* (Hanoi: Foreign Languages Publishing House, 1961).

20. Among the vulnerabilities of the state to revolutionary challenges were the "praetorian" nature of the Batista regime; the absence of solid support in any major sector of the society; the lack of a strong, indigenous upper class that could provide a firm basis for the regime or a replacement in time of crisis; the absence of a strong middle class and meaningful electoral tradition; and the political dependence of the regime on an outside power, the United States. The particularities of Cuba's social relations that made it vulnerable to revolt included a highly unequal distribution of land, with a large proportion owned by foreign companies; a tradition of rebellion in Oriente province where the guerrilla war was launched; a large rural proletariat work-

ing mainly in the sugar mills; and a large squatter population that was susceptible to revolt. See, for example, Wickham-Crowley, *Guerrillas and Revolution in
Latin America*, 96–97.

21. The most notable failure was that of Che Guevara and his guerrilla
band in Bolivia in 1967. Guevara viewed Bolivia as ripe for revolution despite
the reforms that had taken place following the country's (incomplete) 1952
revolution.

22. See Samuel P. Huntington, *Political Order in Changing Societies* (New
Haven, Conn.: Yale University Press, 1968), 315–324.

23. See Selbin, *Modern Latin American Revolutions*, 37–43.

24. See Jeff Goodwin and Theda Skocpol, "Explaining Revolutions in the
Contemporary Third World," *Politics and Society* 17, no. 4 (December 1989),
489–509.

25. Edward N. Luttwak, *Strategy: The Logic of War and Peace* (Cambridge,
Mass.: Belnap Press of Harvard University Press, 1987).

26. See, for example, James DeNardo, *Power in Numbers: The Political
Strategy of Protest and Rebellion* (Princeton: Princeton University Press, 1985).

2

The Origins of
El Salvador's Crisis

By the late 1970s El Salvador was embroiled in a revolutionary crisis that threatened the continuance of the country's traditional economic and political order. The root causes of this crisis lay in economic, political, and strategic factors.

An elitist economic structure and the expansion of an export-crop economy dramatically worsened the conditions of life for the peasantry and forced the majority of the population into an untenable and deteriorating economic situation by the late 1970s. The country's political order excluded the majority from participation and proved incapable of instituting reforms that might have brought meaningful change through democratic means. A transformation occurred in the consciousness of many peasants from the early 1970s. A large number were influenced first by activist Catholic clergy and laypeople and then organized by revolutionary groups that provided structures for collective peasant action. (Others were recruited into the right-wing peasant organization.) Strategies implemented by revolutionary organizations—particularly the decisions to launch a political-military struggle to overthrow the regime, focus organizing efforts in the rural areas, and build mass grassroots organizations—maximized pressure on the regime and precipitated an increasingly violent response. El Salvador's dominant class and its political representatives failed to find a model or develop effective strategies to resolve the country's political and economic problems. Finally, the impact of the Nicaraguan revolution helped raise the crisis of the Romero regime to a new level, generating actions that ultimately deepened the crisis rather than resolved it.

This chapter examines the ways in which each of these factors contributed to the crisis of the late 1970s.

Economic Roots of the Crisis

Several of the theorists discussed in Chapter 1 stressed certain socio-economic factors as critical in explaining why peasant revolutions occur: for Moore, whether the landowning class has made the transition to capitalist agriculture; for Wolf, the impact on peasant society of the expansion of the capitalist market; for Paige, noncultivators who rely on land for income confronting cultivators who rely on wages for their income. In El Salvador the economic roots of the crisis fit none of these models neatly. A landowning class that was economically progressive but politically ultraconservative was unwilling to share any of the burden of economic change with a peasantry that was increasingly pauperized, marginalized, and dislocated by the expansion of the export-crop economy. Deteriorating social and economic conditions, exacerbated by failure to bring change through democratic means, led to increased polarization. Revolutionary groups and their allies sought to overthrow the government while the incumbent regime tried by all means to stay in power.

The core of the Salvadoran economy is agriculture; at the center of the agrarian system is coffee. In 1978 agriculture contributed 25.7 percent to the nation's gross domestic product (GDP), while manufacturing contributed 18.7 percent.[1] In 1969 coffee accounted for 9.1 percent of GDP, 35.8 percent of agricultural production, and 44.2 percent of exports. The area sown with coffee increased from 8.8 percent to 10.1 percent of all agricultural land, and export volume increased by 3.6 percent between 1961 and 1971.[2] By 1978 coffee accounted for 53.2 percent of the value of all exports.[3]

Coffee rose to prominence in El Salvador in the middle to late nineteenth century and replaced indigo, which had been the major export crop of the colonial and early postindependence periods. Between 1859 and 1875 coffee rose from 1 percent to 33 percent of exports.[4] The state played a major role in encouraging coffee growing by reducing production taxes, exempting the coffee labor force from military service, granting land to those who agreed to grow coffee, distributing coffee saplings free through local authorities, and even fining landowners who refused to plant coffee.[5]

The expansion of coffee growing had a dramatic impact on the rural economy and social relations. Lands that had been communal property (*ejidos,* municipal commons; and *comunidades,* communal lands) were transferred to private ownership through laws of 1879, 1881, and 1882 that abolished collective property. It is estimated that a quarter of the cultivable land in the country, almost one and a half million acres, was affected by these laws. Peasants were forced off their lands and into the cash-crop labor force.[6]

Salvadoran coffee growing is highly efficient and productive. The system of coffee farming, according to Browning, "is second to none in terms of techniques of cultivation, adaptability to terrain, and consistently high yields. . . . The per acre yield of Salvadorian *fincas* increases in proportion to their size, and the yields gained from some of the largest properties are the highest not only in the country but in the world."[7] When speaking of coffee farming in El Salvador, it is thus "difficult to find evidence of the charges often made against latifundia in Latin America or against plantation agriculture in the tropics,"[8] of backwardness, waste, and inefficiency.

Coffee is harvested from November to March under conditions that are favorable to maximizing profits. In the 1970s, the laborers in the harvest were mainly subsistence farmers from the northern departments where land was poorest. The coffee grower was responsible for paying the laborers' wages only during the harvest. For the rest of the year the workers engaged in subsistence farming on small plots (at least until the subsistence crisis deepened in the 1960s and 1970s). The importance of seasonal labor in the coffee harvest is indicated by the fact that a third of the money made by agricultural laborers was earned in coffee in the 1960s.[9]

The other two main cash crops, cotton and sugar cane, in 1978 accounted for 11.2 percent and 2.9 percent, respectively, of exports. The expansion of cotton production on the flat coastal plain and in some interior valleys dates from the World War II period, and the importance of sugar as a Salvadoran export crop increased in the 1960s with the ending of the U.S. sugar quota for Cuba. The main food crops grown in El Salvador are maize, sorghum, beans, and rice. These are grown singly or in combination, mainly on land that is unsuitable for export crops.[10] Food crops are grown overwhelmingly on tiny plots of land: In 1979, 48.9 percent of agricultural properties averaged one and a half acres in size and in total covered 4.8 percent of the cultivable land.[11] Small plots of less than twenty-five acres produced 72.2 percent of the maize, 82.2 percent of the sorghum, and 77 percent of the beans grown in the country in 1971.[12]

The expansion of export crops—coffee from the late nineteenth century and cotton from the mid-twentieth century—forced peasants off their lands and into the export-crop economy as seasonal laborers, or onto ever smaller plots to maintain subsistence production of food crops. A population of just over three and a half million that was growing by 157,000 a year in the 1960s exacerbated the crisis of subsistence agriculture.[13] From the 1950s the traditional agrarian relationships in the Salvadoran countryside were sharecropping and *colonato* (a system wherein peasants are given a small plot of land in exchange for work on the landowner's estate); this gave way increasingly to money rent as opposed to rent in kind. Lands dedicated to the main cash crops grew by 43,000 hectares between 1960 and 1972, while the total land in colonato dropped by 3.8 percent and lands held by tenants paying money rent rose by 2.3 percent.[14] After the 1969 "soccer war" with Honduras, this critical situation was worsened by the return from Honduras of 100,000 to 300,000 Salvadoran peasants.[15]

The reciprocal dynamic of concentration of land ownership for export crops, and shrinking plots for subsistence-food production, intensified in the 1960s and 1970s. Between 1961 and 1971 the number of properties increased by 19.4 percent while the available land area fell by 8.2 percent. Most striking of all was the increase in landlessness in this period: In 1961, 19.8 percent of families were without land; in 1971, 41.1 percent were landless.[16] At the other end of the scale, by 1966, 3,000 families controlled 43 percent of the land, and 463 properties covered 29 percent of cultivated land.[17] The skewed distribution of land was paralleled in income distribution: In 1970 the poorest fifth of the population earned 3.7 percent and the richest fifth 50.8 percent of national income; by 1980 the poorest fifth earned just 2 percent and the richest fifth 66 percent of national income.[18]

Following World War II, a state-encouraged process of limited industrialization advanced, peaking during the 1960s period of the Alliance for Progress and the Central American Common Market. During this time El Salvador was able to take advantage of its relatively better developed infrastructure and the enlarged regional market to expand its manufacturing production. The rate of growth of value added in the industrial sector was 11.7 percent per year in the period 1962–1967.[19]

During its expansion, however, industrial development in El Salvador did not bring about structural changes in the Salvadoran economy—for example, by being able to absorb into the workforce peasants who had lost their land. Nor did it give rise to a new class or fraction of a class independent enough to push for the changes that might have staved off political and economic crisis. Industrial production was capital intensive: The proportion of the economically active population engaged in manufacturing fell from 12.9 percent in 1961 to 11.2 percent in 1971. Over the decade of the 1960s, manufacturing production rose by 7.9 percent, while employment grew by only 2.6 percent.[20] And industry was tied to agrarian capital: "The majority of domestic, industrial capital either came directly from or was closely allied to the landed oligarchy. . . . In 1971, 38 per cent of El Salvador's top 1,429 firms were controlled by the 36 largest landowners, who owned 66 per cent of their total capital."[21] The landowning class also controlled the country's finance market and its four leading banks. In a period of rapid growth and change, economic power in El Salvador therefore remained highly concentrated.

Ownership of land and production of export crops were the core of capital accumulation, the jumping-off point for expansion into other sectors of the economy, and the basis for control over El Salvador's political system. The leading families were involved in coffee production, processing, and export; sugar and cotton production, processing and export; manufacturing industry; and/or finance.[22] Twenty-three of the twenty-six family groups producing ten thousand quintals (one quintal = 46 kilograms) or more of coffee were also engaged in coffee processing. These twenty-six large-scale coffee producers included twelve of the fourteen largest producers of cotton and nine of the top ten sugar growers.[23]

If one examines the nature of the Salvadoran landowning class according to the categories used by Moore, Wolf, and Paige, one can see that the landowners had made the transition to capitalist agriculture: Salvadoran coffee growing was among the most efficient and productive in the world, and landowners had branched out into other areas of the economy and did not rely solely on land for their income. But an independent bourgeoisie with an interest in economic reforms to expand the market and political reform to solidify its influence, which has been much emphasized in the literature on revolutionary change and modernization, did not develop. Baloyra argues:

> A bourgeoisie did indeed emerge in El Salvador, but it remained bound to the traditional groups or at least dependent on them for the finance of major projects. The bourgeoisie remained unable to secure the resources necessary to embark on the type of economic projects that would have made it socially and politically hegemonic. A democratic regime would not have been the inevitable result of bourgeois dominance, but without that dominance a new coalition could not be formed to challenge the traditional oligarchy from a solid economic footing.[24]

Whereas the expansion of export crops and demographic pressures created a crisis in the subsistence economy, and the expansion of industry was insufficient to absorb displaced peasants, there was no strong and independent force within the dominant class committed and able to press for the types of changes that might have averted crisis.

There were different factions within El Salvador's economic elite whose competing interests gave rise to intense conflict within the dominant class and between the agrarian faction and the state in the early and mid-1970s, particularly around the question of agrarian reform.[25] But, argues Dunkerley,

despite a number of brushes within the oligarchy, no major shift to
Alliance [for Progress]–type industrial and agrarian reforms was ever
permitted and there existed no faction of the capitalist class that was
strong enough to push it through. Industrialisation neither stemmed
from nor produced a "national bourgeoisie" with its own economic
project or political independence.[26]

In El Salvador, economic factors played an essential role in generating a revolutionary crisis in the late 1970s. But the elements stressed
by Moore, Wolf, and Paige are of only limited value in providing an
explanation. In the Salvadoran case one could not apply the model of
an intransigent and reactionary class unable to make economic
change or allow political reforms because its interests rested only on
land ownership. The Salvadoran oligarchy was undoubtedly reactionary, but explanations of its intransigence must go beyond purely
economic structures and interests. The roots of the Salvadoran oligarchy were in land ownership and the production of export crops,
but the production methods were modern and this class had broadened out to dominate industrial production and the financial system.
Thus, there appear to have been no insurmountable economic barriers to a reform project. Wolf's focus on the expansion of capitalist mar-
kets and its effect on the peasant economy captures elements of the
Salvadoran case but only in broad strokes. A fuller picture of the causes of El Salvador's revolutionary crisis of the late 1970s requires an
examination of the political and strategic factors that interacted with
these economic elements to generate social upheaval.

Failure of the Political System

Chapter 1 explored the importance of political factors to revolutionary outcomes. Theda Skocpol argued that social revolutions result
from state political crises, often exacerbated by international factors,
that may then be taken advantage of by revolutionary vanguards.
Timothy Wickham-Crowley stressed the convergence of a specific pair
of conditions: a peasant-supported guerrilla movement confronting
an isolated dictatorial regime. The following sections demonstrate the
converse of Skocpol's proposition in the case of El Salvador:
Revolutionaries played a major role in generating a state political crisis rather than merely taking advantage of a crisis that had arisen from
other causes. Wickham-Crowley's emphasis on the need for a "patrimonial praetorian regime" receives some support in the Salvadoran
case because one factor in the failure of revolutionaries to take power
in 1979–1980 was that the state rested on a class that largely main-

tained its cohesion and solidarity rather than on a dictator or regime that became isolated from the dominant economic classes.

From 1932, when a major peasant revolt was put down by security forces, to the period of the civil war, the Salvadoran political system was characterized by military rule backed by, and largely for the benefit of, the landed oligarchy. Some of the major features of this system were (1) a weak state that never succeeded in challenging the interests of the dominant class, even when a challenge might have benefited the long-term interests of that class; (2) a division of labor between the armed forces, which controlled major positions in government, and the landowning class, which dominated positions concerned with the economy; (3) a limited opening of the political process to the middle class and some urban workers (particularly after 1960) accompanied by the exclusion of independent political organizing in the countryside and repression directed against radical challenges to the system, both urban and rural; and (4) weak institutionalization of a political party and electoral system that never reached the point of a democratic transfer of power prior to 1980, though it possessed some of the trappings of a democratic process.

The modern Salvadoran political system dates from 1932 and the defeat of a peasant revolt inspired by the Communist Party under the leadership of Farabundo Martí. In a period of deep economic crisis following the U.S. stock market crash, and in the wake of a coup and fraudulent elections in January 1932, the Salvadoran Communist Party (Partido Comunista Salvadoreño, or PCS) called for an insurrection. Before the date of the insurrection, however, the major PCS leaders, including Farabundo Martí, were captured. The insurrection went ahead and some towns in the west of the country were taken by the insurgents. The revolt was put down in three days and Anderson estimates that about 100 people were killed by the rebels. In the weeks that followed, "some twenty-five thousand peasants and workers were rounded up and executed, many times the number who had actually participated in the rebellion,"[27] an event that has become known as "La Matanza" (the massacre).

Following the defeat of the 1932 rebellion and the subsequent massacre, the new shape of the political system and its relationship to the landowning class took form. Between 1932 and 1979 the core of the system rested on an alliance between the landowning class and the armed forces within which military leaders were guardians of the political order, defining the limits of political reform, while the landowning class oversaw the economic order and set tight limits on any change in this area. The military institution was responsible for maintaining the conditions of order necessary for capital accumulation, based primarily on export-crop production. Military presidents could be ousted when they failed to maintain, in White's terms, the appropriate balance between repression and concession, as was the case with the coups of 1944, 1948, and 1960. The military governments never succeeded in taking on the landowning interests on issues of major importance to the oligarchy and imposing a larger vision of class or national interests. Prior to El Salvador's civil war, the military institution did not develop into a major economic power that could provide a counterweight to the dominance of the landowning class.

The regimes that ruled El Salvador from 1932 relied on a very narrow social base of support. The vast majority of the population, living in the countryside, was excluded from political participation until the 1960s, when the military and its allies organized a counterrevolutionary peasant movement, the Democratic Nationalist Organization (Organización Democrática Nacionalista, or ORDEN). Urban workers and an expanding middle class could participate in popularly based political parties from the 1960s, but under controlled conditions. Class relations in the countryside were seen by the rural elite as a zero-sum game in which concessions promised to lead to a complete loss of control. Questions of land redistribution, higher wages for agricultural workers, and political organizing in the countryside were subjects for military or police action rather than political negotiation. Greater flexibility was permitted in urban areas and in relation to other subordinate classes—urban workers and the middle class—because the core of the power of the dominant class, land, was not directly threatened. Thus, at least from 1948 to 1979, the Salvadoran system was characterized by rigid control to maintain order, repression against any threats to oligarchic rule in the countryside, and oscillation between repression and concession in the cities and toward the working and middle classes.

Prior to the 1960s the political parties in El Salvador did not represent interests of social groups in the society or provide alternative programs for governing the country. Rather, they were personalistic vehicles, often organized around a given individual running for office, which were dormant in the period between elections. Elections were invariably won by the candidate chosen by the military, and the official party was the vehicle for getting out the vote for the candidate and maintaining the necessary level of patronage to keep the system functioning smoothly. The ruling party from 1960 to 1979, the National Conciliation Party (Partido de Conciliación Nacional, or PCN), was a patronage organization that dispensed favors to guarantee the loyalty of its cadre and votes at election time.

From the early 1960s to the early 1970s the party system in El Salvador became more pluralistic as the period of industrialization,

associated with the Alliance for Progress and the Central American
Common Market, increased the influence of the middle and urban
working classes, and the military and its allies in the landowning class
accepted an opening up of the political process that did not immediately challenge their power. The Christian Democratic Party (Partido
Demócrata Cristiano, or PDC) and social democratic parties won seats
in the Legislative Assembly, and the PDC controlled the mayor's office
in San Salvador for eight years. During the 1960s, with increasing
enrollments and growing activism in the wake of the Cuban revolution, the country's universities became a focal point for antiregime
activity. With increased urbanization and the expansion of industry
during the Common Market period, labor organizations challenged
the status quo, and teachers' strikes in the late 1960s played an important role in galvanizing opposition to the regime.

The challenge to the rule of the military-oligarchy alliance coa-
lesced in the elections of 1972. But, as in the economic arena with the
1976 attempt at agrarian reform, the system failed its first major test:
The military and its landowning allies were unwilling to hand over
power to a broad coalition (including the PDC, the social-democratic
National Revolutionary Movement [Movimiento Nacional Revolucionario, or MNR], and the Communist Party–linked Democratic
Nationalist Union [Unión Democrática Nacionalista, or UDN]); its
electoral victory in 1972 was overturned by the military. This failure to
bring about change in the political system through elections and other
legal means convinced many would-be democrats that reforms could
only be achieved through extralegal methods.

This closing off of the possibility of democratic change was crucial
to expanding the viability of the revolutionary option. But the model
presented by Skocpol of objective political conditions creating a crisis
that is then capitalized upon by revolutionaries is inadequate to
explain the Salvadoran process. The strategies of the revolutionaries
and of the regime played an essential role in generating the revolutionary crisis of the late 1970s. However, developments in El Salvador,
at least in a negative sense, support Wickham-Crowley's emphasis on
the need for a weak and isolated "praetorian" regime before a strong
guerrilla movement can succeed. In El Salvador the regime was certainly isolated from the majority of the population, but unlike in
Nicaragua and Cuba, the dominant economic class maintained its
cohesion and though weakened was able to regroup and recover from
the events of 1979–1980 (discussed in the next chapter). And the revolutionary opposition was not able to consolidate a broad cross-class
movement that could focus its efforts on overthrowing an isolated dictator or dynasty. When the reformist military coup of October 1979
overthrew General Romero and forced into exile some major military

figures, the class that had dominated El Salvador for generations still remained, along with key supporters in the military, and was able to regroup and return to power under changed conditions.

Transformation of Peasant Consciousness

Peasant consciousness, institutions, and solidarity play an important role in explanations of peasant revolution. Scott stresses the breach of a "moral economy" and the attempt to restore it as a key factor in explaining peasant revolution. Moore and Skocpol emphasize the importance of peasant solidarity and autonomy. Paige points to the role played by wage-earning peasants in sharecropping and migratory labor systems, while Wolf emphasizes the greater likelihood of middle peasants and those in peripheral areas becoming involved in revolutionary upheaval. Popkin argues that peasants decide whether to support revolutionary challengers or incumbent regimes on the basis of rational assessment of the likely costs and benefits, the levels of trust developed, and prospects for success. Finally, the majority of the theorists stress the importance of outside agents in mobilizing and providing direction to peasant grievances. How do these explanations apply to the Salvadoran experience?

Three factors appear to be primary in explaining how a quiescent and repressed peasantry became one of the strongest peasant movements in Latin America in a period of less than a decade. First, the conditions of life of the majority of peasants deteriorated dramatically and laid the foundations for the rise of a revolutionary peasant movement. Second, the consciousness of many peasants was transformed by outside agents, particularly priests and religious activists but also teachers and students. This transformation of consciousness succeeded because real peasant grievances were addressed (rather than peasants being mobilized behind outsiders' agendas) and peasants built their own organizations and leadership to confront their worsening situation. Third, a viable alternative vision was offered to continued existence under deteriorating political and economic conditions. Catholic clergy and activists played a major role in the transformation of consciousness. Revolutionary organizations also contributed to this change and were instrumental in providing direction and an alternative program behind which to mobilize peasant support.

An economic system in El Salvador that marginalized the majority in the society and precipitated a dramatic decline in conditions of life and future prospects of the peasantry was an essential ingredient of the revolutionary crisis that developed in the late 1970s. Political

exclusion and repression that closed down legal and electoral chan-
nels of political change also fueled the desire to challenge the regime.
But these deteriorating conditions in themselves would not have
threatened the continuation of the existing order had there not been
a profound change in the consciousness of the peasant majority
regarding their conditions and the prospects for change.

Prior to the early 1970s, memories of the events of 1932, harsh
repression at the hands of landowners and the National Guard, and
legislation banning union organizing in the countryside helped keep
the lid on peasant discontent. A perceptive observer, Alastair White,
writing in 1973, noted of the peasantry that

> the immense majority make no connection between the existing
> political régime and their poverty, and . . . the lack of any sign of
> rebellion, protest, or even much opposition voting since 1932 is not,
> as is claimed in some left-wing writings, simply a matter of fear of a
> repetition of the holocaust that occurred then. There is discontent,
> but it is vaguely focused on the rich or on landowners rather than
> sharply focused against the government.[28]

At that very time, however, a process of change was beginning in rural
areas of El Salvador that would be a critical component of the revolutionary crisis that evolved in the following years. Two main catalysts—
activist Catholic clergy and lay people and the recently formed political-military (guerrilla) organizations—were crucial in the transformation of peasant consciousness in the 1970s.

The Catholic Church in Latin America, which had been a partner
in colonial and later elite domination in the region since the Spanish
Conquest, underwent significant changes following the Second
Vatican Council in the early 1960s and the Latin American bishops'
conference in Medellín, Colombia, in 1968. The Latin American
church addressed directly the issue of social justice and argued that it
was its duty to take the part of the poor and most oppressed sectors of
society—the "preferential option for the poor"—and work to change
the conditions that gave rise to extremes of wealth and poverty. In El
Salvador the role of activist clergy was critical to the transformation of
the peasantry in the 1970s. Their role in bringing a new social reading
of Christ's life and the scriptures to a peasantry that was deeply
imbued in religion—albeit of a passive, fatalistic, and magical kind
that had benefited the status quo—had the effect of transforming the
consciousness of a large part of the peasant population in the areas of
their pastoral work.[29] Parish structures, as well as the new roles and
functions created in the pastoral work, helped provide the initial bases
for collective peasant action and support and also provided some
defense against repression from the state and landowners who, initial-

ly at least, had more reservations about attacking the church than they had in targeting independent organizations.[30]

Catholic clergy and lay activists brought to the peasantry another way of viewing religion and its relationship to daily life. They also provided training of lay leaders who could then play organizing and leadership roles in their own communities, so that in a short time much of the country was affected by this transformation. Between 1970 and 1976, Montgomery notes, seven centers were established in El Salvador to train catechists and delegates, and through the 1970s approximately 15,000 leaders were trained.[31] Major areas of the church's pastoral work, carried out by Salvadoran and a number of European priests, included Chalatenango, San Vicente, Morazán, and many poor neighborhoods of San Salvador.

An important initiative in this process of transformation was taken in 1972, when a pilot program for a new pastoral approach was launched in Aguilares, a city of 35,000 located 30 kilometers north of San Salvador in a sugar-growing area. A large mission from September 1972 to June 1973 was organized in the area, where the priests spent two weeks in each of the villages compiling political and economic data and talking about the liberating message of Christ. Thirty-seven centers, or mission zones, were organized. The local communities elected lay "delegates of the word"—fifteen to twenty per community—for a total of about 300. Their duty was to serve the community and to search for "truth, unity, action and organization."[32] The priests maintained contact with the communities, animating them and assessing the effectiveness of the pastoral mission.

The pastoral team brought to the communities a new vision of God, the life of Christ, and the role of Christians that had an extraordinary impact. The message paved the way for the creation of a revolutionary peasant movement that integrated a liberating view of Christianity and the duties of the faithful with a deepening analysis of the structural, class basis of inequality and injustice, and the action that would be required to transform social conditions. A second phase of the mission was held from June 1973 to March 1974. "Preparers" (*preparadores*) were elected as intermediaries between the community, and the larger zone and the basis was laid for a movement that could have an impact well beyond the parish level.

The steps in the transition from a sense of powerlessness and the inevitability of the existing arrangements to involvement in a revolutionary movement may be simplified as follows. Faced with a severe and deteriorating social and economic situation, the world view gained through the socioreligious transformation empowered many peasants to believe that change could happen and that they were the agents of that change. They saw that organization was essential for change to occur, and with the aid of students, intellectuals, and other outside advisers they built the vehicles—the radical peasant organizations—through which they could defend and advance their interests. Peasants' awareness of the systemic nature of their problems was expanded by the experience of fighting for their rights on a day-to-day level, confronting the authorities who had made all peasant organizing illegal, facing the counterrevolutionary peasant group ORDEN that was an organized force in many villages, and attempting to win improvements in wages in the mills and haciendas. Many of those affected grew to understand that if change were to occur it could not just be local, could not just involve the peasantry, and given the determination of the landowners and the authorities not to make concessions, could not be won without a violent struggle. The revolutionary organizations were crucial to the transition of the peasantry from apathy to rebellion in their ability to place the local situation of the peasantry in a larger context, in facilitating contact with other sectors and groups in society, and in providing vehicles through which the peasants could organize to win change.

The organizational form the radical peasant movement took varied in different parts of the country. In the central departments of San Vicente and Usulután, peasants revived an organization, the Christian Federation of Salvadoran Peasants (Federación Cristiana de Campesinos Salvadoreños, or FECCAS) that had existed since the 1960s, as the vehicle for defending and advancing their interests. In Chalatenango, peasants built a wholly new organization, the Union of Rural Workers (Unión de Trabajadores del Campo, or UTC), with strong involvement from the Popular Liberation Forces (Fuerzas Populares de Liberación–Farabundo Martí, or FPL). In the east of the country, the Peoples's Revolutionary Army (Ejército Revolucionario del Pueblo, or ERP) built upon the activities of European priests in San Miguel, La Unión, and Morazán and created peasant leagues that formed the base for the area (particularly Morazán) that became the military rearguard of the ERP during the civil war. The peasant organizations played a central role in the creation of the mass popular organizations that became prominent in the revolutionary crisis of the late 1970s. FECCAS was instrumental in 1974, along with the teachers' union, the National Association of Salvadoran Education Workers (Asociación Nacional de Educadores Salvadoreños, or ANDES), in the formation of the United Popular Action Front (Frente de Acción Popular Unificada, or FAPU), the first of the popular organizations linking different sectors and groups. After an internal struggle in which FECCAS argued for a move to political activity rather than remaining focused purely on economic issues, FECCAS, along with ANDES, left FAPU, and the following year helped form the Popular

Revolutionary Bloc (Bloque Popular Revolucionario, or BPR), which was linked to the FPL and became the largest of the popular organizations.

The main catalysts for the "second conversion"—channeling a large number of peasants, who had been awakened to the reality of their condition and the potential for changing it, into revolutionary activity against the regime—were the political-military organizations that grew up from 1970. Their strategies, especially that of placing a major focus on organizing among peasants and other rural workers, were another essential component of the development of the systemic crisis of the late 1970s.

There has been significant sensitivity, particularly during the war years, to the relationship between the organizing carried out by progressive clergy and lay activists, on one hand, and the work of the guerrilla groups, on the other. A large number of priests, including many Jesuits, were tortured, exiled, or murdered by the security forces or related paramilitary bodies because they were viewed as the masterminds of the revolutionary strategy, the intellectual authors of the alienation of the peasantry from their loyalty to the regime. Others have viewed the priests and lay activists as dupes of the revolutionaries, while the insurgents tended to deny any organic connection between the two forms and moments of organizing.

The reality is more complex. The pastoral religious project in El Salvador and elsewhere in Latin America predated the creation of the Salvadoran political-military groups and had distinct objectives. The theology of liberation with its preferential option for the poor looked to a transformation of peasant consciousness and social organization as steps to a realization of Christ's teachings in the world through an empowerment of the powerless and voiceless in society. The religious workers did not come with models of peasant organization but would support forms of organizing that were appropriate to the conditions faced by the peasantry. The problems in El Salvador were the extremity of the conditions, the refusal of the powerful to allow even reformist change, and the existence of a revolutionary project with very defined long-term objectives, within which the peasantry would play a central role.

Organizing by the revolutionary groups, particularly the FPL, began in many places at the same time or very soon after the pastoral religious missions.[33] Some peasants were brought into organizing work directly by the guerrilla groups or by other actors, such as teachers or students, without first being "awakened" by the social teachings of the Catholic Church. For the majority, however, the first step into peasant organizing came through study, reflection, and action within the church's base communities. The next step often involved joining a radical peasant organization and beginning to work collectively for such demands as better wages, improved working conditions, and access to credit. It was the repression almost invariably resulting from this organizing that made the political-military groups—with their ability to provide self-defense, links to other groups, and a society-wide strategy—an appealing option for many peasants.

The development of the peasant movement beyond that envisaged by many religious workers caused crises on an individual and institutional level. Individual priests had to decide whether to support the choices made by the communities and whether to deepen their own involvement. Some priests joined the revolutionaries, many others kept their distance and maintained the separation between the two forms of organizing while respecting the choices made by the peasants, and yet others, such as Rutilio Grande, were killed before they resolved the dilemma.

The Catholic Archdiocese, under Archbishop Oscar Romero, and the Jesuit Community in El Salvador were accused of responsibility for the wave of peasant activity in the countryside. Leaflets appeared reading "Be a patriot. Kill a priest." Between 1977 and 1980 eleven priests were murdered and many more beaten, tortured, and exiled.[34] As the violence increased, Archbishop Romero called for an end to the repression, supported the right of peasants and others to build popular organizations, criticized the institutional violence of the state as fundamentally responsible for the society's crisis, and accepted, in extreme circumstances, the legitimacy of counterviolence.

Theories of Peasant Revolution

When the issues associated with the theorists of peasant revolution are examined in the light of developments in El Salvador, both strengths and limitations are visible. Wolf argued that middle peasants and those in peripheral areas were most susceptible to the call of revolutionary movements. A study by Cabarrús reaches the opposite conclusion in relation to the middle peasants, who were found to be more likely to be apolitical than to join either a revolutionary or counterrevolutionary peasant movement, and were more likely to join the counterrevolutionary ORDEN (31 percent) than the radical FECCAS (19 percent).[35] On the other hand, it is well established that the base areas of the two largest guerrilla organizations, where the revolutionary movement was most strongly implanted among the peasantry, were in Morazán (ERP) and Chalatenango (FPL) and that these departments were the poorest and most peripheral areas in the country as well as the major sources of migrant labor in the export-crop harvests.[36]

When the broader question of why peasants rebel is examined

according to the moral-economy and political-economy approaches, there are aspects of the Salvadoran experience that tend to reinforce elements of each approach. Though it is difficult to argue that Salvadoran peasants rebelled to restore a moral economy based on reciprocal rights and obligations that had previously existed, it is certainly the case that the expansion of export agriculture and the capitalist market wreaked havoc on the peasant economy, broke down landlord-tenant systems based on reciprocity, and denied access to a minimum subsistence to many. More relevant than a breakdown of the moral economy of the peasant, as Wickham-Crowley points out, may be the physical dislocation of peasants from their lands as a key factor in explaining peasant radicalism.[37] By 1975 an estimated 30 percent of the rural, economically active population had less than two months of work a year, and another 19 percent had between two and six months. Thus, as Vilas points out, almost half the rural population was "profoundly underemployed, and itinerant as well."[38]

There are two areas in which Popkin's approach, based on rational choices made by the peasants, is helpful for understanding the process in El Salvador: what the revolutionaries (and others) have to offer to the peasants, and the role of political entrepreneurs. The study by Cabarrús of peasants in the central region of El Salvador reinforces the view that peasants made choices to side with revolutionaries, or not, based on a rational calculation of the likely costs and benefits and the probability of success. The counterrevolutionary peasant group ORDEN and the radical peasant organization FECCAS competed for the allegiance of the peasants in hundreds of villages, and factors such as the greater ability of ORDEN to provide economic resources, the difficulty of obtaining work if identified with FECCAS, and the ability of each organization to provide some degree of social mobility were important in peasants' decisions to affiliate with one or the other group.

Popkin also stresses the importance of political entrepreneurs who are willing to invest their "own time and resources to coordinate the inputs of others in order to produce collective action or collective goods."[39] This conception of outside agents lending assistance that can facilitate peasant organization is an important theme in Popkin's work and is borne out by the Salvadoran experience. The "consciousness raising" provided by activist clergy in their pastoral work brought about a religious-ideological change in a large section of the peasantry, and church structures, particularly the new roles of "delegates of the word" and "preparers," helped facilitate initial organizing efforts and aided in reaching new people, while church sponsorship provided a degree of protection from state and landowner violence. In the subsequent phase, the structures provided by the revolutionary organizations, including national peasant groups, mass popular organizations, and political-military groups, helped develop the revolutionary challenge to the regime.

El Salvador's experience leads to different conclusions on the relationship of peasant solidarity and autonomy, and the maintenance of peasant institutions to peasant revolution, stressed by Moore and Skocpol. What appears to have been most important in El Salvador was not the maintenance of peasant institutions but rather the development of peasant solidarity and the creation of new institutions inspired first by the catalytic role of Catholic clergy and laypersons and later by the revolutionary organizations.

Strategies of the Revolutionary Organizations

A highly unequal economic system that brought about a deterioration in the conditions of many Salvadorans and a political order that denied meaningful access to those seeking reforms were critical elements in the revolutionary crisis that developed in the country in the late 1970s. But in themselves these conditions would likely have contributed only to changes within the system (as had occurred with coups in 1944, 1948, and 1960) rather than to a revolutionary crisis. Key elements in deepening the regime's crisis and threatening its survival were the strategies adopted by revolutionary groups that formed from 1970. The major strategic choices made by these groups were (1) to embark on a political-military struggle to overthrow the regime, prioritizing armed struggle and rejecting elections and other democratic attempts to secure change; (2) to link guerrilla warfare with broadbased political organizing and to create mass popular organizations to incorporate diverse sectors into the struggle for a new society; and (3) to place a major emphasis on organizing peasants and rural workers as a key to bringing about change in a largely agrarian society.

During the 1970s it was the largely nonviolent strategies of mass political organizing that posed the greatest challenge to the regime and generated extremely violent responses from the state. However, the violence of the regime was met by the strategy of the revolutionaries—linking violent and nonviolent methods of struggle—as well as their effectiveness in gaining control or influence in wide sectors of the opposition movement, so that the conflict in El Salvador moved toward greater polarization and confrontation as the crisis of the regime intensified.

Profile of the Revolutionaries

The five organizations that would in 1980 form the Farabundo Martí National Liberation Front (Frente Farabundo Martí para la

Liberación Nacional, or FMLN) developed into what U.S. analysts called the strongest guerrilla army in Latin American history and engaged the United States in its largest counterinsurgency effort since Vietnam. They were characterized by great similarities in the social origins and composition of their leaders but varied dramatically in their strategies for defeating the incumbent regime.[40]

Party leaders point to two distinct origins of the revolutionary groups that may explain much about differences in vision, objectives, and strategies before, during, and after the civil war. Three of the groups—the PCS, the FPL, and the Central American Revolutionary Workers' Party (Partido Revolucionario de Trabajadores Centroamericanos, or PRTC)—had their origins in more traditional forms of Marxism-Leninism, with roots in the PCS.[41] The leaders of the ERP and the Armed Forces of National Resistance (Fuerzas Armadas de Resistencia Nacional, or FARN) had their origins in the youth movement of the PDC, were influenced mainly by the social teachings of the Catholic Church, and also included some nonaligned Marxists and independents.[42] These differences apply to the leadership of the parties rather than to the base, which was predominantly peasant and influenced in the main by the religious teachings of progressive elements within the Catholic Church.

Whereas the ideological origins of the leaders are distinct, their social origins are much more homogenous. With one or two important exceptions,[43] the activists who came into the top echelons of party leadership by the mid- to late 1970s continued to lead the FMLN groups during the civil war and were largely still the leaders in the mid-1990s. Many of these leaders became active in high school or university, in their teens or early twenties. They were influenced by major developments in the world during a volatile period of history, including the Cuban Revolution and attempts to replicate it in other parts of Latin America, the Vietnam War, Third World liberation movements, and the student movements in Europe and the Americas. They were mainly lower-middle class or middle class in social origin, neither from the most privileged sectors nor from the most marginalized. (There was a small number of leaders of peasant origins.) Most were well educated relative to the majority of Salvadorans, having progressed to the upper levels of secondary or into tertiary education, though many put aside their educational objectives to join the guerrillas. By the mid-1990s the top leaders had been in positions of direction for twenty to twenty-five years and were in their early to mid-forties. The majority were male. Their reasons for becoming involved were largely political: opposition to dictatorship, the lack of genuine democracy, and the oppression meted out to regime opponents, and seeing (as opposed to experiencing themselves) the abject conditions in which the majority of Salvadorans lived.

By contrast, the base that was organized by these parties and their leaders was largely the peasantry in the 1970s and overwhelmingly so in the civil war years. One senior FMLN commander estimated that more than 95 percent of the guerrilla combatants were from the peasantry by the end of the war, as were four out of every five intermediate military commanders.[44] The original reason for becoming politically involved also differed for the base of the movement: Economic conditions—lack of access to land, poor working conditions, low wages—tended to be the initial impulse for many peasants to get involved in the opposition movement.

Another important characteristic of El Salvador's revolutionary movement was the development of some very innovative and effective strategies for challenging the regime, hand in hand with a high level of sectarianism and dogmatism that weakened the effectiveness of that challenge. A related contrast was between the inflexibility that the leaders of the revolutionary parties demonstrated in their competition with each other for hegemony—which led to schisms and even armed actions—while they exhibited extraordinary patience, dedication, and a willingness to learn in their relations with the peasants, workers, and other parts of the poor majority that formed the base of the revolutionary movement. Though the relationships of leaders to base were vertical and hierarchical, the success of the parties, particularly in organizing the peasantry, was linked to the fact that the peasants felt themselves to be struggling for their own interests and not merely mobilized as foot soldiers in another's social project.

Strategies of the Revolutionary Opposition

The first and largest of the guerrilla organizations that developed in the 1970s, the FPL, arose out of divisions within the PCS over the means to achieve change in El Salvador. Following a limited effort to launch an armed struggle in 1961–1963 in the wake of the Cuban Revolution, the PCS hewed to a Moscow-oriented political line that a "bourgeois-democratic" revolution would be needed to create the conditions for socialist transformation. The party believed that it should therefore ally with and support those progressive elements (of the bourgeoisie, in the armed forces, and middle-class parties) that could break the power of the landed oligarchy and take power after a brief armed uprising. In practice, the party focused on organizing in the trade unions, and on electoral strategies that could create the conditions for winning power from the landowning classes.

When the party defended the Soviet occupation of Czechoslovakia in 1968 and supported the war against Honduras the following year, the divisions in the PCS came to the forefront. A minority group, led by the party's secretary-general, Salvador Cayetano Carpio, a long-time organizer and militant, left the party to launch an armed struggle against the regime in 1970.

The FPL oriented itself toward armed struggle but from the start rejected the foquismo that had been so popular yet unsuccessful in Latin America in the 1960s. Influenced by General Giap and the Vietnamese experience, the FPL saw a "people's war" as providing the best strategy for defeating the incumbent regime. Armed struggle would be necessary to overthrow a regime that was unwilling to accept any modification in its mode of domination, but military activities had to be linked with and support the political movement, rather than political organizing having as its fundamental purpose military recruitment. The FPL characterized El Salvador as a dependent capitalist society, lacking an independent bourgeoisie that would confront the landed oligarchy, and saw change coming only after a prolonged political and military struggle under the leadership of a worker-peasant alliance.[45]

In 1972 the FPL developed its "line toward the masses" that led to the formation of small nuclei of cadre working in different social sectors and building support for the group's political-military struggle.[46] These small groups grew rapidly and in 1974 the FPL pushed for the creation of an open mass front uniting different sectors. Fearing that premature creation of the front could lead to the movement's being "beheaded," the FPL held back until 1975. In 1973 the group began to focus on organizing in the countryside. Guerrilla leaders visited communities, getting to know peasant families, learning from them, and beginning a process of recruiting individuals and increasing its influence in the peasant movement that was expanding rapidly at that time. When leaders of the ERP created the mass organization FAPU in 1974, cadre of the FPL participated, but differences of conception of the role of a mass front (and the struggle for hegemony within it) led the FPL to form a second mass organization, the BPR, in mid-1975. The BPR would become the largest of the mass popular organizations, with 80,000 to 100,000 members by 1979. The key sectors within the BPR were peasants organized in FECCAS and the UTC, the teachers of ANDES, and high school and university students. The FPL had more difficulty organizing urban workers, who formed a relatively small proportion of the economically active population, had low rates of unionization (about 20 percent), and were more likely to be organized already, for example, by the PCS.

In 1972 a group of intellectuals, university students moved by the social teachings of the Catholic Church, and some workers formed a second guerrilla organization, the ERP. The group was influenced by foquismo and convinced that change in El Salvador could be achieved rapidly through a strategy emphasizing military activity.[47] From the beginning they linked up with priests who were working in the eastern part of the country, in La Unión, San Miguel, and Morazán. The ERP focused on building a military challenge to the regime. They put less emphasis on developing an independent peasant movement and more upon harnessing the grievances of the peasantry into military action against the regime. The eastern part of the country, particularly Morazán, was viewed as a potential region for building a military rear-guard, due to the Christian values of the peasantry and their small-holding status that allowed them the freedom to engage in political activities to improve their lot.[48] After an initial period of limited military actions, a conflict developed in the organization between proponents of the military-oriented approach and a group led by poet Roque Dalton that argued for a greater orientation to the masses. The conflict deepened, and leaders of the ERP arrested, tried, and executed Dalton, claiming he was a CIA agent. Following Dalton's May 1975 execution, supporters of the opposition line formed a new organization, the FARN.

The strategic orientation of the FARN was toward a concept of "national resistance" built around "an anti-fascist front in which the guerrilla would act as the military vanguard less for insurrection than for halting the rise of the right while the organisation of the masses was improved and a united movement of the left built."[49] Throughout the late 1970s the FARN developed contacts with a movement of young military officers who were becoming increasingly opposed to the repression and intransigence of the Romero government. This strategy placed much hope in the potential for sections of the military to influence and change the overall direction of the armed forces. The FARN's approach was more defensive in nature than the "prolonged popular war" strategy of the FPL or the insurrectional approach of the ERP; it countenanced alliances with progressive sectors of the bourgeoisie and elements in the armed forces that were not acceptable to the other groups. In its popular organizing strategy, however, the FARN had much in common with the FPL. Each played a major role in building a mass front that carried out radical actions against the regime. The FARN was more successful in building a base of support among the urban working class and had major influence in strategic sectors, such as the electricity workers, and through its control of the National Trade Union Federation of Salvadoran Workers (Federación Nacional Sindical de Trabajadores Salvadoreños, or FENASTRAS). More than any other group, the FARN used the tactic of kidnapping foreign and domestic business people and raised a "war fund" of some $40 million in the late 1970s.[50]

The PRTC was the smallest of the groups that made up the FMLN. Its leaders were part of the ERP from 1971 but left two years later in opposition to what they perceived as the party's militarism. In early 1976 the PRTC was formed as part of a Central America–wide revolutionary movement based on the conception that the region was a single socioeconomic unit and hence organizing could not be restricted to individual countries. On joining the FMLN in 1980, the PRTC had to agree to leave aside the regional structures and organize on a national level.

Until 1979 the PCS focused on bringing about change through legal and electoral means, allied with reformist parties to win power through elections, and rejected the strategies of the political-military organizations as ultraleftist and inappropriate to the realities of El Salvador. In late 1979, with the failure of the reformist military coup, the PCS threw in its lot with the guerrilla organizations, built a military arm, and joined the FMLN in 1980.

The question of violence is central to assessing the effectiveness of the strategies of the revolutionary groups in the 1970s. Revolutionary leaders saw their ability to link military and political action (with armed efforts subordinated, in the main, to political objectives) as a key advance over failed efforts in other parts of Latin America and as instrumental in generating the regime's crisis in the late 1970s. In this view, they were the only ones who fully understood the reactionary nature of the top military leaders and their landowning allies, and who realized that the regime would never countenance significant reforms but would respond with violence or fraud to all challenges. The electoral fraud of 1972—which took place before there was any meaningful military threat to the system—and the frequent massacres of unarmed civilians by the military in the 1970s support the view that eschewing an armed challenge would likely have led to defeat of the opposition at great human cost.

On the other side, the launching of an armed struggle, though by no means initiating the violence, helped to build a cycle of confrontation that resulted in what the UN Truth Commission called a "convulsion of violence" costing the lives of 75,000 Salvadorans. The armed movement was effective in preventing a massacre of the opposition and in intensifying the crisis of the regime, yet it also deepened the military confrontation and left little space or willingness (on either side) to search for a peaceful outcome to the conflict.

An important strategic initiative on the part of the guerrilla organizations was the decision to form mass organizations linking different sectors—workers, students, peasants, slum dwellers, etc.—in which the guerrilla cadre would participate. This strategy, developed most effectively by the FPL and the FARN in the 1970s, allowed a bridge between what had been mutually exclusive forms of organizing throughout much of Latin America: legal and illegal activities, violent and largely nonviolent conflict, and clandestine guerrilla warfare and open political organizing. It also provided a fruitful recruiting ground for the guerrilla groups among the most committed members of the popular organizations. By the late 1970s the mass popular organizations were a major threat to the regime while guerrilla actions, though growing in effectiveness, were still only a thorn in the side of the Romero government.

Finally, the decision (particularly by the FPL and the ERP) to focus major efforts on organizing among peasants and rural workers from the early 1970s proved to be a particularly effective strategy: The country was still largely agrarian and its peasantry was becoming politically active in response to deteriorating conditions and the activities of religious workers. The ability from the mid-1970s to bring together peasants and rural workers with urban workers and other sectors was also important in broadening and intensifying the challenge to the regime and preventing the government from utilizing an effective "divide and rule" strategy. The impact of the strategies of the left-wing groups is indicated in a declassified secret U.S. intelligence document from late 1979:

> Since 1977, militant group activities—marches, strikes, and occupations—have caused monumental problems for the governments in power. Frequently confronted with extreme demands, the administrations have alternated between military response—and an inevitably bloody aftermath that accelerated leftist recruitment—or drawn-out negotiations that tended to undercut and weaken their control.[51]

Among the competing strategies of the four political-military groups that were active during the 1970s, some were clearly more effective than others. From a purely strategic standpoint the approaches used by the FPL were shown to be most successful in combining political and military efforts, and helped to build the largest mass organization, the highly combative BPR. The FPL was also very effective in building a peasant movement that would become the backbone of the war effort, though it was fundamentally a political rather than a military movement.

The FARN also built a strong mass popular organization with a particularly powerful presence in the urban labor movement. Its strategy of reaching out to progressive sectors of the military, however, was less successful in practice. The problem was not so much that the mil-

itary would always play a counterrevolutionary role (in fact, young officers were willing in October 1979 to oust the regime of General
Romero and expel their ultraconservative leaders) but that the FARN
appeared to make this effort too central a part of their overall strategy. It placed excessive hope in (elements of) an institution that had little history of subordinating its interests to those of other sectors of
society.

The strength of the strategies of the ERP lay in their focus, sim-
plicity, and audacity: The goal was to overthrow the regime in the
shortest possible time, and every effort was made to strengthen the
organization's capacity to confront and defeat the regime militarily.
This approach helped the ERP build a powerful military organization
during the civil war that was able to turn much of Morazán into guer-
rilla-controlled territory. The limitation of the approach was that political organizing became the means to a military end, rather than the
reverse; the ERP did not develop the same level of political challenge
to the regime in the 1970s as did the FPL and the FARN through their
mass popular organizations.

Although the FPL developed some of the most effective strategies
in the 1970s, the party's certainty that it had the right answers was a
major barrier to a broader united effort prior to the formation of the
FMLN in 1980. Questions of strategy were of great importance in this
period and the major choices would have an impact on the strength of
the challenge to the regime. But dogmatism, sectarianism, and the
struggle for hegemony prevented the revolutionary groups from combining certain strategies effectively. For example, the attempt to reach
out to middle sectors or to progressive members of the armed forces
was compatible with a strategy that prioritized organizing the most
oppressed groups in the society, as long as it was clear which was most
central to the objective. Likewise, the complete rejection of electoral
approaches left the largest of the revolutionary groups without a
meaningful discourse with sectors that had not fully broken with the
system. So in effect, the all-or-nothing nature of the struggle between
the positions of the revolutionary groups allowed little space for a
more nuanced approach, and highly innovative and effective strategies were weakened by a lack of unity.

It was not only the strategies of the guerrilla groups that challenged the regime and helped generate the crisis of the late 1970s.
Though the guerrilla groups appear to have had a more realistic view
of the regime's willingness to accept democratic change than their
reformist competitors (the PDC, the MNR, and the PCS), it is unlikely that revolutionary momentum could have built before all democratic and electoral possibilities had been exhausted. In this respect, the
efforts of the PDC, the PCS, and social democrats were essential to the

development of the crisis of the late 1970s even though they were defeated in their objectives. Likewise, the activities of Catholic activists in the countryside after 1972 were crucial in transforming peasant consciousness even though, in the main, these religious workers did not have a programmatic political vision.

By the second half of the 1970s a revolutionary movement had developed in El Salvador that was unlike any the country had seen before and unusual, if not unique, in Latin American history. It was a broad, radical, and class-based movement of the dispossessed of El Salvador linking peasants, workers, students, teachers, slum dwellers, the unemployed, and other excluded sectors of the society in a struggle for change that incorporated demands that ran from the immediate needs of a given group to the call for the overthrow of the government. The movement operated largely outside the formal political system, was not based on the existing political parties, and did not play a significant role in electoral strategies. The peasantry played a central role in the mass movement, both in terms of numbers and in its focus and demands.

Political-military organizations formed from 1970 played a central role in the opposition movement and had a major responsibility for the formation of the mass popular organizations that united a wide spectrum of grassroots groups after 1974. Although the majority of the participants in the grassroots organizations were not members of political-military groups, the demands of the mass movement reflected the politics and objectives of those groups, and by the late 1970s the popular organizations were calling for revolutionary action to overthrow the government.

The mass movement employed a variety of strategies and tactics to achieve its objectives, such as marches, strikes, workplace sit-ins, land takeovers, and embassy occupations. The tactics became more radical as the crisis of the regime deepened and repression increased. The political-military groups carried out a low-level guerrilla war throughout the 1970s, ambushing military forces, kidnapping businesspeople to gain funds and publicity, and bombing offices of the ruling party or other targets associated with the regime. By the end of the decade, the breadth and radicalism of the legal mass movement posed a greater threat to the Romero regime than did the military capability of the guerrilla groups. The more radicalized members of the mass movement, however, provided a large pool of potential recruits for the guerrilla groups.

The main weakness of the revolutionary movement was that it was divided among organizations, each of which had its own assessment of the nature of the system and the proper strategies for weakening the regime. Each organization had its own political-ideological links with a mass organization and with specific base groups (e.g., trade unions, peasant groups, and student organizations). Divisions between the groups were deep. Military capacity was still weak in relation to the Salvadoran army and security forces, and by the end of the decade, the guerrilla groups did not pose a direct military challenge to the continued existence of the regime. There was a fundamental and seemingly irreconcilable divide between the revolutionary organizations and those parties and groups that believed in reform of the system. The movement faced a powerful and cohesive adversary in the class that had controlled Salvadoran society for over a century, even as the political order descended into crisis. And influence among other sectors, particularly the middle class, was limited, making a broad, multiclass alliance against the regime (as against Somoza in Nicaragua) more difficult.

Strategies of the Regime

Theorists of revolution in recent years have given greater emphasis to the types of regime most susceptible to a revolutionary challenge, but little systematic attention has been paid to the significance of strategic choices made by regimes in confronting opposition movements, or to the relationship between those choices and the development of revolutionary crises and outcomes. Just as the strategies of opposition movements may strengthen revolutionaries and further marginalize the regime, so may appropriate regime choices undercut the support of a rebel movement. In El Salvador in the 1970s three regime strategies appear to have strengthened the opposition while undercutting the regime's base of support: rejecting any meaningful economic reforms, thus removing a possible safety valve for the regime; closing down political avenues of change (by overturning the elections of 1972 and 1977), thus making the revolutionary alternative more viable; and embarking on a campaign of repression as the mode of defeating the opposition, which only galvanized the growing movement for change.

During the 1970s, as the conditions of life deteriorated for peasants and rural workers with little expansion of urban opportunities, El Salvador's military-oligarchic regime faced two distinct but related choices. The first was either to embark on a process of economic reform, particularly agrarian reform, that could ease tensions in the countryside and undercut support for militant opponents, or to reject reforms and fight at all costs to maintain the existing economic order and the privileges of the dominant class. The second choice was either to accept a democratic transformation of the political order by carrying out free and fair elections and accepting their results, or to guarantee elite domination of the system by preventing democratic change. A third strategic choice—to respond to political challenges with flexibility and openness or with repression—emerged, to a large extent, from the first two choices made.

The choices made by the regime and the social class it represented helped create the political crisis of the late 1970s. The rejection of a limited land-reform measure in 1976, following an intense intra-elite struggle, ensured that the land question remained a central point of contention and class struggle and bolstered the argument of revolutionaries that reforms would only follow a revolutionary victory. The regime's rejection of the opposition's apparent electoral victories of 1972 and 1977 helped polarize the political process, marginalized moderate politicians, and strengthened the arguments of radicals on the need for armed struggle to overthrow the regime. An almost inevitable consequence of these choices was for the regime to opt for repression as the means to defeat the growing opposition movement. By 1977, when this strategy reached its high point under the regime of General Romero, the opposition was strong and sufficiently organized to withstand the campaign of repression that was unleashed, and the violence of the regime and its backers tended only to motivate opponents and convince them of the need for revolution to change the society.

Why was El Salvador's landowning class unwilling to accept change when well-timed reforms might have undercut the momentum for revolution? Theorists such as Moore and Paige link the type of intransigence shown by El Salvador's landowning class to economic backwardness or complete reliance on land for income. But in El Salvador the major landowners were economically efficient and had branched out into industry and finance. There appear to have been no structural impediments to reform as a strategy for maintaining power. The roots of intransigence seem to lie more in history and ideology than in economic structures and relations per se.

The oligarchy had obtained its wealth less than a century earlier from a wholesale expropriation of peasant land. The response to this expropriation had been initial rebellion, a major outbreak of peasant revolt in 1932, and the continued practice of the Salvadoran peasantry to squat on land to grow maize and beans, whoever the owner might be. Order had been maintained in the countryside through repression—the National Guard was paid by local landowners on an everyday level—and the massacre following the 1932 uprising was the ultimate example of the price to be paid for revolt. The ideology of the landowning class reflected this reality. El Salvador's elite saw two incompatible systems confronting each other: a modern, progressive system of agriculture underlying the nation's wealth and culture; and a primitive, unproductive system of subsistence food production by illiterate peasants. Any expansion of the latter would have to come at the expense of the former and would threaten the entire system and way of life of the elite. Add to this the specter of international communism backing peasant insubordination, and the basis for landowner recalcitrance becomes clearer. It was not that the landowning class was economically unable to make concessions to the peasantry but that, given its history and ideology, it was unwilling to countenance a different or better way to protect its interests.

Toward a Revolutionary Crisis

The defeat of the agrarian-reform law of 1976 weakened the Molina regime and the military institution, but strengthened the most conservative elements of the landowning class, which were determined to respond with maximum force to the threat posed by the reformist political parties, the popular organizations, and the guerrillas. These conservative sectors, represented in the National Association of Private Enterprise (Asociación Nacional de la Empresa Privada, or ANEP) and the Eastern Farmers Front (Frente de Agricultores de la Región Oriental, or FARO), which had vociferously opposed the agrarian reform, were able to ensure that the military picked for the 1977 elections a successor to Molina who would rule with an iron hand. The candidate was found in the defense minister, General Carlos Humberto Romero, a friend of the landowners who could be trusted to take a hard line against the growing popular opposition.

The February 1977 elections were contested again by the National Opposition Union, or UNO (Unión Nacional Opositora)—made up of the PDC, the MNR, and the UDN—whose 1972 victory was overturned by the military. Once again the elections were marked by fraud—stuffed ballot boxes, intimidation of voters—and General Romero was declared the victor over the UNO candidate, Colonel Ernesto Claramount Rozeville. Supporters of UNO came out to protest the fraud and occupied the main plaza in San Salvador for three days. On 28 February government troops attacked the protesters, killing some 200 people.[52]

Over the next two years the level of confrontation and violence intensified. The tactics of the popular organizations became more militant while the actions of the guerrilla groups grew more frequent and effective. Repression directed against the popular organizations and the Catholic Church increased, and the church under its new archbishop, Monsignor Oscar Arnulfo Romero, became more critical of the regime. In the countryside many villages became microcosms of an incipient civil war as the radical peasant organizations confronted the counterrevolutionary peasant group ORDEN. El Salvador gained public prominence as international commissions came to investigate the human-rights situation, and the Romero regime became more isolated as the new U.S. administration, under President Jimmy Carter, focused on human-rights violations as a core component of its foreign policy. Finally, the Sandinista revolution in Nicaragua in July 1979 moved El Salvador to the center of U.S. foreign-policy concerns.

In March 1977, soon after the election, attacks against the Catholic Church intensified. Father Rutilio Grande, a Jesuit priest who was a major organizer of the pastoral work in peasant communities in the region of Aguilares, was killed there with two peasants. Jesuits were blamed for instigating rebellion in the countryside and the landowners' group FARO accused the Catholic Archdiocese of fomenting the peasant movement. In June an ultraright-wing paramilitary group, the White Warriors' Union (Unión Guerrera Blanca, or UGB), threatened to kill all Jesuits who did not leave the country. By July, more than thirty priests had been imprisoned, tortured, expelled, or killed.[53] The campaign had the effect of moving Archbishop Romero, whose appointment had been supported by the landowners, to take an increasingly critical stand toward the regime and to support the rights of the popular groups to organize to change their conditions.

Repression also increased markedly against the peasant movement. Aguilares was occupied by the military for a month. In early 1978, the National Guard, the Treasury Police, the National Police, and ORDEN launched a joint operation in an area of 1,000 square kilometers in the departments of Cuscutlán and Cabañas in which six people were killed, fourteen wounded, and sixty-eight disappeared. Marches and demonstrations in the cities received similar treatment. Ten people were killed attending an International Workers' Day demonstration on 1 May 1977. Forces attacked a demonstration on the anniversary of the 28 February killing of 200 people, and detained 192 members of the BPR. In November 1977 the Romero regime passed a Law for the Guarantee and Defense of Public Order suspending constitutional guarantees and providing the government with authority to ban strikes, demonstrations, and a variety of other actions against the regime.[54]

In spite of the law suspending constitutional guarantees, a wave of strikes and factory occupations was launched by the mass organizations of BPR, FAPU, and the Popular Leagues–28 February (Ligas Populares–28 de Febrero, or LP-28), which had been formed to commemorate the killings following the 1977 elections and was linked to the ERP. Forty labor strikes were carried out in the period immediately following passage of the law, and factory occupations, often with the owners or managers held hostage, became a new tactic of the movement. Military actions by the guerrilla groups were also stepped up. Dunkerley summarizes the growing challenge:

> By the autumn of 1978 guerrilla raids were occurring at the rate of at least one a week. In the first two weeks of November the FPL killed six policemen, attacked the US Embassy, destroyed the San Miguel plant of the Bayer pharmaceutical company and blew up an electricity plant; the ERP planted at least 40 bombs in San Salvador and destroyed PCN offices in three towns; RN made its presence known with four spectacular kidnappings early in December, capturing Japanese, Dutch and British businessmen, netting an immediate $1 million from Philips alone, and deriving considerable publicity from paid advertisements in 39 papers around the world. The guerrillas were recruiting well and the skill of their militants was shown to be high.[55]

By the summer of 1979 the Salvadoran regime model that had operated since 1948 was in crisis. The root of the crisis lay in the economic structure of the society and the mode of political control perpetuating the economic order. But the factor that precipitated the political crisis of the regime was that popular opposition had risen to the level of open rebellion that could not be controlled by the most severe repression. Baloyra addresses the problem of the popular organizations from the standpoint of the regime:

> The basic problem of the people that these organizations served was a living wage, and their best weapon was to organize. Once they were organized, the exclusionist formula had to be changed or they had to be crushed, à la 1932. The reasons were simple. The Salvadoran oligarchy did not want to readjust its living standards or to share economic power. The Salvadoran military saw any attempt to organize outside the control of the government as inherently dangerous and popular class organizations as simply subversive. Under the model with which it was working, the military could not allow the popular classes to become a political actor.[56]

But if internal conditions created the crisis in El Salvador, an external event, the Sandinista revolution in neighboring Nicaragua, magnified the urgency of resolving the crisis. Despite clear differences in the nature of the two societies and regimes, the parallels between Nicaragua and El Salvador—notably their repressive governments and mass (including armed) opposition movements—were obvious to all. The opposition movement, inspired by the success of the Sandinistas, saw the possibility of a quick victory in El Salvador. The Romero regime believed that an iron hand could defeat the opposition, but sectors within the armed forces, among business people, and a section of the landowning class (encouraged by the United States) believed action had to be taken to avoid a revolution in El Salvador.

The U.S. role in El Salvador had historically been limited, compared to its involvement in other countries in Central America and the Caribbean. However, during the period of the Alliance for Progress, U.S. agencies had played a major part in creating the security structures, particularly the Salvadoran National Security Agency, or ANS-ESAL (Agencia Nacional de Seguridad Salvadoreña), that laid the basis for the "dirty war" from 1979. There had been no direct military interventions. U.S. investments in the country were low and the conduct of El Salvador's rulers in running the country had not been a major concern of U.S. administrations. However, when the Carter administration came into office, with human rights as a central element of its foreign policy, the Molina government refused U.S. military aid that was linked to observance of human rights, and throughout the period of the Romero regime the United States exerted pressure for improvements in human rights. The victory of the Sandinistas in Nicaragua, along with the Soviet invasion of Afghanistan, brought a fundamental reappraisal of U.S. interests in the Central American region and increased the urgency of resolving the crisis in El Salvador.

In the period between the Sandinista victory in Nicaragua in July 1979 and the reformist military coup in El Salvador in October, U.S. policymakers sought to pressure the Romero government to institute reforms that would undercut the revolutionaries and prevent "another Nicaragua." The approach adopted by the United States was to offer to allow military sales, intelligence sharing, and modest military aid to the Romero regime in exchange for improvements in human rights, early legislative elections, and political liberalization.[57] Although Romero made accommodating noises, no real changes were forthcoming and, as late as the first days of October 1979, the Carter administration was still debating whether to continue to pressure Romero to carry out reforms or to play a more active role in supporting coup plots that had been under way for almost a year.[58] The dilemma for the administration was that though it was becoming increasingly obvious that the Romero government was unwilling to make substantial changes, it was not clear that the planned coup would succeed; a failed coup with which the U.S. government was associated could be damaging to U.S. interests. The approach of the Carter administration was to wait and watch, avoiding any public identification with the coup plotters and their objectives, but to move quickly to support it and influence its direction if it succeeded. When it was clear that the 15 October reformist military coup against Romero was successful, the U.S. moved expeditiously to provide it with support.

Summary

The crisis that developed in El Salvador by the late 1970s had a variety of causes, all of which appear to have been necessary for social revolution to arise at that time.[59] Economic and political factors associated with the theorists discussed in Chapter 1—such as the increased squeezing of the peasantry, a narrow and repressive political order, and a growing (including armed) opposition movement—were essential to the creation of the crisis of the late 1970s. But factors more under the control of the competing forces in El Salvador were also indispensable elements in the upheaval of this period. The strategies of revolutionary groups—opting for armed conflict with the regime; combining military actions and mass political organizing; and placing a major emphasis on mobilizing peasant support—and of the regime—rejecting any meaningful political or economic reforms, and opting for violence as the way to defeat the left—contributed equally to the crisis of the late 1970s. Without the choices (appropriate and inappropriate) made by the revolutionaries and the regime, it is highly unlikely that the economic and political factors, serious as they were, would have brought the country to the verge of revolution.

Notes

1. United Nations, Economic Commission for Latin America (ECLA), *Economic Survey of Latin America, 1978* (Santiago, Chile: United Nations, 1980), 235.

2. James Dunkerley, *The Long War: Dictatorship and Revolution in El Salvador* (London: Verso Editions, 1983), 60.

3. United Nations, ECLA, *Economic Survey of Latin America, 1978*, 240.

4. Dunkerley, *The Long War,* 11.

5. Alastair White, *El Salvador,* Nations of the Modern World Series (New York: Praeger Publishers, 1973), 80.

6. Dunkerley, *The Long War,* 12.

7. David Browning, *El Salvador: Landscape and Society* (Oxford: Clarendon Press, 1971), 223–224.

8. Ibid.

9. White, *El Salvador,* 127.

10. In 1975–1976, 351,700 manzanas (1 manzana =1.73 acres) of land were sown to maize, 189,000 to sorghum, 79,800 to beans, and 24,200 to rice, totaling some half of the cultivable land in the country. Carlos Rafael Cabarrús P., *Génesis de una revolución: Análisis del surgimiento y desarrollo de la organización*

campesina en El Salvador (Mexico, D.F.: Ediciones de la Casa Chata, 1983), 84.

11. Ibid., 58.

12. Ibid., 61.

13. Italo López Vallecillos, "Rasgos sociales y tendencias políticas en El Salvador (1969–1979)," *Estudios Centroamericanos* 372/373 (October/November 1979), 867.

14. Dunkerley, *The Long War,* 62.

15. Cabarrús, *Génesis de una revolución,* gives the lower figure, 351; López Vallecillos, "Rasgos sociales y tendencias políticas," gives the higher, 864.

16. See Cabarrús, *Génesis de una revolución,* 59–61: In 1961, 226,896 properties covered 1,581,428 hectares; in 1971, 270,808 properties (19.4 percent more properties) covered 1,451,894 hectares (8.2 percent less land).

17. Dunkerley, *The Long War,* 62, citing Santiago Ruíz, "La modernización agricola en El Salvador," *Estudios Centroamericanos* 330 (April 1976), 154.

18. Carlos M. Vilas, *Between Earthquakes and Volcanoes: Market, State, and the Revolutions in Central America,* translated by Ted Kuster (New York: Monthly Review Press, 1995), 68.

19. White, *El Salvador,* 226.

20. Dunkerley, *The Long War,* 54, citing T. J. Downing, "Agricultural Modernization in El Salvador, Central America," Occasional Paper 32 (Center for Latin American Studies, University of Cambridge, 1978), 7.

21. Dunkerley, *The Long War,* 53, citing Mauricio Domenech et al., "The Basis of Wealth and Reaction in El Salvador" (mimeo, San Salvador, 1976).

22. Dunkerley, *The Long War,* 53.

23. Enrique A. Baloyra, *El Salvador in Transition* (Chapel Hill: University of North Carolina Press, 1982), 25.

24. Ibid., 30.

25. Rafael Guidos Véjar, "La crisis política en El Salvador, 1976–1979," *Estudios Centroamericanos* 369/370 (July/August 1979), 507–526, points to two main groups: an "agrarian front" identifying more narrowly with the interests of agrarian capital, and "industrializing groups" that strove to make their own faction dominant politically and economically. Italo López Vallecillos, "Fuerzas sociales y cambio social en El Salvador," *Estudios Centroamericanos* 369/370 (July/August 1979), 558, identifies an agro-financial faction opposed to any attempt to transform social relations in the countryside, and an agro-industrial-financial faction seeking to impose new patterns of agricultural diversification.

26. Dunkerley, *The Long War,* 54.

27. A. Douglas Kincaid, "Peasants into Rebels: Community and Class in Rural El Salvador," *Comparative Studies in Society and History* 29, 3 (1987), 476; Thomas P. Anderson, *Matanza: El Salvador's Communist Revolt of 1932* (Lincoln: University of Nebraska Press, 1971), 136, gives a figure of 10,000 "rebels" losing their lives in the uprising, with 90 percent killed in the massacre following the uprising.

28. White, *El Salvador,* 208.

29. See Rodolfo Cardenal, *Historia de una esperanza: Vida de Rutilio Grande* (San Salvador: UCA Editores, 1987), 235–241, for a discussion of the "magical consciousness of the peasantry."

30. Cardenal, *Historia de una esperanza,* 297–298, for a discussion of the protection provided by the Catholic Church to the incipient peasant movement, and 458, where the role of parish structures in the development of the movement is outlined.

31. Tommie Sue Montgomery, *Revolution in El Salvador: From Civil Strife to Civil Peace* (Boulder, Colo.: Westview Press, 1995), 87. Chapter 3 provides an excellent discussion of the role of the Catholic Church in the transformation of the peasantry in El Salvador. See also Teresa Whitfield, *Paying the Price: Ignacio Ellacuría and the Murdered Jesuits of El Salvador* (Philadelphia: Temple University Press, 1995); Cabarrús, *Génesis de una revolución;* Cardenal, *Historia de una esperanza;* and Jenny Pearce, *Promised Land: Peasant Rebellion in Chalatenango, El Salvador* (London: Latin America Bureau, 1986) for discussion of the role of the church in the transformation of peasant consciousness in the 1970s in El Salvador.

32. Cabarrús, *Génesis de una revolución,* 142–148.

33. The FPL began sending people out to the countryside to live beside and work with the peasantry from 1973: Gerson Martínez, interview by author, tape recording, San Salvador, 11 July 1995.

34. Whitfield, *Paying the Price,* 119.

35. Cabarrús, *Génesis de una revolución,* 183–184.

36. The importance of migrant workers in building the revolutionary peasant movement in El Salvador is emphasized by Facundo Guardado, a peasant leader who went on to head the BPR and later became an FMLN commander: interview by author, tape recording, San Salvador, 19 February 1993.

37. Wickham-Crowley, *Guerrillas and Revolution in Latin America,* 94.

38. Vilas, *Between Earthquakes and Volcanoes,* 57.

39. Samuel L. Popkin, *The Rational Peasant* (Berkeley: University of California Press, 1979), 259.

40. This section is based on interviews and discussions with about half of the top leadership of the parties that made up the FMLN during the civil war and secondary information about many others.

41. The PRTC, the smallest of the five groups in the FMLN, fits this model least clearly. Its leaders were members of the ERP but broke with the party for political reasons in 1973: Nidia Díaz, interview by author, San Salvador, 14 July 1995. Ideologically, however, their approach was closer to traditional Marxism than to that of the ERP and RN. Roberto Roca, the party's leader, was close to, though not a member of the Communist Youth, according to a leader of the PCS, Miguel Saenz: author interview, tape recording, San Salvador, 11 July 1995.

42. Author interviews with Ana Guadalupe Martínez, Eduardo Sancho, and Juan Ramón Medrano, tape recordings, San Salvador, 12, 13, and 14 July 1995.

43. The major exception to the points made regarding the social origins of the movement's leadership was Salvador Cayetano Carpio, the leader of the FPL, who played a central role in the guerrilla strategies of the 1970s and in the early years of the war. Carpio had a long history of political activity in the leadership of the Communist Party and as a trade-union organizer. His second in command, Mélida Anaya Montes ("Ana María"), was also of a different generation from the majority of the movement's other leaders. The top leaders of the PCS, which did not play a revolutionary role in the 1970s, were also of an older generation.

44. Facundo Guardado, author interview, tape recording, San Salvador, 15 July 1995.

45. See Fuerzas Populares de Liberación, *Revolutionary Strategy in El Salvador* (London: Tricontinental Society, 1980).

46. This section relies on author interviews with FPL leaders Gerson

Martínez, Milton Mendez, Leonel González, and Facundo Guardado, tape recordings, San Salvador, 11, 13, 14, and 15 July 1995.

47. Leaders of the ERP and the FARN, which split from it in 1975, stated that they wanted to create a single guerrilla organization but that FPL leader Carpio refused to work with groups influenced by Christian teachings. Eduardo Sancho (Fermán Cienfuegos) discussed a meeting on 24 December 1969 to plan the launching of armed struggle in El Salvador attended by Sancho and Carpio, among others. Carpio, according to this view, refused to accept a joining of Marxist and Christian influenced groups, thus requiring two organizations: Sancho, author interview, 13 July 1995. However, within a relatively short time, the FPL would be working closely with groups and individuals moved by teachings of the progressive wing of the Catholic Church and in 1975 would send a letter pointing out the necessity for Christians to play a central role in the revolution. See Pearce, *Promised Land*, 128–129.

48. Juan Ramón Medrano, author interview, 14 July 1995.

49. Dunkerley, *The Long War*, 95.

50. Eduardo Sancho, author interview, 13 July 1995.

51. *U.S. Declassified Documents II*, CIA, "Growth and Prospects of Leftist Extremists in El Salvador," interagency intelligence memorandum, January 1980.

52. Dunkerley, *The Long War*, 107.

53. Cabarrús, *Génesis de una revolución*, 285.

54. See Cabarrús, *Génesis de una revolución*, 298–303 for a summary of events in this period.

55. Dunkerley, *The Long War*, 117.

56. Baloyra, *El Salvador in Transition*, 72.

57. *U.S. Declassified Documents II*, Department of State, Part 1, "Ambassador Bowdler's Talking Points for El Salvador," memorandum from Viron P. Vaky to the acting secretary, 21 August 1979.

58. See *U.S. Declassified Documents II*, Department of State, Part 2, "Situation in El Salvador," telegram #264095, from Assistant Secretary Vaky for Ambassador Devine, 9 October 1979: "We must now decide whether we should—or can—involve ourselves more deeply in attempting to shape an outcome compatible with our interests, and if so how and in what direction."

59. In late 1979, U.S. intelligence analysts gave the Salvadoran rebels at least a 50 percent chance of taking power in the following six months. See, for example, *U.S. Declassified Documents II*, National Security Council, "U.S. Policy to El Salvador," memorandum for the president from Zbigniew Brzezinski, 29 January 1980: "The extremists in El Salvador have a better-than-even chance to seize and hold power after the anarchy and violence they will sow," citing CIA conclusions.

3

Preparation for War

The 1979 coup was a defining moment in El Salvador's history. It brought about significant changes in the economic and political order. It was the last opportunity to effect a democratic transition in the country short of civil war. And it "shook out" the sides that went on to fight the civil war, in ways that could not have been predicted prior to October 1979.

Many actors with different and contradictory motives and interests were involved in the coup or in forming or supporting the juntas that arose from it: progressive and conservative military officers, reformist politicians, businesspeople and progressive landowners, the Catholic Church, and the U.S. government. But the underlying purpose of its main organizers was to preempt leftist revolution by breaking the domination of a narrow landed oligarchy and incorporating democratic politicians and parties into a reformed political system alongside forward-looking representatives of the capitalist class. The military would play a central role in guaranteeing this transformation. U.S. intelligence documents available to policymakers in the weeks leading up to the coup defined its orientation clearly:

> A coup [excised words] will take place no later than the weekend of 13–14 October 1979. [Excised words] the governments of Chile, Argentina, Brazil and Panama have already given their approval to the coup and have promised their immediate recognition of the new government which will be formed. [Excised words] the new government will be leftist during its early days, and attempt to destroy the influence of the El Salvadoran oligarchy over the government and the economy. This move will be for the purpose of allowing significant social and institutional changes which would not be possible as long as the oligarchy is allowed to exist in its present form. . . . The military will, however, maintain control at all times to ensure that the government will not become extreme leftist as is expected will be the case in Nicaragua.[1]

CIA cables made clear that the junta would begin by attempting to win the support of leftist elements and then move to the right:

> Initially the coup will be announced as a "people's revolution" and may appear in its first days to be a leftist takeover. The rhetoric to be used in initial press releases and speeches has been carefully prepared to reinforce this impression.[2]

> The political stance of the junta following the takeover will be drastically shifted to the left. A prompt and strong plea will be made to both moderates and leftists (such as the Popular Revolutionary Block, BPR) to join the "revolution." It is believed it would be easier to gain the support of the left from the start, then gradually move to the right than to risk an open confrontation with the "popular groups." Significant social reforms and political accommodations will be made from the start to gain popular support.[3]

The coup was carried out by reformist army officers led by Colonel Adolfo Majano, and supported by a conservative group of officers led by Colonels Jaime Abdul Gutiérrez and José Guillermo García, with links to the U.S. Embassy. Plans for the coup originated among the more progressive younger officers, but Gutiérrez and other senior officers got wind of the plot and managed to include themselves in the planning.[4] The United States pressured the reformist wing to include Gutiérrez, in place of a progressive officer, on the first governing junta along with Majano. García became defense minister.[5] Three civilians, Guillermo Ungo of the social-democratic MNR, Román Mayorga, rector of the Jesuit-run Central American University (Universidad Centroamericana "José Simeón Cañas," or UCA), and Mario Andino, a businessman, made up the remainder of the five-person junta. The government consisted of members or supporters of reformist political parties, progressive capitalists, army officers, and people close to the UCA. The mass organizations were not included in the government or junta, and they continued to press their demands (particularly regarding the repression and the freeing of political prisoners) to test the bona fides of the junta. Reactions from the guerrilla groups varied, with the ERP calling for insurrection, the FPL viewing the coup as merely an attempt to improve the system of domination and calling for stepped-up pressure, and the FARN taking a more optimistic view of the potential for change. However, as the repression increased and the first junta collapsed, the revolutionary groups moved closer to unity and joint action to overthrow the government.

The junta passed decrees banning ORDEN and closing the military-intelligence organization ANSESAL, and prevented land transfers in preparation for agrarian reform. But at the same time, state repression increased dramatically, with more people killed in the two weeks following the coup than in the rest of the entire year.[6]

Assessment of the Strength
of Major Actors Following the Coup

The reformist coup was intended to break the power of the landed *oligarchy* through removal of right-wing military officers most identified with the economic elite. The coup would also institute economic reforms, particularly land reform, that would take from the oligarchy control of much of the land, the financial system, and the marketing of export crops. Phase 1 of the land reform was to expropriate properties over 1,250 acres and would affect 15 percent of El Salvador's farmland. The beneficiaries would be former employees and *colonos* who would form cooperatives to farm the land. Phase 2, the heart of the reform, was to expropriate properties between 375 and 1,250 acres and would cover 1,700 to 1,800 properties, 23 percent of the country's farm land. Most significantly, Phase 2 would affect over 60 percent of coffee production. Phase 3, the "land-to-the-tiller" program, was to convert renters of plots under 18 acres into owners, subject to payments for the land. But though the economic reforms weakened the traditional landowning class, its economic power was not broken, because the land-reform measures were only partially implemented and political and military power was retained through relations with conservative active-duty and former military officers. Immediately following the coup, landowners threatened with expropriation began plotting with conservative military officers and right-wing civilians to restore the economic and political dominance of the traditional elite.

The Salvadoran *military* was weakened significantly by the coup. Its traditional symbiotic relationship with the landowning class was fractured and it was divided into two factions. A progressive group identified with Colonel Majano sought to deepen the social and economic reforms and modernize the country's economic and political systems. A conservative group associated with Defense Minister García focused on repressive actions to defeat the left while publicly supporting the reforms to maintain U.S. support. With the prospect of civil war looming against a growing Marxist-led insurgency, U.S. analysts in late 1979 took a pessimistic view of the future of the armed forces: "We have by now been able to bring in some visitors to assess intelligence and [the] military situation here. In both cases, visitors have been appalled at inadequacies of human, organizational, and other resources which they have unearthed."[7] And according to a secret 1980 U.S. military intelligence assessment:

> The Salvadoran Armed Forces will be sorely pressed to contain a sustained, large-scale insurgency campaign against the threat now emerging, particularly one that receives strong foreign support.

Under such conditions, the military could probably hold out for no
more than six weeks without outside assistance.[8]

Military aid was viewed by U.S. policymakers as crucial to the survival
of the government and the prevention of another perceived defeat in
the geopolitical struggle against communism.

The *traditional political parties* had been weakened by their inability to bring about change through electoral means and had lost much
of their membership to the popular organizations and allied guerrilla
groups. A leader of the PDC in discussions with General Romero in
mid-1979 agreed that

> traditional and legally recognized political parties are largely inoper-
> able . . . and have lost their popular following to more radical groups.
> . . . BPR and other so-called popular front groups have moved into
> the vacuum and garnered increasing public support and de facto
> political power as the only organizations capable of assuming a dis-
> senting political role vis-à-vis the government.[9]

The incoming U.S. ambassador in March 1980 saw the PDC as being
"out of touch with the people for many years and . . . lack[ing] the
power to end officially sponsored, encouraged or tolerated violence."[10] Yet along with the more conservative elements in the
Salvadoran military, the PDC would be the primary vehicle of the
United States to defeat the left through the implementation of a
reform strategy.

Other *democratic political parties,* notably the social-democratic
MNR and the PCS-linked UDN, sought to achieve change through
reform during the first junta following the coup. But they threw in
their lot with the guerrilla groups in early 1980 on concluding that the
reform strategy was incapable of resolving the country's crisis and that
real power remained in the hands of conservative military officers.

By late 1979 the U.S. Embassy and Southern Command concluded that "without U.S. military advice and materiel the present government will fall."[11] The guerrilla groups were seen as having the momentum in the period following the Sandinista victory in Nicaragua:

> The radical, revolutionary, extremist left is growing in size, boundless
> in its confidence and enthusiasm, and has multiplied its effectiveness
> through control of the "popular organizations" which have been
> demonstrating their capabilities by occupying farms, embassies, pub-
> lic buildings, factories, etc.[12]

The guerrillas were estimated to have collected about $53 million
through kidnappings and, following arms purchases, to have as much
as $20 million still available in January 1980. The U.S. Embassy viewed

the level and quality of guerrilla training to be equal to that of Nicaragua's core guerrillas in late 1978 and the number of guerrillas to be about equal to Nicaragua in spring 1979.[13] The CIA concluded in early 1980 that "if external support for the insurgents is half of what it was in Nicaragua, the extremists in El Salvador have a better-than-even chance to seize and hold power after the anarchy and violence they will sow."[14]

The picture looked very different from the guerrilla side. At the time of the coup in October 1979 there were fundamental strategic differences among the major guerrilla groups and deep divisions between these groups and the reformist parties and their allies. Although the largely unarmed mass movement was extremely combative, and a popular uprising of the kind that had been seen in Nicaragua was not beyond the bounds of possibility, the military readiness of the guerrillas to engage in large-scale conflict with the armed forces was extremely limited. During late 1979 and 1980 thousands of members of popular organizations were ready and willing to take up arms but the number of weapons available was minuscule.[15] It was not until very late in 1980, and more strongly following the FMLN's January 1981 offensive, that large quantities of arms began to flow into the country, mainly from the Soviet bloc through Cuba and Nicaragua.[16]

Strategies of the Major Actors

The reformist coup of October 1979 forced from political power the representatives of El Salvador's landowning elite and began the process of breaking the economic dominance of the traditional oligarchy. A group of major landowners residing in Miami and Guatemala—in alliance with right-wing military officers and civilian allies, and under the leadership of cashiered Major Roberto d'Aubuisson—adopted the strategy of launching a "dirty war" against all those suspected of supporting the left and moving to regain power by attempting military coups against the civilian-military juntas.[17] The structures with which to wage a dirty war had been put in place in the 1960s and 1970s with the civilian intelligence networks and vigilante organizations that were part of the rural paramilitary group ORDEN and the national intelligence agency ANSESAL. Both these groups were suppressed following the coup, but d'Aubuisson, a high official in ANSESAL, with the support of conservative members of the high command, took the intelligence files and used them as a basis for identifying death-squad targets.

Right-wing death squads were organized (or already existed) in all of the security forces—the National Guard, the Treasury Police, and the National Police—as well as in the intelligence sections of army units. Civilian squads were formed as well, the most significant being organized by d'Aubuisson's Broad National Front (Frente Amplio Nacional, or FAN) and its successor, the Nationalist Republican Alliance Party (Alianza Republicana Nacionalista, or ARENA). Support for the dirty-war strategy came from anticommunist groups and military establishments in Argentina, Venezuela, anti-Castro Cubans, and "six enormously wealthy former landowners who lost estates in Phase 1 of the agrarian reform" and who had assets in the range of $200–500 million.[18] But what was most crucial to their effectiveness was the collusion and active support of military officers at the highest levels of the Salvadoran armed forces. A declassified secret CIA document highlights the role of the minister and the vice-minister of defense in supporting death-squad operations:

> "García and Carranza gave him [d'Aubuisson] their most suitable men in each part of the country for his squads," the Salvadoran said. "The goal was to make it seem that the revolutionary junta was incapable of governing, to create chaos so they could push Majano out." The former military official said he had direct knowledge of the participation of Mr. d'Aubuisson, General García and Colonel Carranza in the process of selecting death squad victims.[19]

In mid-1980 the U.S. ambassador acknowledged the connection between the far right and the military high command and the consequent obstacles to U.S. policy: "The reality is that the principal threat to the stability of this government comes from the officers of the high command who are secretly in the right's corner."[20]

The first junta formed following the reformist coup was unable to stabilize the situation in the country. The members of the junta and government associated with the UCA and social-democratic parties, as well as progressive military officers, sought to institute reforms and to end the violence against the popular organizations. Conservative military officers and their civilian allies, however, were determined to defeat the left and were prepared to use whatever levels of violence were necessary. The mass organizations demanded an end to the repression and the release of political prisoners who had been captured by the previous regime. The junta was neither able to end the violence nor to release the political prisoners. An October 1979 cable from the U.S. Embassy highlighted the problem:

> Gutiérrez and Ungo then outlined difficulty Junta is encountering in coping with continuing violence and nearly insoluble problem of disappeared persons. Regarding latter, Junta has searched jails and now

verified that alleged 300 political prisoners no longer exist, but it does not know how to reveal and admit this fact publicly without provoking public outcry.[21]

As violence against the mass organizations increased, two civilian members of the junta, nineteen cabinet members, and other government officials resigned in early January 1980, claiming that real power did not lie with the junta and government but rather with the armed forces, which had moved to the right in the months since the coup.[22]

Following the resignation of the junta and government members, the PDC entered into a pact with the leaders of the armed forces and took positions in the second junta. A group of leading members left the PDC in protest of the party's continued presence in the government. Led by Rubén Zamora, they formed a new party, the Popular Social Christian Movement (Movimiento Popular Social Cristiano, or MPSC), which later joined the Democratic Revolutionary Front (Frente Democrático Revolucionario, or FDR).

From January 1980 until elections were held for a constituent assembly two years later, El Salvador was governed by a civilian-military junta that was held together by mutual need and U.S. pressure and persuasion. A declassified secret U.S. Embassy cable from early 1980 assessed the situation:

> The PDC-military coalition is still a highly tenuous one driven by a sense of mutual need but with important differences of orientation and method still to be resolved: the strains in this marriage of convenience are aggravated by the strong pull of the two extremes as they maneuver to strengthen their position. . . . The PDC, recognizing that it no longer has the broad popular base it once enjoyed, is trying to appeal to the mass of underprivileged by advocating reform policies, stiff-arming the private sector, and seeking some drastic changes in the leadership of the military who are regarded as a liability in trying to broaden its base.[23]

At the same time, the conservative military members of the junta viewed the PDC as adding little to the government but were constrained in their ability to force out the PDC by the U.S. belief that the party was crucial to the defeat of the left and a resolution of the crisis.

From the time of the October 1979 coup to the end of 1980 a struggle went on between the liberal and conservative members of the armed forces. Almost from the beginning the conservative elements took the initiative. The escalating violence forced liberal junta and government members out and left the progressive military members isolated from their erstwhile civilian allies who moved to join with the guerrillas. In May 1980 soldiers loyal to Colonel Majano arrested Major d'Aubuisson and his associates as they were planning a coup.

Documents in d'Aubuisson's possession linked him to the murder of Archbishop Romero. An internal struggle within the armed forces over d'Aubuisson's fate ensued, with progressive officers wanting him shot or imprisoned and conservatives calling for his release. D'Aubuisson was released and Majano, while remaining in the junta, was demoted from his position as joint head of the armed forces. By the end of 1980 Majano was forced off the junta and his military supporters were relieved of key responsibilities.

The strategy of the conservative military leaders during 1980 was to wage an uncompromising campaign of violence to defeat the left, in alliance with d'Aubuisson and the far right. At the same time, these officers presented themselves as supporters of the U.S.-backed reforms because U.S. military aid was seen as crucial both to defeating the left and to maintaining the integrity and ensuring the survival of the military institution. U.S. officials were aware of this double role but appeared to believe that with sufficient aid the conservative military officers could be wooed away from their dirty-war tactics.

For the Carter administration the fundamental objective in El Salvador following the success of the Sandinistas in Nicaragua was to prevent a leftist victory. There were differences of strategy within and between agencies in the U.S. government. Military and intelligence agencies were more willing to support General Romero against the left prior to the coup and to countenance a right-wing military regime after the coup. Ambassador Robert White, who took up his post in El Salvador in March 1980, was more inclined to view the far right as the major enemy of democracy and stability in El Salvador. In practice, however, preventing a leftist victory remained the major priority during the Carter administration's last year in office. The key to achieving this objective was the provision of sufficient U.S. military aid and training to turn the Salvadoran military into a viable fighting force. From January 1980 this involved convincing the PDC (who were fearful of being attacked as "tools of imperialism") that they should accept U.S. military aid. Military aid and training were used as an inducement to Salvadoran military leaders to clean up the way they were conducting the war against the left and end egregious human-rights violations. Declassified U.S. documents illustrate these priorities.

U.S. ambassador Frank J. Devine laid out his position on military aid to the junta in two January 1980 cables to the State Department:

> My own feeling is that this [military aid] may be crucial to survival of JRG [Revolutionary Governing Junta] and that we should find ways and means of making this as palatable and politically feasible as possible for JRG to accept.[24]

How to overcome PDC hangup on USG [U.S. Government] military assistance. . . . PDC members of the Junta . . . fear that presence of MTT's [U.S. mobile training teams] would give left strong base for arguing that PDC had sold out to imperialists. . . . I doubt that we can overcome PDC resistance . . . without some multilateral cover.[25]

Regarding inducements to the armed forces to improve their conduct, Ambassador Robert White reported on his discussions with Defense Minister García:

I conceded [to Junta member Colonel Gutiérrez] I had told Col. García that if "land to the tiller" received the backing of the high command I could see my way clear to press for immediate delivery of the helicopters.[26]

A declassified State Department document, originally classified as secret/sensitive, confirms the importance at the highest levels of the Carter administration of military aid as an inducement to the Salvadoran armed forces to improve human rights:

A memorandum approved by the President asked Ambassador White to try to use helicopters and training teams as inducements to the El Salvador military to bring under control elements of their own forces who are participating in indiscriminate violence and excessive use of force.[27]

Ambassador White reported on discussions with Salvadoran civilian and military leaders regarding the deal:

Comment: while we did everything we could to soften the presentation, there was no way to disguise that the deal consisted of helicopters in exchange for a measurably improved performance in determined areas over a fixed time span.[28]

The other core element of U.S. policy in El Salvador following the coup of October 1979 was to break the power of the landed oligarchy and carry out social and economic reforms that would take away the left's banners and win support for a "centrist" and "reformist" government. Thus, in March 1980, with strong pressure and support from the United States, the junta announced a three-phase agrarian reform and the nationalization of banking and credit institutions, following the earlier nationalization of the domestic and export trade of coffee. These reforms were accompanied by a state of siege suspending constitutional guarantees.[29]

The strategy of the left-wing organizations in the fifteen months following the reformist coup was relatively straightforward: to create the conditions for a showdown with the junta and the Salvadoran military that would lead to the seizure of power by the left. In the months after the coup the primary emphasis was on political organizing leading to a popular insurrection. But as the process became more prolonged, with greater U.S. involvement and continued military and death-squad repression against the grassroots organizations, the guerrilla groups accelerated the process of military training and obtaining the arms necessary to defeat the Salvadoran military in a political-military offensive. Throughout this period, unification of the political-military groups, the popular organizations, and the political parties that had participated in the first junta became a priority.

The process of unification of the left began publicly with the creation of a broad front of all the mass organizations, the Revolutionary Coordination of the Masses (Coordinadora Revolucionaria de Masas, or CRM), in January 1980. This was followed by the unification in the FDR of the mass organizations and the parties and groups that had taken part in the first junta, excluding the PDC, behind a platform for a democratic revolutionary government.[30] At the same time, the guerrilla organizations were being unified and a Unified Revolutionary Directorate (Dirección Revolucionaria Unificada, or DRU) was formed in May 1980 by the FPL, the ERP, the FARN, and the PCS.[31] In October these organizations and the PRTC created the FMLN.

In June 1980 the CRM organized a general strike that was reported to be 80 percent effective in shutting down factories, construction, transport, schools and universities, the commercial and banking sector, and public employment.[32] A second general strike called for three days in August was less successful, with 40 percent of businesses open and traffic functioning. Divisions opened up within the revolutionary organizations over processes of decisionmaking in the DRU and on whether to form a single party. The FARN, which wanted to form a single workers' party, left the DRU, rejoining again in October.[33]

By the second half of 1980 the stage was set for civil war. The conservatives in the military moved progressive officers out of command positions in September and Majano was forced from the junta in December. José Napoleón Duarte was named president, with Gutiérrez as commander-in-chief of the armed forces. The guerrilla front shifted its focus to the countryside and moved many of its militants out of the mass organizations into military roles in preparation for an offensive to overthrow the regime. During the second half of 1980 intensive efforts were undertaken to provide military training to cadre and to assemble the materiel required to launch an offensive that, accompanied by a popular insurrection, could overthrow the government.

Assessment of Competing Strategies

In the period between the reformist coup of October 1979 and the FMLN's January 1981 offensive, the major protagonists attempted to resolve the country's political crisis in their own favor. The successes and limitations of their strategies defined both the composition of the forces that would fight the eleven-year civil war and the overall character of that conflict.

The right wing associated with the old order sought military support for coup attempts to restore the prior economic and political arrangements, and conspired with conservative military officers to carry out a dirty war against the left. During 1980 an estimated 15,000 people were killed, two-thirds at the hands of the army and security forces.[34]

Conservative military officers tried to oust progressives from key positions and conducted a campaign of terror to defeat the left while maintaining U.S. aid by supporting the economic reforms.

The U.S. government sought to reframe Salvadoran politics around a civilian-military alliance that could carry out reforms to break the power of the oligarchy while providing sufficient arms and training to the Salvadoran military to defeat the armed left, and ensuring that violations of human rights were limited to guarantee public and congressional support for the policy.

The left worked to overthrow the civilian-military government through a political-military strategy that focused on winning international support, arming and training their military forces, and launching an offensive that, accompanied by an insurrection and a general strike, could bring to power a "democratic-revolutionary government."

The Success of the Strategies

Intensive efforts by U.S. officials helped thwart at least three right-wing coup attempts during 1980.[35] Conservative military officers appeared to understand the danger of a withdrawal of U.S. arms and other support if a coup succeeded, and therefore resisted right-wing calls for support. The effectiveness of the death-squad strategy, however, is more complex. Guerrilla leaders have tended to minimize the importance that the right-wing campaign of violence against suspected leftists and sympathizers had on their efforts to win power in El Salvador. However, the campaign of terror, particularly in the capital, appears to have instilled fear into the population and contributed to a move from a near-insurrection in early 1980 (at the time of the formation of the broad front of mass organizations, the CRM, and the 22 January march) to much stronger reservations about demonstrating active opposition to the government by the time of the January 1981 FMLN offensive. Whereas much of the killing was relatively indiscriminate— directed against people who fit the broad profile of leftist sympathizer or those only peripherally involved in the opposition movement— right-wing intelligence also scored some successes. Two FMLN leaders acknowledged to the U.S. ambassador soon after the end of the war that serious losses had been suffered to death-squad attacks:

> [FMLN commander and ERP leader, Joaquín Villalobos said] the FMLN lost most of its urban network to death squad counter-terror-ism in the 1981–1983 period. According to [Commander Ana Guadalupe] Martínez, in a 30-day period in 1982, the FMLN lost over 100 urban commandos to death squads.[36]

Overall, however, the dirty-war strategy failed in its objective of defeat-ing the insurgents. The FMLN was able to make accommodations and maintain its viability as a military and political force. The massive use of terror to defeat the left also had huge political costs that were never fully overcome: It was the image and scale of death-squad killings, par-ticularly from 1980 to 1982, that imprinted El Salvador on the inter-national consciousness and made human-rights violations a key issue in the political and propaganda war over El Salvador.

The strategies of conservative military officers in this period were effective. Through a campaign of violence against any public opposi-tion, they were able to force reformist politicians to leave the first junta and government. This left progressive military officers more iso-lated, and a campaign to marginalize reformers in the military was suc-cessful in weakening, then forcing out, Colonel Majano and isolating his supporters. Conservative military leaders were able to maintain U.S. support by accepting the need for land reform and other eco-nomic reforms, and by making periodic promises to improve their per-formance in the area of human rights. Thus, by the end of 1980, con-servative officers were in a stronger position than a year earlier, with progressives weakened and levels of U.S. aid growing. The survival of the military institution looked more assured, in spite of military involvement or collusion in the killings of Archbishop Romero in March, six FDR leaders in October, and four U.S. churchwomen in December 1980, as well as large-scale massacres of civilians in the countryside.

The area in which the conservative military strategy was least suc-cessful was in the attempt to defeat the armed left. Although death-squad terror helped to quell popular organizing in the cities, the guer-rilla groups were able to expand their hold over territory and population in the rural areas, where an incipient civil war raged through much of 1980, and were able to lay the basis for a major offensive and a prolonged war. The dirty-war strategy, moreover, had major political costs, internationally and particularly in the United States, that would in the years ahead place considerable constraints on the ways in which the U.S. government and its Salvadoran allies could conduct the war.

U.S. strategy in El Salvador in this critical period had several major flaws, some of which would be carried through to the end of the war. The Carter administration, responding to international events and concerned with the geopolitical struggle against the Soviet Union and its allies, defined El Salvador as a crucial place to prevent a revolutionary victory. In the months following the July 1979 Sandinista victory in Nicaragua, U.S. policymakers vacillated over the best ways to prevent revolution in El Salvador: how much to support the Romero government in exchange for reforms, and whether to aid moderates planning a coup. Once the coup had succeeded, however, the U.S. government positioned itself as a major player in Salvadoran politics. But because it was intervening in a process that was already well advanced, the United States was constrained in what it could accomplish and in the forces at its disposal. Some of the problems with U.S. strategy were as follows.

1. In defining the left as the major danger in El Salvador, the Carter administration underemphasized the danger of the right wing and did little to stop the massive violations of human rights during 1980. Although the role of the military in such killings as those of the FDR leaders and the four U.S. churchwomen was well known, the U.S. response was little more than symbolic. Cutting off military aid could weaken the Salvadoran armed forces and lead to what the United States strove to prevent: a leftist victory.

2. In allying itself with the conservative Salvadoran military (and apparently doing little to support progressive military officers), the United States essentially became their prisoners. As Schwarz has argued, having defined the defeat of the left as a critical national-security interest, U.S. administrations had little leverage over the Salvadoran armed forces.[37] During 1980 the Carter administration portrayed the government as centrist and reformist, the military as a transformed institution, and human-rights violations as being carried out by unknown or renegade elements. But the U.S. government's own documents from that period show that the Salvadoran High Command was in league with the ultraright, major human-rights violations were being carried out under the command of military leaders, and junta president Duarte was covering up for the military's violations of human rights to increase his own influence with them.[38]

3. At the behest of the United States and with significant U.S.

advice and support, the Salvadoran junta carried out a major land reform in March 1980, the goal of which was to break the power of the traditional oligarchy and in the process to win the support of large sections of the peasantry from the insurgents. The dilemma of the land-reform strategy for the United States was that for it to succeed in weakening the left it would need to be profound and far reaching, providing scores of thousands of landless peasant families with land and the technical assistance to make their crops viable. However, whereas the United States wanted to break the power of the traditional oligarchy, it also wished to ensure that the economic elite remained part of the system and joined in efforts to defeat the left, rather than conspiring to overthrow the government. The Carter administration chose to accept a more limited land reform in which Phase 2, which would have affected the majority of land used for export crops, was postponed to the distant future. Ironically, this had the effect of weakening the land reform and its prospect of undercutting the insurgents while the economic elite remained implacably opposed to the junta and the PDC and their policies.

4. The Carter administration appears to have made very little effort to incorporate the popular organizations into a solution to the crisis in El Salvador. Although it is understandable that the armed left was viewed as beyond the pale, the lack of any serious attempt to incorporate the base of the mass organizations (which in early 1980 appeared to represent a majority of Salvadorans) into a solution to the country's crisis meant that a successful outcome for the United States would be a center-right one. This would increase the prospects of war if the left were not defeated in short order.

The strategies of the guerrilla organizations to resolve the crisis in their favor—arming, training, building domestic and international support—were relatively effective in building the strength of the insurgents to challenge the regime, but these groups were hampered by problems of unity and lack of arms at the time that a confrontation with the regime would have generated most popular support. In early 1980, U.S. intelligence agencies viewed the guerrillas' prospects of victory as about equal to those of the junta.[39] During the first half of the year momentum and popular support appear to have been in the guerrillas' favor. Yet with U.S. support the junta held on and, though still weak, was in a stronger position at the end of 1980 than at the beginning of the year.

The major factor that prevented the left from taking power in early 1980 appears to have been timing: The revolutionary movement was unprepared to take advantage of the opportunity offered. The period following the fall of the first junta was the time of the regime's

greatest weakness. On one side, the military and the PDC were isolated and even had difficulty in finding members to fill government positions. On the other side, the mass organizations had united by early
January, and the level of popular enthusiasm for change reached its
greatest expression in the march of 22 January 1980.

But the unification process of the guerrilla organizations was in its
early stages. There were still major hurdles to overcome in defining
the nature of the unity among these groups and the modalities of taking power. The process advanced rapidly in the following months but
it was difficult to maintain the level of enthusiasm and commitment of
the organized people under conditions of increasing repression, and
the guerrilla organizations were not ready militarily to take on the
regime. These groups had been engaged in small-scale conflict with
the forces of the regime, but a political-military offensive (e.g., an
insurrectional general strike accompanied by a military offensive)
would require more weapons and logistical support, training, and military cadre than the guerrilla organizations possessed in early 1980.
Through the rest of the year these conditions were put in place, but
meanwhile conditions for a popular uprising had changed. One rebel
leader described the problem:

> We had a race to catch up. That was a difficult time. . . . We didn't
> have arms. And we had setbacks in the unity process. There was a
> great popular surge. If we had been able to rise on that wave, things
> would have been much more successful. But we weren't ready. And
> we were ready when the wave had already passed.[40]

The second factor was the effect of the coup of October 1979.
Although it unified the opposition, following the fall of the first junta,
it also resulted in a new actor, the United States, coming into the center of the Salvadoran process and helping to consolidate the center-
right and right-wing forces behind a project that responded primarily
to U.S. geopolitical interests. The entry of the United States into the
process helped bring together two political forces, the PDC and conservatives in the military, that had been enemies throughout the previous decade, behind a project to weaken the oligarchy and defeat the
left. The U.S. Embassy also played an important role in holding off
coups from the far right that would have further polarized the situation and weakened the counterrevolutionary side. The U.S. role was
an important factor, though not the decisive one, in preventing a successful revolutionary outcome in early 1980.

The third important factor in preventing a leftist overthrow of the
government was the determination of the alliance of the ultraright,
led by d'Aubuisson, and the conservative military leaders who dominated the junta, led by Colonel García, to unleash a campaign of

extreme violence to defeat the left. In 1980 an estimated 15,000 people were killed, the vast majority by the military and security forces or
by death squads linked to those bodies, on suspicion of supporting the
left. This wave of repression did not defeat the revolutionary movement, but military attacks on demonstrations and strikes, a state of
siege banning political activity, and death-squad terror did succeed in
limiting the forms of mass action that the left could organize. The revolutionary movement was forced to shift its emphasis to building its
military capability, and shift the locus of the conflict from the cities to
the countryside.

A final factor that impeded a revolutionary outcome in 1980 was
the high level of cohesion maintained by the dominant class. As a
result of the coup of 1979 the military lost its most right-wing elements, while a progressive faction, for a time, was the main protagonist within the armed forces. But the conservative group that
remained in the military soon regained hegemony and was able to
exclude the more liberal sector within a period of a year. The conservative landowners were displaced from their central economic position following the coup, but through their connections with former
and active-duty military officers they were able to regroup to press for
a rollback of the reforms resulting from the 1979 coup. The resilience
and consolidation of the dominant class contrasted with the brittle-
ness of the Batista regime in Cuba and Somoza's in Nicaragua, and
provided a greater obstacle to the opposition movement's ability to
turn a revolutionary crisis into a successful revolution.

The revolution missed its most opportune moment and was held
at bay, but it was not defeated. Rather, the form of conflict changed
from a classic revolution—a short, sharp struggle for the seizure of
power—to a revolutionary civil war in which two conflicting armies
and political-military projects contested over a prolonged period for
control of the state.

The Cycle of Violence and Confrontation

As 1980 drew to a close, the space for negotiation and compromise
appeared nonexistent and a full-scale war imminent. The country's
military leaders and their elite landowning allies had rejected any
meaningful changes through peaceful, democratic methods in the distribution of wealth and income and in access to political power. This
intransigence helped ensure that when movements for change developed and were repressed, the option of counterviolence appeared to
many Salvadorans as the only, or at least the most viable, method of
bringing about needed reforms. In the 1970s the response of violence
and fraud to all challenges—electoral, economic and social, or armed

guerrilla—failed to quell the movement for change and even empowered it and strengthened the revolutionary element within it. By the end of the 1970s, popular opposition threatened the continued existence of the country's political and economic order and brought about two crucial escalations in the cycle of violence and confrontation.

Right-wing military leaders and civilian allies made the decision to undertake a massive campaign of violence to eradicate the left. The U.S. government, fearful of another leftist revolution following that in Nicaragua, entered El Salvador's political equation determined to prevent a rebel victory. The left, politically on the ascendant but still fragmented and militarily weak, moved to unify and build its military capacity to defeat the government and its U.S. backers by violent means. Military escalation proceeded rapidly on both sides and each saw its own future and the potential for achieving its social, economic, and political goals as being tied to the defeat of its enemy. Compromise was not in the vocabulary of either side and negotiation, when discussed, was only a code word for the surrender of the adversary. The left believed it had the popular support and momentum to overthrow the government. Forces on the right were confident that the U.S. government would not permit a leftist victory. As the sides moved toward war, the room for alternative positions and programs narrowed and the potential for dialogue diminished. With the election of Ronald Reagan in the November 1980 U.S. elections, the prospect of compromise between a militantly anticommunist president and a Marxist-led insurgency grew even more remote. Strategies of violence became the central means to resolve the country's economic, social, and political problems.

Notes

1. *U.S. Declassified Documents II*, CIA, "Final Stages of Coup Planning by El Salvadoran Military," 11 October 1979.
2. *U.S. Declassified Documents II*, CIA, "Final Phase of Coup Planning by Moderates Within the El Salvadoran Army," 3 October 1979.
3. *U.S. Declassified Documents II*, CIA, "Coup Planning by Moderate Middle Grade El Salvadoran Officers," 1 October 1979.
4. See William Stanley, *The Protection Racket State: Elite Politics, Military Extortion, and the Origins of El Salvador's Civil War*, draft of forthcoming book to be published by Temple University Press, 218–226.
5. James Dunkerley, *The Long War: Dictatorship and Revolution in El Salvador* (London: Verso Editions, 1983), 135–136, citing interview with Salvadoran officer in Carolyn Forché, "The Road to Reaction in El Salvador," in *The Nation*, special issue, *El Salvador: The Roots of Intervention* (1981), 7–8.
6. Dunkerley, *The Long War*, 143.

7. *U.S. Declassified Documents II,* Department of State, Part 21A, "Survivability of Revolutionary Governing Junta (JRG)," telegram #07283, from U.S. Embassy, San Salvador, to Secretary of State, 19 December 1979.

8. *U.S. Declassified Documents II,* Defense Intelligence Agency, "DIA Assessment of Threat and Indigenous Capabilities," n.d. [late January/early February 1980].

9. *U.S. Declassified Documents II,* Department of State, Part 2, "Former Christian Democratic Party (PDC) Candidate Analyzes National Political Scene," memorandum of conversation, 15 June 1979.

10. *U.S. Declassified Documents II,* Department of State, Part 5, "Preliminary Assessment of Situation in El Salvador," telegram #02038, from U.S. Embassy, San Salvador, to Secretary of State, 19 March 1980.

11. *U.S. Declassified Documents II,* Department of State, Part 5, "Augmentation of U.S. Military Personnel in El Salvador," memorandum, 21 December 1979.

12. *U.S. Declassified Documents II,* Department of State, Part 1, "El Salvador in the Post-Somoza Period," telegram #04175, from U.S. Embassy, San Salvador, to Secretary of State, 26 July 1979.

13. *U.S. Declassified Documents II,* Department of State, Part 18, "Outside Assistance to Guerrillas in El Salvador," memorandum, 4 October 1979; and Defense Intelligence Agency, "DIA Assessment of Threat and Indigenous Capabilities," n.d. [late January/early February 1980].

14. *U.S. Declassified Documents II,* National Security Council, "U.S. Policy to El Salvador," memorandum for the president from Zbigniew Brzezinski, 29 January 1980.

15. Leaders of all of the FMLN parties refer to an extreme shortage of arms and trained combatants and give examples of a hundred combatants training of whom only a dozen had (very old) weapons and the rest carried sticks. Author interviews with Ana Guadalupe Martínez, Nidia Díaz, Gerson Martínez, Facundo Guardado, Juan Ramón Medrano, July 1995.

16. There are serious discrepancies between the assessment of U.S. intelligence agencies regarding the threat posed by the guerrillas and the insurgents' assessment of their own military strength. Possible explanations are a lack of good intelligence on the armed left and a tendency to overestimate their threat in the wake of the Sandinista victory in Nicaragua; or that intelligence agencies inflated the threat to help justify immediate U.S. military aid to the junta. Whatever the reasons, the figure of 2,000 armed and trained insurgents in late 1979 that appears in intelligence documents bears very little relationship to the reality presented by FMLN leaders interviewed.

17. This information on the use of death squads by the right wing as a strategy to defeat the left is based on multiple sources including recently declassified U.S. documents, particularly, *U.S. Declassified Documents I,* CIA, National Foreign Assessment Center, "El Salvador: The Right Wing," 18 March 1981; CIA, "Rightwing Terrorism," 17 April 1981; CIA, "Briefing Paper on Right-Wing Terrorism in El Salvador," 27 October 1983; CIA, Directorate of Intelligence, "D'Aubuisson's Terrorist Activities," 2 March 1984; CIA, Directorate of Intelligence, "Controlling Rightwing Terrorism," February 1985; Department of State, memorandum, "Possible Leads on Rightist Terrorist Activities," 11 December 1980; Department of State, "El Salvadoran Rightists Allegedly Receive Assistance of Argentine Right-Wing Civilians," memorandum of conversation, from U.S. Embassy, Buenos Aires, Argentina, 5 January 1981; and Allan Nairn, "Behind the Death Squads," *The Progressive* 48, no. 5 (May 1984), 20–29.

18. *U.S. Declassified Documents I*, Department of State, ER 4b vol. 4, "Millionaires' Murder Inc.?" telegram #00096, from U.S. Embassy, San Salvador, to Secretary of State, 6 January 1981.

19. *U.S. Declassified Documents I*, CIA, no title [García and Carranza and death squads], 5 March 1984.

20. *U.S. Declassified Documents II*, Department of State, Part 5, "Call on Minister of Defense, May 20," telegram #03590, from U.S. Embassy, San Salvador, to Secretary of State, 21 May 1980.

21. *U.S. Declassified Documents II*, Department of State, Part 2, "Meeting with New Civilian/Military Junta of El Salvador on the Continuation of Relations," telegram #06150, from U.S. Embassy, San Salvador, to Secretary of State, 25 October 1979.

22. See *Estudios Centroamericanos* 375/376 (January/February 1980), 120–123, for texts of resignations.

23. *U.S. Declassified Documents II*, Department of State, Part 5, "Salvadoran Situation: Next Step," telegram #00529, from U.S. Embassy, San Salvador, to Secretary of State, 24 January 1980.

24. *U.S. Declassified Documents II*, Department of State, Part 5, "Current Political Crisis in El Salvador and Status of Proposed Programs of USG Assistance," telegram #00037, from U.S. Embassy, San Salvador, to Secretary of State, 15 January 1980.

25. *U.S. Declassified Documents II*, Department of State, Part 21B, "Salvadoran Situation: Next Step," 24 January 1980.

26. *U.S. Declassified Documents II*, Department of State, Part 6, "Foreign Minister and JRG Member Gutiérrez Discuss Current Issues," telegram #03632, from U.S. Embassy, San Salvador, to Secretary of State, 22 May 1980.

27. *U.S. Declassified Documents II*, Department of State, Part 21E, "Helicopters for El Salvador," memorandum to the acting secretary, 20 June 1980.

28. *U.S. Declassified Documents II*, Department of State, Part 21E, "Ambassador and COMUTILGP [*sic,* COMUSMILGP: Commander, U.S. Military Group in El Salvador?] Presentation of Helicopter Proposal to JRG and High Command, August 21," telegram #05810, from U.S. Embassy, San Salvador, to Secretary of State, 23 August 1980.

29. See *Estudios Centroamericanos* 377/378 (March/April 1980), 384–396, for text of government decrees.

30. See *Estudios Centroamericanos* 377/378 (March/April 1980), 343–345, for the platform of the democratic revolutionary government.

31. See *Estudios Centroamericanos* 379 (May 1980), 537–539, for manifesto of the DRU.

32. "Paro Nacional de la Coordinadora Revolucionaria de Masas," in *Estudios Centroamericanos* 380 (June 1980), 595–596.

33. See *Estudios Centroamericanos* 383 (September 1980), 921–922, for FARN communiqué.

34. *Estudios Centroamericanos* 387/388 (January/February 1981), 4.

35. *U.S. Declassified Documents I*, Department of State, ER 4b vol. 4, "Millionaires' Murder Inc.?" telegram #00096, from U.S. Embassy, San Salvador, to Secretary of State, 6 January 1981.

36. *U.S. Declassified Documents I*, Department of State, ER 5n vol. 9, "Dinner with Joaquín Villalobos," telegram #01355, from U.S. Embassy, San Salvador, to Secretary of State, 5 February 1992.

37. Schwarz, *American Counterinsurgency Doctrine*, xiii.

38. "It is Duarte's strategy to increase his authority by continuing to cover

up for the military's wave of killings thereby winning their gratitude and confidence." *U.S. Declassified Documents I*, Department of State, ER 1m, no title [Ambassador White's meeting with junta member Duarte and Foreign Minister Chavez Mena], 30 November 1980.

39. *U.S. Declassified Documents II*, National Security Council, "U.S. Policy to El Salvador," memorandum for the president from Zbigniew Brzezinski, 29 January 1980.

40. Gerson Martínez, author interview, tape recording, San Salvador, 9 November 1992.

4

Fighting Different Wars: Insurgent and Counterinsurgent Strategies from the January 1981 FMLN Offensive to Mid-1984

In early October 1979 El Salvador was ruled by a military regime in alliance with a small landed oligarchy that was threatened by a growing leftist insurgency and a powerful grassroots opposition, and viewed internationally as a pariah for its gross human-rights violations. By the end of 1980, as the long-heralded FMLN offensive approached, the political, social, and military contours of El Salvador had been changed in fundamental ways.

The country was governed by a civilian-military junta that united conservative military officers with representatives of the PDC. The interests of these two groups differed greatly: The PDC emphasized reforms to regain the popular support it had lost in the previous decade and to undercut the left; the armed forces focused on military and paramilitary violence to defeat the left. But they were held together by U.S. pressure and the aid provided to hold off attacks from the left.

Significant economic reforms had been implemented giving land to thousands of peasants and taking the commanding heights of the economy out of the hands of the traditional elite. Although it was weakened, however, the economic and political power of the oligarchy was not broken. Phase 2, the major element of the agrarian reform that would have affected properties between 375 and 1,250 acres and taken over 60 percent of the coffee land, was postponed to the distant future.

Right-wing opponents of the junta and its reforms, funded by very wealthy landowners and in collusion with the military High Command, unleashed an unprecedented wave of violence against suspected leftists. Although this campaign of terror did not achieve its objective of defeating the left, the killing of some 15,000 civilians, including prominent citizens, made public political activity a hazardous undertaking.

The left, which had been fragmented in late 1979, undertook a process of unification leading to the creation of the FMLN, an alliance of five guerrilla organizations, and its political wing, the FDR, in 1980. Throughout 1980 the guerrilla organizations scrambled to obtain sufficient arms and training to challenge the junta, worked to strengthen their internal unity, and sought to win international support. But by the time the FMLN had created the conditions to challenge the junta militarily, the wave of popular opposition in the cities had ebbed as a result of legal and extralegal repression as well as the left's own decision to shift leading cadre and members of the mass organizations from political to military roles.

The economy deteriorated dramatically during 1980 as a result of the political and military turmoil. The country's gross domestic product dropped by 9 percent for the year. Gross domestic investment diminished by 50 percent and imports fell by 25 percent. The national unemployment rate rose from 7 percent to 17 percent, and the value of exports declined by 15 percent for the year.[1] At the end of 1980 the economy was a major point of vulnerability for the governing junta. Economic recovery was essential to implementing programs that could undercut the left. But lack of investor confidence in the government's ability to resolve the country's crisis, and attacks on the economic infrastructure by the left, placed major obstacles to an economic recovery that could fuel political-military success in the war.

Following the October 1979 coup, the United States became a major actor in Salvadoran politics. Desperate to avoid a repeat of Nicaragua in El Salvador, the Carter administration played a central role in devising the major political and military strategies, including the economic reforms, discouraged coup attempts from the right, and consolidated the major actors to create a legitimate government that could be supported against the left.

Revolutionary and Counterrevolutionary Strategy: Interests, Objectives, and Resources

By the beginning of 1981, as the war began, the makeup of the two conflicting sides could be clearly defined. On one side, a coalition of often-conflicting actors, including the Salvadoran military, the PDC, and the far right, was being held together by the United States. On the other side, the guerrilla groups and their political allies sought to maintain the momentum and support that had brought them close to revolution in early 1980.

The major Salvadoran counterrevolutionary actors and the United States each had their own interests but were united in their desire to defeat the insurgency and in the assessment that the FMLN-FDR was the primary enemy. The United States had taken on the role of molding these disparate interests into a coherent bloc to defeat the rebels. This proved a difficult task. The far right, determined to recover land and prevent further losses, attempted a number of coups that were viewed by the U.S. as highly counterproductive in the battle against the left. The military was engaged in a dirty war against the guerrillas and their social base that, over time, came to be seen by U.S. policymakers and advisers as threatening to the overall war effort because it placed continued U.S. aid to El Salvador in jeopardy. The United States did not control these actors but, as the main source of external funding for the war, exerted significant influence, attempted to mediate conflicts between them, and played the central role in plotting the strategic direction of the war: in developing the land reform, the elections strategy, and the major military strategies.

U.S. interests in the country were laid out in the annual integrated assessment of security assistance for El Salvador for 1981 as:

> 1. Prevention of the takeover of a friendly neighbor of the U.S. by a Communist guerrilla army in good measure trained and equipped by Havana, with support from Moscow and its allies. We also have an interest in avoiding an extreme right coup which among other things would greatly complicate the already difficult problem of mobilizing U.S. and international support for measures necessary to avoid power passing to Leninist-Castroite forces.
>
> 2. The maintenance in El Salvador of a government which shares our ideal of democracy and of change through reform and institutional modification rather than by further revolution and destruction
> . . .
>
> 3. As a necessary condition for advancement of interests 1 and 2 above, prevention of further deterioration of the economy of El Salvador, early resumption of economic growth, and the creation of a social, political, and economic atmosphere that will reinstill in El Salvador's citizens confidence and hope for the future.[2]

The PDC, the armed forces, and the far right shared the U.S. interest in defeating the guerrillas, but each had its own interests as well. The military, which had shifted from its century-old relationship with the landowners, was primarily concerned with the survival of the military institution and, in the face of the threat from the left, saw a close relationship with the United States, and U.S. military aid, as a way of ensuring survival and growth. The PDC, which had been thwarted in its attempts to reach power through elections, saw an alliance with the armed forces behind a reform program, and a close relationship with the United States, as a means to rebuild a base of popular support and win power. The far right, with its base in the landowning class, saw the insurgency as a threat to its survival and, in alliance with the military, sought to wipe out the social base of the opposition. The right also viewed the agrarian and other social and economic reforms as "communistic" and plotted coups, first, and electoral strategies, later, to attempt to recover its power and influence. The challenge, particularly for the United States, was to ensure that the shared interest in defeating the left overcame the significant differences that, on occasion, threatened to destroy the entire counterrevolutionary operation.

The resources available to the counterrevolution were potentially substantial but were contingent on the success of the program and the methods used to implement it. The Reagan administration had defined El Salvador as a geostrategic issue of great importance to the United States and was willing to provide the necessary military and economic aid and other forms of advice and support to defeat the insurgency. However, the track record of the military, particularly in the area of human rights, the destabilizing actions of the far right, and questions regarding the capability and commitment of the government, placed aid levels in jeopardy. Public and congressional opposition to U.S. policy in El Salvador, resulting in restrictions and conditions placed on aid, put a premium on controlling the actions of the far right and the military, and in ensuring that the war was fought in ways that could guarantee continued aid.

Though divided at times over strategies and tactics, the revolutionary side was more united in its overall interests and objectives, but it also had access to significantly fewer resources. The FMLN maintained an alliance with the FDR, made up in practice of the social-democratic MNR and the social-Christian MPSC. From late 1980, the FDR operated in exile and played a major role in diplomatic activity. Military strategy was developed and implemented by the FMLN while the overall direction of the political-military effort was developed in consultation between the two fronts. The objectives of the FMLN-FDR were laid out in the Platform of the Revolutionary Democratic Government:

> The decisive task of the revolution on which completion of all its tasks and objectives depends is the conquest of power and the installation of a revolutionary democratic government, which at the head of the people will undertake the construction of a new society.[3]

The revolution would put an end to the "power and political, economic and social control of the great lords of land and capital," end the "dependence of our country on Yankee imperialism," and "assure democratic rights and freedoms for all the people." The government would be made up of "representatives of the revolutionary and people's movement, as well as of the democratic parties, organizations, sectors, and individuals who are willing to participate in the carrying out of this programmatic platform." The programs carried out by the government would include nationalization of the banking and financial system, expropriation of monopolistic enterprises, a deep agrarian reform, substantial increases in social services, job creation programs, and a massive plan for low-cost housing.[4]

For the FMLN-FDR, the key to realizing any changes was to win power. This could come through a combination of political, military, and diplomatic strategies, but given El Salvador's history and the resistance of their adversary, military means would have to play a central role. By the end of 1980 the parties of the FMLN believed that the conditions existed in El Salvador to take power through a political-military strategy that combined a military offensive with a general strike and popular insurrection, and they launched what they termed a final offensive on 10 January 1981.

The resources at the disposal of the FMLN-FDR were significantly less than those available to their enemies. Joaquín Villalobos of the FMLN's General Command estimated that the advantage enjoyed by the armed forces over the guerrillas was between ten and twenty-seven to one.[5] But the FMLN possessed a base for command and control, logistics, and the transport of military and other supplies in Nicaragua; access to training and arms from Cuba, Vietnam, and other Soviet bloc countries; financial support from these nations and some nonaligned states; and a base of solidarity and opposition to U.S. policy in the United States, Latin America, and Europe.

Perhaps most significant for the FMLN in waging its revolutionary war was the strategic unity it maintained throughout the conflict at the level of its General Command, which consisted of the leaders of the five constituent organizations. For the entire duration of the war, the five parties that made up the FMLN maintained their own structures, organizations, and party finances. There were significant differences in ideology among the parties, as well as struggles over strategy, tactics, and access to funds, that prevented the development of ongoing, unitary leadership bodies (e.g., for finances, logistics) below the level of the General Command. Only this body and the Political-Diplomatic Commission (formed in early 1981) continued to function as unitary bodies throughout the war. This meant that the General Command was often called on to resolve even fairly minor tactical matters that had reached an impasse at lower levels. But most important, the General Command continued to provide strategic direction to the five parties in their conduct of the war, even if those directions were at times general enough to allow the parties to carry out actions that appeared counterproductive to the others.[6]

In contrast, the chain of command on the counterrevolutionary side was much more complex. Though U.S. political and military leaders had great influence with their Salvadoran counterparts due to the high level of military and economic aid provided, their role was normally one of cajoling and persuading rather than enforcing policies. For a decade U.S. military advisers tried to persuade the Salvadoran armed forces to wage a small-unit war and to limit gross violations of human rights, with only limited success. At the same time, the U.S. Embassy worked to consolidate antagonistic groups and individuals behind a common strategy, with mixed results. Even among the major U.S. political and military strategists there was at times lack of clarity as to objectives, as in the early 1980s when Ambassador Hinton argued that his job in El Salvador was to "hold on" while General Nutting, head of U.S. Southern Command, claimed that "we're here to win."[7]

Military Strategy

Between the offensive they launched in January 1981 and the inauguration of José Napoleón Duarte in June 1984, the FMLN employed at least four major political-military strategies. In January 1981 it launched an offensive that was designed to resolve the question of power in the shortest time possible. When the offensive failed to spark a general insurrection, the FMLN moved into a strategy of "resistance, development and advance"[8] that began in February 1981 in a defensive period and moved to consolidation of a rearguard and increasingly toward offensive actions through 1981 and the first half of 1982. With the victories achieved during this period and the evident weakness of the armed forces, the insurgents entered a period of almost continuous offensives designed to defeat El Salvador's armed forces (ESAF) militarily. By late 1983, when the limitations of an almost exclusively military strategy based on concentrated forces and regular combat became apparent, the FMLN made a fundamental shift to a prolonged war strategy designed to wear out its enemy politically and militarily and prepare the conditions for a strategic counteroffensive to take power.

During the same time period, the military strategy of the ESAF was contradictory. U.S. policymakers and military advisers encouraged the armed forces to employ an offensive approach to defeating the guerrillas through small-unit tactics that would take the war to the FMLN. The armed forces would go behind guerrilla lines and wage an irregular counterguerrilla war with air support, keeping the FMLN off balance and preventing the rebels from taking the initiative in the war. The military would focus on protecting key economic areas and population centers and force the insurgents into the poorer northern and eastern areas; this would lay the basis for restricting the scope and threat of the insurgency and turn the guerrillas into bandits over a short period. Civic-action programs would win support for the government and armed forces in the countryside, while civil defense units would help deal with the security threat, tie the population to the government and armed forces, and free the military to confront the guerrillas directly. The buildup of the armed forces following the Woerner Report (discussed in the following section) of late 1981 was based on this conception of how the war should be fought and won, and drew on the lessons of counterinsurgency from Vietnam, Latin America, and elsewhere.[9]

In practice, the armed forces fought a different kind of war. Half the troops were occupied in static defense of infrastructure.[10] The normal mode of offensive operations was to engage in sweeps with thousands of troops through rebel areas, moving slowly with heavy equipment on the main highways. The guerrillas, with advanced warning of the offensive, would leave the area, taking with them, in the early period, their civilian supporters. Contact with the enemy was infrequent and normally occurred at a time and place chosen by the insurgents. Military casualties were high, averaging twenty per day in early 1981,[11] as were civilian losses at the hands of the armed forces.[12] Outside of these major sweeps the troops tended to stay close to their barracks for fear of attack and rarely sought engagements with the rebels. Senior officers were reputed to be more interested in the money they could make from nonexistent soldiers' pay, in waging a "nine-to-five" war, and in controlling their own departments as fiefdoms, than in defeating the insurgents.[13]

Throughout this period the best approach for winning the war remained a matter of conflict. U.S. advisers supported and built up the reputations of officers who took an offensive approach to the war, such as Colonel Sigifredo Ochoa in Cabañas and later in Chalatenango, and Colonel Domingo Monterrosa in the eastern departments, and tried to persuade Salvadoran military commanders to focus their efforts on the central economic region of the country rather than on pursuing the guerrillas through the northern and eastern regions they dominated.

Undoubtedly the major strategic military initiative on the counterrevolutionary side in this period was the implementation of the recommendations of the Woerner Report, which resulted in the doubling of the size of the armed forces between 1981 and 1984, with similar increases in the number of battalions, fixed-wing aircraft, and helicopters.[14] This buildup helped prevent an FMLN victory in 1983 and contributed to a change in guerrilla strategy the following year. The other main counterinsurgency initiative in this period, much less successful, was the launching in mid-1983 of the National Plan, a multifaceted program to consolidate government and military support in the key economic region of San Vicente and Usulután.

Military Conflict in El Salvador: January 1981–June 1984

On 10 January 1981 the FMLN launched the long-awaited offensive that formally began the civil war in El Salvador. The initiative was projected by FMLN leaders as a final offensive that would overthrow the government and present the incoming Reagan administration with a fait accompli when it took office. The offensive was intended to combine direct military attacks with a general strike and insurrection to defeat the armed forces.[15]

The three-week-long offensive failed to achieve its objectives of defeating the military and overthrowing the government. The populace in the cities, particularly San Salvador, did not rise in insurrection. Government troops did not mutiny, except in the Santa Ana barracks, where seventy soldiers killed their commander and joined the rebel forces.[16] And although twenty-six factories heeded the call to strike and 20,000 government workers walked off their jobs in support of the rebel initiative, the government's preparations for the offensive, and its awareness of many of the plans, allowed the security forces to move against union leaders in the preceding weeks and militarize workplaces to prevent strikes.[17]

Although the offensive did not achieve its ultimate objectives and the guerrillas fell victim in the propaganda war to their own triumphalism, it was not a failure militarily. A study by the Jesuit-run UCA reported that there were 516 military actions by the FMLN in all fourteen departments, including eighty-two takeovers of villages or cities and eighty-one attacks on military posts and garrisons.[18] During the offensive the FMLN occupied four departmental capitals and twenty cities and population centers. According to Raúl Benítez Manaut, one of the major results of the January offensive was "the consolidation of one of the tendencies of the war: the geopolitical division of the interior of the country. The FMLN tended to consolidate its rearguard in the northern and eastern zones and the civil-military Junta consolidated its in the cities and in the west."[19]

The outcome of the offensive was mixed, failing to spark a general strike and popular uprising but succeeding in stretching the ESAF throughout the country and laying the basis for guerrilla control of large areas of the countryside. According to a U.S. military assessment, a "popular insurrection" which the insurgent leaders recognized would be needed for lasting military gains, did not occur. Government forces were severely strained by the offensive. Nonetheless, after two weeks of heavy fighting, they forced the insurgents to terminate their coordinated assaults, to evacuate all the struck towns, and to retreat to their sanctuaries along the Honduran border and on rugged volcanic highlands. . . . In the January offensive, the insurgents launched over a dozen large and sustained attacks throughout the country.[20]

The expectation of a general insurrection appears to have been based on a degree of wishful thinking and a failure to examine closely the level of motivation of workers, students, and marginalized sectors, particularly in the capital, who would have formed the mass base of a popular uprising. The level of terror during 1980 that resulted in an estimated 15,000 deaths, the lack of public-protest activities in the second half of 1980, and the fact that many key organizers had been withdrawn from political work into military roles, perhaps ought to have signaled the difficulty involved in generating a popular uprising in the face of daily terror. FMLN leaders later recognized the problem and admitted that they missed the opportune moment.[21] Yet the FMLN continued to return to the vision of a popular insurrection to resolve the problem of power, even in unlikely circumstances.

When the January offensive failed to overthrow the junta, the FMLN moved into a defensive mode with the slogan "resist, develop, advance." The armed forces, U.S. advisers, and much of the press saw the offensive as a major defeat for the FMLN requiring only some mopping-up operations before the guerrillas were defeated. A senior U.S. official, Luigi Einaudi, later expressed a common view of that period:

> I had assumed . . . after the failure of the 1981 offensive, that this guerrilla movement, that had launched it, would probably wind up going historically the way of most Latin American guerrilla movements. That is to say, you had your chance, you made your run at power, you lose it, you blow it, you disintegrate, you disappear.[22]

A rare alternative view at that time was expressed in the *New York Times:* The rebels had "demonstrated that, after decades of political and economic repression, a revolutionary movement in El Salvador has achieved enough power and popular support to take on the army and survive."[23]

During the first half of 1981 the ESAF carried out twenty-eight mass offensives, termed "encircle and annihilate," to wipe out the FMLN; in each of these it used over 1,000 troops, but with scant success.[24] Where conditions were favorable, the insurgents defended their positions in fixed battles and gained tactical military experience. By mid-1981 the U.S. Embassy evaluated the war as essentially stalemated:

> The military situation in mid-1981 is that both sides have fought to a draw. The resources currently available to the government and to the insurgents indicate that there is very little that will change this situation. The guerrillas have the initiative on their side—they can attack when and where they want—and the government has the capacity to contain the insurgent assaults on a case-by-case basis, but not to destroy the insurgents' force. Consequently, as we perceive the situation, there is no military end in sight to the war of attrition in El Salvador.[25]

Between mid-1981 and mid-1982 the main tactics of the ESAF did not change. The number of troops involved in the major sweeps of guerrilla zones increased while the duration of the sweeps decreased.[26] In fall 1981, however, the team led by General Fred Woerner made its assessment of the military situation and worked with senior ESAF officers to develop a military strategy for El Salvador. The recommendations of the Woerner group focused on (1) "preparations for the war": increasing the size of the military force to 40,000, creating ten additional battalions for a force structure of twenty-five, improving command control, communications, the intelligence system, the combat-service support system, and training base, developing a noncommissioned officer structure, and spending $296 million on materiel and equipment to fight the war more effectively; and (2) "fighting the war": changing the way the ESAF fought to a more aggressive and offensive mode. From mid-1981 to mid-1982 the initial steps for augmenting the strength of the ESAF were taken: A new battalion, the Atonal, trained in Panama and El Salvador by U.S. and Venezuelan advisers, came into service in January 1982, and 500 officers and 1,000 troops (the latter forming the Belloso Battalion) were trained in the United States in early 1982.[27]

The Woerner group's assessment of the military situation in El Salvador in late 1981 was not positive:

> The internal defense principle of the offensive through aggressive small unit operations, both day and night has been overshadowed by a defensive mentality. . . .
> [There is] a severe shortage of junior leaders and the compromise of formalized training, which occupies a low priority and, consequently, is seldom accomplished. In a spirit of national survival, the Armed Forces High Command has adopted a strategically defensive posture, forsaking long term capabilities for short term urgent requirements. This posture does not provide for winning; to the contrary, it reinforces the insurgent strategy of protracted warfare. Time,

within the critical context of popular support, seems to favor the insurgent. The continued attrition of national resources increase [sic] the possibility of military defeat via economic and political collapse.[28]

For the FMLN the period from mid-1981 to mid-1982 was a time of consolidation and expansion. The rearguard of the insurgent forces was built. One FMLN leader described the process:

> We consider an internal rearguard a political-military zone of control where the local power of the enemy has been expelled; where our troops, installations, workshops, hospitals, schools of instruction, command, were located. At that time, 1981–1983, we were in the midst of insurrectional masses who organized their own forms of self-management.
> These rearguards were built on a base of highly organized and radicalized zones where practically the whole population had risen up and broken with the regime. . . .
> In the period 81–82 we began to build the social base of support of the guerrillas; a base which provided food, gave information, and shared our lives.[29]

Two other developments of the FMLN in this period were the systematic use of economic sabotage to undercut the government's "war economy," and the implementation of commando actions that dealt material and psychological blows to the armed forces and government. These attacks included the destruction in October 1981 of the Puente de Oro, the most important bridge crossing the Río Lempa, connecting the livestock, fishing, and farming centers of the east with the processing and consuming centers of the west; and the destruction of a large part of the Salvadoran air force at the Ilopango base in January 1982.[30]

The major political-military setback for the insurgents in this period was the elections of March 1982, which strengthened the position of the government. The FMLN sought to block elections by generating popular uprisings through a military attack on Usulután that would culminate in the fall of the government. FMLN leader Joaquín Villalobos described the objective as "to try to dynamize the urban mass movement through a victorious action whose fundamental design was military. . . . If this did not happen, our plan was to complicate as much as possible the carrying out of the elections and this we did pretty well. The results were felt within a few days."[31]

But though the elections resulted in a complicated situation for the overall policy of counterinsurgency, this was less a result of the actions of the FMLN than of the internal divisions within the counter-revolutionary camp. The elections themselves were hailed internationally as a step toward democratization and viewed as a defeat for the guerrillas. Perhaps most important, they began a process of legitimation of the government and hence of the counterrevolutionary strategy that the FMLN found difficult to challenge directly and successfully.

Despite the setback in the elections, Colonel Domingo Monterrosa, who was viewed as one of the ESAF's most capable commanders, conceded that the FMLN was stronger and more effective than ever, and diplomats and intelligence sources estimated that between one-quarter and one-third of the land surface was under rebel control or outside government control.[32] In the annual military assessment, the U.S. Embassy estimated the strength of the guerrillas in mid-1982

> at approximately 5,800 armed first line forces. . . . Insurgent training appears to be excellent in areas of communications, demolitions, resupply operations, base camp security, commando operations, propaganda and intelligence. Past guerrilla performance in large-scale coordinated operations is rated as being slightly lower. Weaknesses, as of this date, include 1) some recent decline in morale among combatants and mass followers caused by a lack of adequate supplies of food and medicine as well as a loss of faith in the proximity of a victorious outcome; 2) voluntary recruiting difficulties; and 3) erosion of popular support for the cause. These weaknesses became manifest at the time of the 28 March elections when the insurgents were defeated politically and repulsed militarily. . . . They are prepared for a prolonged war of attrition designed to wear down the military, undermine the economy, and destroy the resolve of the population. . . . The insurgents have still the initiative to select the time and location of their attacks.[33]

From mid-1982 to the end of 1983 the FMLN moved to the offensive, having determined that conditions existed to defeat the armed forces, and set out to win a military victory. According to Villalobos: "Our fundamental problem came to be: how to break the army militarily. . . . We had to achieve a greater efficacy in the military terrain: to move from the defense of positions to a war of movement, to move from the dispersion to the concentration of forces."[34]

Leonel González, also a member of the FMLN's General Command, described developments in this period:

> First we began to build large units, we moved from simple platoons to build battalions [300 troops] and even brigades [3 battalions; 1,200 troops including special forces]. From January and February of 1982, we moved to a situation of greater initiative, on the basis of a better knowledge of the terrain and with more consolidated armed guerrilla units.

> That is what allowed us to change the military correlation of forces in certain areas of Chalatenango, Morazán, San Vicente, Cabañas, Usulután, where on building larger units and having a superiority of forces, we were able to begin to hit them, wipe out small posts and recover a large quantity of arms, at the same time we took a great number of prisoners and this hurt the morale of the army.[35]

Between mid-1982 and the end of 1983 the initiative in the war shifted dramatically toward the guerrillas. The FMLN launched a series of offensives from June 1982 that took over towns and overran military posts throughout the northern, eastern, and central regions of the country.[36] They defeated the armed forces in major confrontations, such as the battle of Moscarrón in June 1982 in which 100 troops were killed or wounded in an ambush and 44 captured.[37] They also took over key towns—Berlín in February 1983—and laid siege to San Miguel, one of the country's largest cities, in September 1983.[38] In one two-month campaign in late 1983, U.S. advisers reported that the FMLN killed more than 800 ESAF troops, captured 400, and attacked more than sixty towns from central El Salvador to the Honduran border, and that the fighting affected nine of the country's fourteen provinces.[39] In northeastern El Salvador, rebels controlled a 1,000-square mile area and 100,000 people, allowing new opportunities for recruitment, training, and deployment of forces.[40] The year 1983 ended with the successful assault on the Fourth Brigade barracks at El Paraíso with 180 government casualties and the destruction of the country's major bridge, the Cuscutlán.[41] At the end of 1983 the State Department reported that the guerrillas had attacked more than seventy-five towns and garrisons and had retaken the initiative in the war.[42]

The period from mid-1982 to the end of 1983 saw the Salvadoran military at its lowest ebb. By May 1983, the *Miami Herald* reported that "Top Pentagon military officers say bluntly that the U.S. supported government in El Salvador is losing its war against guerrilla opposition."[43] With 40 percent to 50 percent of the troops deployed to guard fixed positions—barracks, bridges, industrial plants, coffee plantations, etc.—the FMLN's offensive strategy placed the ESAF in a dilemma.[44] They could attempt to defend every small town and village by deploying twenty to thirty troops and stretch their human resources to the limits. The FMLN could then concentrate its forces and attack these posts, recover weapons, and take prisoners. Or the military could focus its resources on defending the economically and politically strategic areas, as the U.S. advisers proposed, and give up control of many small towns and large swathes of the countryside. The guerrillas would then be in control of much of the country's territory, which they would use as a rearguard to arm, train, and provision their forces and strengthen political ties with the local population. Differences over strategy and tactics, compounded by personal and political divisions, led to a mutiny in early 1983 by Colonel Sigifredo Ochoa against the defense minister, General García, resulting in the resignation of García in April of that year.

The U.S. military advisory group in El Salvador ["Milgroup"] had been attempting to get the ESAF to take a more aggressive approach to the war—focusing on small units that could patrol day and night, take the war to the enemy, and go behind guerrilla lines with air support—rather than carrying out multibattalion operations without ever confronting the FMLN. They argued that the ESAF should concentrate on defending the richest and most highly populated areas and leave the rebel strongholds to be dealt with last. The advisers developed, and convinced the government and military to take up, a National Plan to defend and consolidate support for the government in the key departments of San Vicente and Usulután. These departments were selected for their economic importance as producers of coffee, cotton, and sugar, their central position, their function as the highway, electric, and communications link to the eastern part of the country, and their high concentration of displaced people.[45]

The National Plan focused first on San Vicente in June 1983 and was to begin by clearing the guerrillas out of the area, followed by a massive civic-action campaign—to reopen schools, pave streets, and restore electricity—administered by a National Commission for Restoration of Areas (Comisión Nacional de Restauración de Areas, or CONARA) made up of a number of government agencies and funded by the U.S. Agency for International Development (AID). Another core component of the program was the creation of civil-defense units to provide security to the area. In practice the plan failed. After much initial optimism, brought on by a reduction of guerrilla activity as the rebels reorganized to deal with the new government strategy, the armed forces withdrew many of their troops to deal with a major FMLN attack on the barracks in San Miguel in early September 1983.[46]

The *New York Times* reported in December 1983 that U.S. officials saw the National Plan as in danger of failing:

> The project, which United States officials said last spring was the "make-it-or-break-it" test for the Salvadoran military, has been damaged by a guerrilla counteroffensive and by unwillingness of the Government army to pursue insurgents who have returned to the province, San Vicente. "The plan is at a stage where it needs reinvigoration after the guerrilla counteroffensive," Ambassador Thomas R. Pickering said. "The army has not shown the capacity to deal with the counteroffensive and the area of the plan. We had said that was a key test." . . . Most of the rich land in the northern part of the province

has been left uncultivated, and even the army has not been to the far northeastern area in three months. . . . Many of the specially trained forces that were in San Vicente when the plan got under way have left to reinforce troops in other areas.[47]

By late 1983 the military situation was at a low point. U.S. ambassador Thomas Pickering later recounted: "There were days at the end of 1983 when we wondered whether we would make it through the next two or three months because of that offensive and where things were taking us."[48]

It appears, however, that the FMLN strategy of building a quasi-regular army, which brought the ESAF to the brink of defeat, extended the forces of the FMLN beyond what Clausewitz termed the "culminating point of victory": the point at which advances turn into reverses through overextension. The concentration of forces and their deployment in near-regular combat played into some of the growing strengths of the Salvadoran military—principally its air mobility, intelligence, and movement toward more irregular tactics.

The FMLN's move to concentrate its forces made the guerrilla columns vulnerable to attack, particularly from the air, and increased its casualties, at a time when the air power of the ESAF was coming into heavy use. The large units required a great number of support people and used significant quantities of munitions, the supply of which was not inexhaustible. And the concentrated units left open wide spaces of the territory for penetration by army patrols. These factors caused the FMLN to rethink its fundamental political-military strategy beginning in late 1983. But perhaps the most important realizations were that the development of a regular army separated the FMLN from its popular base and that to win the war against the Salvadoran army and its U.S. backers would require a more political strategy that played to the strengths of the guerrilla forces. An FMLN analysis from mid-1985 characterized the weakness of the earlier strategy:

Our first and most important weakness was to have forgotten the decisive importance of the incorporation of all the people into the revolutionary war, as the principal arm of our revolution. . . . [This led to] a linear strategic development of the revolutionary war towards a quick victory according to which the key was to construct and arm more and more battalions and brigades, supposedly possible through the rapid incorporation of the masses, of new combatants, supported with a permanent and continuous logistics and financing—[which was] impossible in our conditions.[49]

From early 1984 the FMLN moved to a strategy that sought to combine the armed struggle with the "political struggle of the masses" to weaken the regime, and to launch "at the most critical moment for the

enemy, the strategic military counter-offensive with the popular insurrection."[50] Some of the main components of this strategy were to
break up the rebel forces into small units dispersed throughout the
territory with the ability to concentrate at short notice to engage in
large and medium attacks; to wear down the enemy with ambushes
and harassing attacks with the minimum use of materiel and rebel
casualties; to move back to the cities and rebuild the mass movement
that had been decimated by the terror of the early 1980s; to destroy
the local power of the government and create a vacuum of power, and
put in its place a local power of "double face" (*doble cara*) with both an
open and a clandestine character; and to take the war to the "deep
rearguard of the enemy with special operations against the strategic
infrastructure and the military forces."[51]

By the middle of 1984 the Salvadoran government and armed
forces, and U.S. policymakers and advisers, believed the war had
been turned around. The army had weathered the heaviest FMLN
assault of the war and had pushed the guerrillas onto the defensive particularly through its expanded air capability, more irregular
tactics, and improved intelligence. Captured rebel documents and
increasing numbers of deserters from the FMLN, many of whom
had been forcibly recruited, provided evidence that the guerrillas
were going through a difficult period.[52] The elections of March and
May 1984 that brought José Napoleón Duarte to the presidency provided hopes that sufficient U.S. funds could be obtained to win the
war.

The War in the Political Arena

Strategies of Counterinsurgency

During the period from 1981 to 1984, the United States and its
Salvadoran allies did not develop a unified political-military strategy to
defeat the FMLN. Rather than adopt a single approach that would
integrate political, military, and economic strategies and tactics to
achieve the overarching objective of defeating the insurgents, the
counterrevolutionary coalition developed a series of piecemeal
approaches to advance its interests. By contrast, the FMLN and its
allies were able to develop a more integrated strategy to attain power,
but in practice they focused heavily on military activities as the key to
attaining their goals.

Militarily, the counterrevolutionary strategy focused on expanding, arming, and training the ESAF so that it could fight the war from
an advantageous position; ensuring that the Salvadoran military

fought an aggressive, irregular, small-unit war; and building popular support for the army and government through civic-action programs and civil defense. Politically, the strategy of the United States and its allies prioritized generating domestic (Salvadoran) and international backing for the government and depriving the insurgents of support, nationally and internationally. As a fundamental necessity for any political or military advance, the United States sought to ensure economic stabilization and growth through direct aid, multilateral assistance, and measures aimed at economic recovery.

A government with strong domestic and international support was seen as the best guarantee against the guerrillas' success. In early 1981 the government was not popular within El Salvador or internationally. The main political strategies developed to legitimate the government were (1) a public-relations campaign to present the guerrillas as Communists backed by the Soviet Union and the Eastern bloc, and the government and military as committed to democracy, so as to ensure sufficient public and congressional support to generate the aid required to win the war; (2) diplomatic initiatives to mobilize international political and material support for the government and armed forces and to isolate the insurgents; (3) a strategy of elections to involve the majority of Salvadorans in the political process and present the government as a product of the will of the Salvadoran people, thereby ensuring enhanced assistance and support; and (4) measures to maintain a government in power that could continue to justify U.S. support, pressure on the government and armed forces to ensure minimum observance of human rights, and a continuation of the economic reforms to merit continued aid.

PUBLIC RELATIONS AND DIPLOMACY.   The strategy of public relations and diplomacy was not a success in the first year. Despite numerous attempts at the highest levels of the Reagan administration to present a rebel victory in the war in El Salvador as a strategic threat to the United States, the majority of Americans appeared more afraid that U.S. involvement would lead to another Vietnam than they were of a guerrilla victory. Many saw El Salvador more as a human-rights concern than as a major challenge to national security. The U.S. Congress mirrored public concerns about El Salvador and, though it granted the majority of assistance requested by the administration, placed restrictions on the aid that called on the administration to certify every six months that progress was being made in key human-rights cases, that economic reforms were continuing, and that the government was gaining control over the actions of the armed forces. A declassified secret National Security Council memo from the first month of the new administration illustrated the problem:

U.S. Public and Congressional Constraints: The full panoply of concerned activist and church groups (with the Roman Catholic hierar-
chy in the forefront) is beginning efforts to mobilize public opinion
to demand an end to U.S. support for the Salvadoran government.
This campaign can be expected to have growing effect—particularly
in Congress—unless our intelligence on international communist
intervention orchestrated by Moscow and Havana convinces the
American public that the East-West factor and El Salvador's proximi-
ty to the U.S. have assumed overwhelming importance in determining U.S. interest.[53]

Internationally the campaign of public relations and diplomacy
was no more successful. A "white paper" purporting to document massive Communist-bloc military aid to the guerrillas was later revealed by
its author to contain serious flaws.[54] Despite an international campaign to build support for the Salvadoran junta, France and Mexico
recognized the FMLN-FDR as a "representative political force" in
August 1981, according the opposition a level of recognition just short
of a "state of belligerency." Though the Reagan administration was
able to neutralize the impact of the declaration to some extent by
mobilizing nine Latin American allies to protest it as an interference
in El Salvador's internal affairs, José Napoleón Duarte called the
Franco-Mexican recognition the "lowest point for the Junta
Government."[55]

ELECTIONS.   The attempt to frame the war in El Salvador as an extension of the East-West conflict continued, but it had only limited success
in convincing those who were not already believers. Of much greater
significance in changing perceptions of the Salvadoran government,
particularly outside the country, was the strategy of guaranteeing legislative and presidential elections in 1982 and 1984. The strategic role
of elections in countering the threat from the left was highlighted by
U.S. Deputy Secretary of State Warren Christopher in August 1980:

An important element of our policy toward the JRG has been to
encourage the initiation of a political process leading toward elections. . . . We view [the elections] as vital to success of the JRG in
countering its radical opponents. Once a political process is
announced . . . the ground will be cut from under the terrorist
groups. The JRG and the military will be given a propaganda weapon,
both domestically and abroad. It would become much easier for foreign governments to justify providing assistance to the JRG. . . .
    The JRG is engaged in a political struggle as well as a military
and security struggle. Announcement of an electoral process would
help immeasurably in this struggle.[56]

A year later, under a new U.S. administration, a similar view of elections was expressed:

> Their purpose, as described by U.S. Ambassador Deane R. Hinton in a recent interview, is to discredit and isolate the Marxist-led insurgents. . . .
> "How are they going to go around the world saying they represent the people of El Salvador if the people of El Salvador are on record as supporting somebody else?" . . .
> "The more a government is legitimized," said one prominent Christian Democratic politician, "the more possibilities it has of aid."[57]

During 1981 the call for elections provided a response to those in El Salvador and internationally who were pressing for negotiations as a way to resolve the civil conflict. The Salvadoran and U.S. governments were able to present the elections as a potential solution to the crisis, invite observers from around the world to witness that they were free and fair, and call on the political and military opposition to take part in them. Carlos Andres Pérez, former president of Venezuela, argued that "the United States is insincere," and the "call for elections to solve El Salvador's problems is madness and stupidity. It has no chance."[58] The FMLN-FDR claimed that elections were meaningless under conditions of civil war in which tens of thousands of opponents of the junta had been murdered.

The elections held in March 1982 for a Constituent Assembly, which would draw up a constitution and choose a provisional president, were a great public-relations success. U.S. policymakers projected the results as a massive repudiation of the guerrillas and a critical moment in the war. For U.S. ambassador Deane Hinton, "Those elections were a turning point in history. In one day the impression of most Americans switched. . . . It was of major importance for turning the situation around politically."[59] Acting Archbishop Rivera y Damas called the large turnout a "vote in favor of peace, democracy and justice," and urged the guerrillas to "accept the judgment of the people" and lay down their arms.[60]

The 1982 elections were an important step in the process of legitimating the Salvadoran government in the eyes of the U.S. Congress and international opinion. This process would receive a greater boost with the 1984 and 1985 elections that brought Duarte to the presidency and gave the PDC the majority in the Legislative Assembly.

The results of the elections were more complex, however. Although the PDC won a plurality of votes, the right-wing parties—ARENA, led by Roberto d'Aubuisson, and the traditional governing party, the PCN—won a majority of the seats and appeared set to name d'Aubuisson as president and to end the land reform. Only intense pressure from the United States, including a congressional threat to cut off aid, ensured that the land reform was not gutted and that the PDC formed part of a coalition government. General Vernon Walters brought a letter from Secretary of State Haig warning that a reversal of the reforms and continued disagreement on who should be president would jeopardize the flow of U.S. economic and military aid.[61] Ultimately, pressure from the United States and the Salvadoran military ensured that an acceptable candidate, Alvaro Magaña, a banker who was close to the armed forces, was chosen as provisional president and that U.S. aid could continue.

The elections were a political victory for the United States and the counterrevolutionary bloc in El Salvador. They were also effective in encouraging the right-wing forces, now represented by the ARENA Party, to attempt to bring about change through the electoral process rather than through coups and other extralegal means. They did not, however, resolve the divisions, particularly between the right wing and the civilian and military supporters of the reform strategy, that made more difficult the effective prosecution of the war.

The period between the elections of March 1982 and those of March 1984 saw no major advances in the consolidation of the counterrevolutionary bloc; the main achievements, beyond writing a new constitution, consisted of surviving in power with the land reform still on the books, human-rights violations kept within limits acceptable to the U.S. Congress, formal steps taken to show an openness to negotiations, and preparations laid for the 1984 elections. The war was the defining issue of Salvadoran politics, although the capital, San Salvador, remained relatively calm, and the central political issues—land reform, negotiations, and human rights—were all closely linked to the question of how best to ensure continued funding for the war. Throughout this period the U.S. Embassy played a central role in mediating disputes among the major actors and attempting to consolidate the bloc of counterrevolutionary forces—ARENA and the far right, the military, and the PDC—behind a coherent political-military strategy to win the war.

LAND REFORM.   The Reagan administration was politically and philosophically opposed to land reform as an interference in the free play of market forces and hence a barrier to economic expansion. In the Salvadoran case, however, administration strategists saw the potential for land reform to undercut the insurgents, and were aware of the importance attached to the socioeconomic reforms by liberal members of Congress and labor leaders. Whereas the administration made no attempt to expand the land-reform program or even ensure that its original purposes were fulfilled, it was careful to ensure that the program was maintained against threats from the Salvadoran right wing.

NEGOTIATIONS.   During the period from 1981 to mid-1984 intensive efforts were made to seek a negotiated solution to the war in El Salvador. These efforts failed primarily because both sides felt they were winning or could win the war. Negotiations thus were used more as a tactic to support the central military efforts, and as a public-relations vehicle, than as a strategy for ending the war.

The Reagan administration viewed negotiations as a face-saving way of losing the war and strongly opposed negotiating with the FMLN except as a tactical device to divide the rebel alliance.[62] The right wing in El Salvador was adamant in opposing negotiations; when informal, exploratory talks began, death-squad killings increased.[63] The military High Command believed that it could win the war and saw no reason to negotiate. The FMLN made a number of calls for negotiations as early as the January 1981 offensive but was divided over the strategy through most of 1981 and 1982. Once it had taken the military offensive by mid-1982 the FMLN saw negotiations as a subsidiary element within a predominantly military strategy for winning power. Under these circumstances any moves toward negotiations were designed to respond to congressional and international pressure and to avoid the appearance of seeking only a military resolution to the conflict. In February 1983, the U.S. ambassador to the United Nations, Jeane Kirkpatrick, indicated that the administration's foreign-policy team was unswervingly opposed to negotiations as a way to end the Salvadoran civil war.[64] Another report stated: "'The feeling never was that we could negotiate an agreement on El Salvador or Nicaragua,' a high [U.S.] official said. 'Notwithstanding, we decided in February that we needed to move on the diplomatic side to deflect the perception of our only going for a military solution.'"[65]

During 1983, steps were taken to open contacts between the U.S. and Salvadoran governments and the FMLN-FDR. A special envoy for Central America, former senator Richard Stone, was appointed to explore political solutions to the conflicts in the region. A Salvadoran government commission was created to open discussions with the rebels, and Stone and the commission held meetings with the FMLN-FDR. But with the government and the United States maintaining that the only matter to negotiate was opposition participation in elections, while the rebel alliance held out for a share of political power, no progress was made toward a political solution in this period.

THE 1984 ELECTIONS.   The major political breakthrough for U.S. policy and the strategy of counterrevolution in El Salvador came with the election of José Napoleón Duarte as president in 1984. The 1982 elections had played an important role in limiting El Salvador's international isolation and in taking the edge off congressional opposition to the administration's policy in the country. But the right-wing majority in the election produced a political result that, if anything, made the prosecution of the war more difficult. Thus, in the 1984 elections, the Reagan administration sought to guarantee not only an electoral process that could help legitimate the government but also a result that could advance the strategies of the United States and its allies to win the war. In practice this meant ensuring that the ARENA candidate Roberto d'Aubuisson, who was linked by U.S. intelligence to the murder of Archbishop Romero and to control of death squads, not be elected president. Because a d'Aubuisson victory was seen as a potential disaster for U.S. policy, the CIA gave $1.4 million to the PDC and the PCN to prevent his victory, and sponsored European and Latin American journalists to travel to El Salvador, where they were given negative information about the ARENA candidate.[66]

The 1984 elections were another political victory for the United States and its major Salvadoran allies. For the guerrillas the elections represented a public-relations defeat but also created a more negative correlation of forces for them. Duarte and the PDC made a social pact with sectors of labor influenced by the American Institute for Free Labor Development (AIFLD) and won the election by 53 percent to 47 percent over d'Aubuisson on a platform that called for peace, an end to the violence, and a resolution of the country's economic problems.[67] The U.S. Embassy and the State Department carried out a serious and sophisticated campaign to present the elections as a true representation of the will of the Salvadoran people and a repudiation of the guerrillas. Internationally, despite the absence of the left and the prevailing war conditions, the elections were viewed as relatively free and fair, and as a rejection of the FMLN.

The election of Duarte in 1984 provided the strongest foundation for the strategy of counterinsurgency since the start of the war. Duarte had been elected and was viewed as a moderate reformer. He had the potential for building a stronger base of domestic support through a continuation of a reformist strategy that could help undercut support for the insurgency. His election and democratic credentials also served to legitimate the government internationally, to increase the likelihood of financial support, and thus to enhance the prospects for winning the war.

From Duarte's inauguration in June 1984, the question of aid to El Salvador ceased to be a highly contentious issue in Congress. Supported by the recommendations of the Kissinger Commission, which issued its report in January 1984, almost all the funds requested by the administration for El Salvador were granted. International support for the government increased. Mexico, which along with France had recognized the insurgents in 1981, upgraded its diplomatic mission to El Salvador, and aid from West Germany was restored. With the military advance of the FMLN halted by early 1984 and the ESAF moving to the offensive, the prospects for defeating the insurgency appeared better in mid-1984 than at any time since the start of the war.

OVERALL STRATEGY OF THE UNITED STATES AND ITS SALVADORAN ALLIES. By early 1983, important actors within the Reagan administration were viewing the situation in El Salvador as desperate, and seeing the need for drastic action to prevent a rebel victory. A declassified National Security Council review of Central America policy, originally classified as "secret-sensitive," highlighted the dilemma facing U.S. policy in the region, and particularly in El Salvador:

> We are committed to defeating the Marxist-Leninists in Central America. We believe that should we fail to do so on the current battlefields of El Salvador and Nicaragua, we shall have to face them in Mexico and on the canal where the stakes will be much higher.
> The American public in its vast majority doesn't want the isthmus to go communist either, but it recoils at the violence of the struggle. And it can become—indeed may now be becoming—impatient with the time it takes to win a guerrilla contest. Moreover, so far post-Vietnam constraints on projection of US power overseas—the War Powers Resolution, policy limits on foreign aid monies, intelligence oversight, and the general aversion to the involvement of US forces in local conflicts—have retained strong constituencies. We have thus not been able "to do it right" because we have had to design a strategy to fit within multiple constraints.

U.S. strategy in Central America was seen to have six basic elements: (1) military assistance to stop and ultimately defeat the Salvadoran insurgents; (2) political and economic reforms in El Salvador and elsewhere; (3) the Caribbean Basin Initiative to win congressional backing and the support of regional leaders; (4) taking the war to Nicaragua; (5) deterring Cuban/Soviet escalation; and (6) the diplomatic track.

Regarding political and economic reforms in El Salvador, the analysis argued that

> we have pressed hard for democratization to legitimize our friends, delegitimize our adversaries, and trump the human rights and pro-negotiations constituencies in the US. We came out hard for land reform in El Salvador—despite its inconsistency with the philosophy of this Administration—for the same reasons, and to assure ourselves one element of organized support at home, the AFL/CIO.

The approach was seen to have worked well for a "constrained strategy," with one key exception: "failure to gain the initiative on the ground in El Salvador."

> In the US our actions have broadened support and reduced tensions. We have been able to turn certification into a means to justify support, rather than to withdraw it.
>
> But in El Salvador our friends have not been able to use the time and the resource[s] to gain the initiative against the insurgents. The guerrillas have been regionalized and have not increased in numbers. But they have more experience, are better armed and coordinated than before, and continue to inflict massive damage on the economy while scoring periodic psychological successes.

Opinions within the administration differed on prospects in El Salvador, with the ambassador seeing the standoff as sustainable with current programs and the commander in chief of U.S. Southern Command in Panama fearing that the Salvadorans "could be defeated in the field, or suffer a catastrophic loss of morale, within the year if much more vigorous support is not provided." Continued guerrilla successes would "stimulate peace initiatives both here and abroad."

Congress and public opinion were viewed as critical to U.S. success in El Salvador by the document's authors.

> What will it take to move the Congress? We believe that present congressional support is neither broad enough nor durable enough to provide the increased resources to keep us in the game for the next two years. . . . It continues to be true that a majority in both houses does not want to have the onus of pulling the plug on neighbors fighting communists. The problem is that at present there is no majority to increase aid, as we must.

Two alternative strategies were seen to be available:

> *First strategy.* Full court press on US national security interests. . . . This is a high risk strategy. . . . [It is not] entirely clear which way the "Who Lost Central America theme" would cut in a [1984 U.S. presidential election] campaign. *Second Strategy.* Develop a centrist bipartisan majority to carry on the struggle—with whatever assistance it takes—through at least the next two years. . . . [This] would require that we show substantial activity on the diplomatic front—either in support of an emerging Latin peace initiative, or on our own. . . . We will have to take extreme care to avoid a Latin-only initiative being seized on by the Congress as evidence the Latins want peace (implicitly: even if we don't) and result in our requests for increased aid being set aside pending its outcome.
>
> *Conclusion:* As our adversaries know well, the struggle for Central America will be decided here, perhaps more than there. We cannot

carry the struggle forward without running major risks. Either we must challenge Congress to put up or shut up on the national security issue—and be prepared to take it to the people. Or we must try to broaden and prolong our support by co-opting the negotiations issue. If we leave things as they are, it is likely that El Salvador will slowly decay confronting us with a defeat, perhaps as early as 1984.[68]

Over the next year the Reagan administration proceeded on both fronts. Every opportunity was taken by the president and his senior advisers to present the issue of Central America as critical to the national security of the United States and to argue that the loss of El Salvador or the consolidation of the Sandinistas in Nicaragua would be a step toward fighting communism on the U.S.–Mexican border, as well as causing thousands of refugees to flee to the United States. At the same time, in mid-1983, the administration began the process of assembling broader support for its policies in the region with the creation of a bipartisan commission, headed by former U.S. Secretary of State Henry Kissinger, to study U.S. options in Central America.

Political Strategy of the FMLN-FDR

In this first period of the war the primary focus of the FMLN was on building the military capacity to defeat the Salvadoran armed forces. An integral part of the FMLN military strategy, once the January 1981 offensive failed to overthrow the government, was to build a social and political base of support in the countryside that provided recruits, provisions, intelligence, and logistical support to make the guerrilla war viable. This social base had its roots in the peasantry that had been radicalized in the 1970s and had long-standing links with the guerrilla organizations. The areas of the FMLN's greatest strength during the war were those regions in which the strongest peasant movements had been built in the 1970s.[69] This base expanded as the FMLN took control of larger areas of the countryside, particularly from 1982 to 1984, although control of territory did not directly correlate with peasant allegiance. A major achievement of the FMLN, and a reflection of the depth of commitment to the cause by its supporters, was the willingness of its rural adherents to maintain their support and stay with the insurgents despite regular and massive army sweeps, massacres, and later, particularly after 1983, the launching of air attacks against rebel zones.

From the FMLN offensive in early 1981 the geopolitical terrain of the war (within El Salvador) began to establish itself. The FMLN formed its strategic rearguard particularly in the northern department of Chalatenango and in Morazán in the east, with bases in San Vicente, Usulután, Cabañas, and on the Guazapa Volcano. The cities, particularly the capital, San Salvador, became the rearguard of the government and armed forces. This had negative implications for the FMLN in a number of respects: The government and armed forces had a monopoly of influence—through information, propaganda, terror, and other forms of social control—upon poorer residents of the capital who had formed one of the strongest bases of support for the revolution up to 1980. This would have an impact on the readiness to engage in political activity of all but the hardiest or most clandestine supporters of the revolution. Second, insofar as the war was occurring mainly in the countryside, many middle-class and wealthy Salvadorans did not need to concern themselves greatly with the conflict and did not provide a source of pressure to end the war. And third, given the difficulty for reporters to go out to the countryside, much of the international news from El Salvador reflected the reality of the capital; as long as San Salvador was quiet and under secure government control, so the country as a whole appeared.

By late 1983 the FMLN recognized the weakness of a strategy that emphasized too heavily the military dimension, that viewed the rural masses as a military more than a political factor in the war, and that overlooked political organizing of workers and marginalized sectors in the major cities under government control. The strategic shift that the FMLN made in 1984 toward a "war of all the people" laid the basis for contending with the government for the allegiance of broad sectors of the urban population.

One of the other main weaknesses of the FMLN's political strategy in the period 1981–1984 was its inability to find an effective way of dealing with the issue of elections. In 1982 the guerrillas sought to prevent the elections from taking place by spurring a popular uprising through successful military actions. In 1984 the attack on the elections was less direct and more a continuation of regular military actions. In each case the military was able to deploy its forces in large numbers to guarantee the vote, particularly in the cities, and was able to present itself as the protector of democracy. On the international level, the FMLN-FDR attempted to combat the U.S.-led public-relations campaign in support of the elections, arguing that the minimum conditions did not exist to hold elections in El Salvador and that only meaningful negotiations could resolve the conflict. The insurgents did not have the resources to compete with the U.S.–Salvadoran government campaign; a combination of effective public relations and a weariness with the war that brought many to the polls in the hope of ending their misery provided the counterrevolutionary side with an electoral outcome favorable to waging the war.

The effectiveness of the elections strategy on the part of the United States and its Salvadoran allies moved the FMLN from a strong and offensive position in terms of international legitimacy in 1981 to a much more defensive situation following the election of Duarte in 1984. The major area of strength of the political work of the FMLN-FDR in this period was its effort to build international support for the revolution, particularly at the grassroots level, and its work to create a movement in the United States that consistently challenged and raised the political costs of a policy of support for the Salvadoran government.

From the mid-1970s the parties that would become the FMLN viewed international support as important to the success of the revolution, and saw raising the international visibility of the conflict in El Salvador as a way of increasing pressure on the Salvadoran government and armed forces. This was a reason for the takeovers of embassies in the late 1970s and the demand for publication of political manifestos in newspapers around the world as part of the price for the release of kidnapped businessmen. With the large exodus of Salvadorans to Europe, Latin America, the United States, and other countries as a result of the dirty war in the late 1970s and early 1980s, supporters of the revolution formed solidarity committees to raise the visibility of the conflict in El Salvador and provide political and material support for the revolution. In the case of the United States this work was particularly important in challenging the U.S. role in the last year of the Carter administration and in building public opposition to the Reagan administration's expansion of U.S. involvement in El Salvador.

Public opposition to Reagan-administration policy, which arose from concerns about the direction of U.S. efforts, the nature of the regime that the United States was supporting, and the perceived parallels with the buildup to war in Vietnam, provided the basis for congressional opposition, and restricted the scope and nature of U.S. involvement in El Salvador. Solidarity organizations, which played a central role in the larger movement in opposition to U.S. policy, carried out demonstrations, civil-disobedience actions, call-ins, and letter-writing campaigns to Congress in opposition to administration policies and in support of the revolution in El Salvador. The groups also raised funds for communities and organizations in El Salvador that were linked to the FMLN or supported the revolution. Faith-based groups played a major role in limiting U.S. involvement and in linking parishes and communities in the United States with their counterparts in El Salvador (and Nicaragua). The movement pressured Congress to place restrictions on U.S. involvement in El Salvador in the early years of the Reagan administration and helped keep the issue of the U.S. role alive in the second half of the 1980s when El Salvador had ceased to be an issue in Congress.

International organizing, and particularly the building of opposition to U.S. policies in El Salvador within the United States, was an
essential political strategy of the Salvadoran insurgents. Half a billion
dollars per year in U.S. aid to a country the size of Massachusetts, with
a budget not much larger than the U.S. aid, could accomplish much
in El Salvador no matter how effective were the FMLN's strategies.
"Broadening the battlefield" by taking the issue of the war in El
Salvador to the American people and the U.S. Congress could limit
intervention and place important constraints on U.S. policy in El
Salvador. The methods used by the FMLN, and implemented most
effectively in the United States by the FPL, mirrored the organizing
model developed in El Salvador. The methods included recruiting
cadre and supporters and building their identification with the
Salvadoran revolution and the particular insurgent organization; carrying out political struggles within key organizations, where necessary,
or recruiting or winning over leading members to ensure that the
plans and activities articulated closely with the strategies and needs of
the insurgents in El Salvador; creating new organizations or coalitions
to respond to particular political or economic needs of the revolutionary movement in El Salvador; and organizing clandestinely with
the maximum compartmentalization of information to prevent effective counterorganizing by U.S. or Salvadoran government agencies or
quasi-independent operators. An important result of this organizing
was that opposition to U.S. policy continued and even grew in the second half of the 1980s despite a large drop in media coverage, a solid
bipartisan consensus in Congress in support of aid to Duarte, and the
apparent shift in the initiative to government forces in the war.

Overall, however, in this first period the political strategies of the
FMLN and its allies were subordinated to the attempt to resolve the
conflict through a predominantly military effort to defeat the
Salvadoran armed forces and their U.S. backers.

The Economic War

One of the most important elements of the Salvadoran civil war in the
period 1981–1984 was the war for the economy between the FMLN
and the Salvadoran government backed by the United States. Each
side saw the health of the economy as crucial to its ability to win the
war. For the FMLN, "The key is to break the capacity of the economy
to sustain the war."[70] For the guerrillas, attacks on the economy—
mainly through sabotage of the electrical and telephone systems,
bridges, dams, power stations, export crops, and processing plants—
had the potential for deepening public opposition to the government

as resources were shifted from social programs to repairing or replacing damaged infrastructure and to higher defense spending. These attacks could also deepen divisions between the dominant classes and the government. According to Villalobos, "Destabilization also plays an important role in generating the conditions for the decomposition of the enemy, through a deepening of the lack of confidence in bourgeois sectors in the capacity of the dictatorship to guarantee for them stability in the functioning of the economy."[71]

The threat of economic sabotage and its potential for disrupting the overall plans of the counterrevolution kept half of the ESAF soldiers tied down in the static defense of infrastructure and unable to take offensive actions against the rebels. The war on the economy also had the potential, the FMLN believed, to stretch the ability and will of the United States to continue funding the war in El Salvador at the level necessary to win.

For the Salvadoran government and the United States, economic stabilization and recovery were essential elements of the political plans to legitimate the government by carrying through the socioeconomic reforms and winning popular support. Economic recovery was also crucial for gaining the support, or at least neutrality, of business sectors on the right, and for guaranteeing adequate funds for the effective military prosecution of the war. In early 1981 the *New York Times* reported that junta president Duarte considered the "economic crisis caused by the guerrilla war was a greater threat than the Marxist guerrillas."[72]

The strategy of the FMLN was to prevent economic recovery through attacks on the "war economy" and through the effects of the war in general. The strategy of the Salvadoran and U.S. governments was to guarantee sufficient funds from the United States and multilateral financial agencies—the International Monetary Fund, the World Bank, and the Inter-American Development Bank—to stabilize the economic situation and then to spur economic growth through advances in the war, political consolidation, and economic measures.

The economic situation in El Salvador was extremely serious in the early 1980s. The country's GDP declined by 9 percent in 1981, following a 9 percent fall in 1980. Between 1979 and 1981 there was a 20 percent decline in productive activity and a 26 percent fall in per capita income. In 1981 almost all investment stopped, industrial production fell by 17 percent, the value of coffee exports declined by 22.1 percent, and that of cotton by 19.3 percent. Between January 1980 and August 1981 employment dropped 27 percent in manufacturing, 56 percent in construction, 25 percent in commerce, and 33 percent in transport.[73] In this situation U.S. economic and military aid, as well as the funds that could be leveraged from international financial institutions, were critical to the survival of the government. In the face of significant congressional opposition, the Reagan administration was able to increase U.S. aid to El Salvador from $64.5 million (including $6 million in military aid) in 1980 to $156 million ($35 million in military aid) in 1981, and $302 million ($80 million in military aid) in 1982.[74] Increasingly, U.S. assistance made up the shortfall between government revenues and expenses while building up the capacity of the Salvadoran armed forces to confront the FMLN.

Economic sabotage and the general costs of waging the war were a critical factor in preventing economic recovery in the first years of the 1980s. A U.S. Embassy study estimated the damage caused by the insurgents in the 1980s at $596.8 million, including lost agricultural production ($235.2 million); budgetary outlays on refugees and defense ($150.5 million); losses to industry and commerce ($97.8 million); damage to infrastructure ($98.1 million); and other minor losses ($15.2 million).[75] The broader assessment of lost production resulting from lack of investment was estimated to be over $1.5 billion; this was compounded by a drop in world prices for coffee and cotton that produced a loss in the 1980s of $2.2 billion from 1976–1980 levels.[76]

The effect of the sabotage and the costs of the war worsened an extremely bad economic situation. By 1982 per capita GDP had fallen by a third from 1978 levels. In 1983 and 1984 the economy began to bottom out, with no growth the first year and only 1.5 percent expansion in the second. In 1984 coffee and cotton production continued to contract significantly. The deficit on the current account was $310 million, or 7 percent of GDP. Manufacturing production leveled off, albeit at 70 percent of 1978 levels. Official unemployment figures rose to 30 percent. However, $400 million a year in U.S. aid for 1983 and 1984 helped keep the economy afloat.[77]

During the period 1981–1984 a higher proportion of government spending was allocated to fund the war: Expenditure for defense and public security rose from 14 percent to 22 percent of the budget between 1980 and 1984, while spending for social programs declined from 55 percent to 37 percent of the government budget during this period.[78] Wages remained frozen, increasing the potential for an explosion of wage demands once the political system opened up. Increasing aid was required from the United States to prevent economic collapse during a period when funds from Congress were by no means guaranteed.

Yet despite the effectiveness of the FMLN's attack on the economy, the Reagan administration was able to convince Congress to appropriate sufficient funds to prevent an economic collapse while financing the military buildup that was intended to turn the war around. By mid-1984 the economic war was a stalemate: The FMLN was able to prevent economic growth while the U.S. government was able to guarantee sufficient funding for the government to prevent economic collapse. As a new period began under the Duarte government there were favorable signs for both sides: External funding for the government would be easier to obtain but real incomes were estimated to have fallen by as much as 45 percent to 50 percent between 1980 and 1985,[79] and the conflict between the PDC and the private sector over the reforms and economic policy remained as bitter as ever.

Evaluation of the Strategies

Strategies of the FMLN-FDR

During the period from January 1981 to June 1984 the military strategies of the FMLN placed the government army on the defensive and brought the war close to a point of resolution in late 1983. With a strategy that sought to respond to and defeat each new stage of the counterinsurgency war, the guerrillas succeeded in building a force that U.S. advisers termed the most effective guerrilla army in Latin American history; consolidated a loyal and reliable social base of support in the countryside; won control of between one-quarter and one-third of the national territory; defeated a much larger and better-armed force in numerous engagements, taking hundreds of prisoners, causing thousands of casualties, and capturing numerous arms; and captured important towns, overran key barracks, and helped prevent economic recovery through continuous attacks on the economic infrastructure of the country.

Among the specific strategies and tactics that helped put the FMLN in a dominant military position by 1983 were the following.

THE OFFENSIVE OF 1981. Though it did not achieve its overall objective of overthrowing the government, the January 1981 offensive laid the basis for consolidating guerrilla control of areas of the countryside, building a rearguard, and forming and training a guerrilla army. The offensive epitomized an effective mode of operation of the insurgents: to concentrate all of their forces at a given time to maximize the impact and the costs to the enemy. The rationale for this approach was explained by FMLN leader Joaquín Villalobos:

> We think that it is preferable at a given moment to make a global review and look for a new strategic objective, using one hundred percent of our forces with the goal of bringing about a significant change, a turnaround of the situation. A combination of actions in

the same period gives better results than a mere quantitative sum of
operations that are not joined in the same maneuver.

The 10th of January [1981 offensive] has that virtue. We could
have used all our armed potential, accumulated for January 10, in
another way, more spaced, continuous, with successive operations.
That would have been a grave error. We would not have stopped the
enemy.[80]

This approach would also be a key part of FMLN strategy in the late
1980s, in which all efforts were focused on a "strategic counteroffensive" ultimately launched in November 1989.

DEFENSE, CONSOLIDATION, AND ADVANCE, 1981–1982.   During this period the FMLN defended areas and populations that would form the
guerrilla rearguard, developed skills in military operations and tactics,
guaranteed the arming, training, and provisioning of the insurgent
army during a difficult period, and took the initiative with attacks
against lightly defended positions, economic sabotage, and the attrition of enemy forces.

This strategy, combining tactical offensive and defensive operations, laid the groundwork for a prolonged war that could play to the
strengths of the insurgent forces: their long-term commitment to a
political vision, strong rural support, mobility, good intelligence,
knowledge of the terrain, training, and growing military experience.

CONCENTRATION OF FORCES AND SEARCH FOR MILITARY VICTORY, MID-1982
TO THE END OF 1983.   The strategy of concentrating forces to bring a
military resolution to the conflict brought major initial successes.
According to all indicators—ESAF casualties, arms taken, prisoners
captured, terrain controlled, major towns and army positions taken,
infrastructure damaged or destroyed, level of enemy morale—the
guerrillas were winning the war. However, the FMLN had military
weaknesses. Its concentration of forces made the insurgents vulnerable to the assets of the armed forces, particularly helicopters, aircraft,
and artillery, supported by greatly improved technical intelligence
available to the military. Though the FMLN had become much more
sophisticated in the military sphere, a quasi-regular war played to one
of the strengths of the ESAF: its access to sophisticated equipment and
extensive funds to wage a high-technology war.

The political weaknesses of this strategy were even more telling.
The focus on achieving a quick military victory had negative political
consequences: Military considerations took precedence over political
ramifications, as, for example, with the decision to forcibly recruit to
the guerrilla army. In this situation, the need for greater numbers of
troops to replace combatants killed and wounded and to engage in

large-scale actions became a more important consideration than the negative consequences for the guerrillas in loss of local political support, high levels of desertion, and a negative international image. The FMLN also acknowledged the political weaknesses of this militaristic focus in undervaluing the importance of political work with the masses in the major cities. The insurgents failed to contest effectively the military, political, psychological, and ideological control by the government and armed forces of the large proportion of the country's population that resided in the urban centers.

In these circumstances a military victory, even if it had occurred, would have placed the FMLN in a very difficult situation. With much of the population not actively committed to either side and the U.S. government determined to prevent a rebel victory, the FMLN would have been in a significantly weaker and more vulnerable position than were the Sandinistas in July 1979, had they succeeded in the military strategy.

"WAR OF ALL THE PEOPLE," FROM 1984.   The change in FMLN strategy from early 1984 was viewed as a sign of weakness by most of its opponents, a signal that the guerrillas were on the ropes and that with the appropriate political and military strategies, and the advantages presented by Duarte's election, the FMLN could be defeated relatively quickly. Even within the guerrillas' own ranks the change in strategy raised doubts and concerns: The shift to a strategy based on smaller units and political-military work with the local population required more initiative and political and ideological commitment. Desertions and defections increased, and the guerrillas moved to purge their ranks of wavering elements and to strengthen the political and ideological core of the revolutionary movement. Within the period 1981–1984, the shift in FMLN strategy could be interpreted in different ways: as a defensive response to the strategies of the ESAF and its U.S. backers, or as a political move that would, in the medium to long term, strengthen the position of the guerrillas. This would only become clear in the next period. What the insurgents had done, however, was to revert to a strategy that focused on dispersion of forces, linking the political and military aspects of the war, and positioning themselves for a prolonged process of "wearing out" what they considered the reformist facade of the counterinsurgency war.

ECONOMIC SABOTAGE.   During the period 1981–1984 the attack on the economy helped prevent the stabilization and growth of the economy that could have lessened the divisions between the government and business groups, and allowed more resources to be channeled into programs that would benefit the majority, thus undercutting the populist appeal of the rebels. In fact, however, even with $400 million a year in aid from the United States, social and economic conditions deteriorated dramatically for the majority, boding ill for the future. Annual per capita income fell by 30 percent between 1978 and 1983, while spending on social programs declined from 55 percent to 37 percent of the government budget between 1980 and 1984.[81]

It was claimed that economic sabotage had negative consequences for the guerrillas because actions such as destroying electrical towers, bridges, and buses hurt the very people whose support the FMLN was attempting to win or maintain. This was a continuous theme of the government and its supporters; the FMLN claimed that while its actions had some negative collateral consequences for the poor, the fundamental damage was caused to a wealthy minority whose support was essential to the continuation of the counterinsurgency war. The rebel position was laid out by Joaquín Villalobos:

> FMLN sabotage strikes at strategic parts of the economy: the electricity that is mostly used by industry, trade and the productive apparatus of the nation's vital areas; export products which generate foreign exchange (coffee, cotton and sugar cane); the telecommunications system, which has military and economic value; the railroad and transportation system. This . . . directly affects the economic structure of the capitalist oligarchic system.[82]

An analysis of the impact of economic sabotage in the *Los Angeles Times* saw the strategy as a "double-edged sword" that could damage the guerrillas' "credibility with the poor majority in whose name the war is being waged." However, the advantages to the insurgents were seen to be significant:

> Attacking the economy strikes directly at the mercantilist right-wing, which has historically ruled the country to its own advantage in collaboration with the army.
>
> It is a strategy that buys time by prolonging the military struggle and tying down the army while there is no clear political mandate for guerrilla victory. More troops are occupied in guarding places and things than are hunting guerrillas.
>
> By stripping rural areas of what few fruits of the 20th Century they do possess, the strategy makes the guerrillas seem omnipresent and the army more incompetent. About 60 percent of the Salvadoran people live in rural areas. Finally, the strategy tends to stretch distances in a small, overpopulated country the size of Massachusetts, again to the benefit of the guerrillas, who go on foot while the army prefers to ride. . . .
>
> A military observer here concluded that the guerrillas "are antagonizing a lot of people who depend on public transportation and those in the country who depend on electricity."

A Salvadoran analyst countered, however: "The guerrillas know what they are doing. In the countryside only a relative handful of people ever had electricity. When they blow a power line, it hurts their enemies, not themselves."

(A Ministry of Planning study shows that in 1978, before the war began, only 18 percent of the country's 460,263 units of rural housing had electricity.)[83]

An advantage of economic sabotage for the FMLN lay in the fact that a single act (e.g., destroying a major bridge) could have political, economic, and military implications at the same time: affecting the political confidence of the dominant sectors, preventing economic recovery and the ability of the government to satisfy political and economic expectations, and forcing the military to adopt more defensive strategies that limited their mobility. The perceived value of the strategy to the rebels is evident from the fact that the FMLN continued to employ sabotage throughout the war as a core element of the revolutionary war.

POLITICAL AND DIPLOMATIC STRATEGIES.   During this period political strategies played an important but subordinate role in the FMLN's attempt to take power. International diplomacy, particularly the role of the FDR, was effective in helping isolate the Salvadoran government in 1981 and to a lesser extent in 1982. In the following years, with the elections of 1982 and 1984, the government and the United States took the offensive in the arena of international public relations and diplomacy. Consistent diplomatic activity and media and public-relations work by the FMLN-FDR helped to offset the enormous material advantages possessed by the U.S. and Salvadoran governments, and prevented propaganda setbacks from having a material effect on the insurgents' ability to wage the war. Work to influence the direction of the activities of international solidarity, particularly in the United States, helped keep the Reagan administration on the defensive in its policies toward El Salvador and the Central American region in the period up to the 1984 elections, when the initiative moved strongly in favor of the U.S. and Salvadoran governments.

The role of negotiations during this period was a subordinate one, given the major differences between the two sides on what was negotiable and the fact that each side thought it could win the war. The FMLN-FDR was able to prevent the issue of negotiations from being subsumed within a debate about elections—to prevent the Salvadoran government from defining the insurgents' participation in elections as the only issue to negotiate. However, the insurgents were not able to coalesce a sufficient body of international support for negotiations that would address the fundamental issues that gave rise to the civil conflict.

Finally, through support from friendly regimes, parties, and international solidarity, as well as military actions that recovered weapons, the FMLN was able to guarantee sufficient economic and military support to prolong the war.[84]

Strategies of the Counterinsurgency

MILITARY STRATEGIES.   The three main military strategies of the United States and the Salvadoran government and armed forces between 1981 and 1984 were (1) rapidly expanding, arming, and training the Salvadoran military to confront the insurgency from a position of strength; (2) waging an aggressive, mobile, small-unit war, to take the conflict to the insurgents, and force them out of the populous and economically important central zone and into the poorer northern and eastern border areas; and (3) launching a counterinsurgency campaign to win popular support for the government and armed forces through civic-action programs, and guarantee security and loyalty through the formation of civil-defense units throughout the country.

The expansion, arming, and training of the military was effective defensively in helping to stave off defeat by the FMLN in 1983. The growth of the armed forces ensured that despite an extremely high casualty rate from mid-1982 the armed forces did not collapse: 2,292 government soldiers were killed in action, 4,195 were wounded, and 328 listed as missing in the twelve-month period ending June 30, 1983.[85] This was just less than double the total figure for the preceding twelve-month period, and more than a fifth of the total force structure of the Salvadoran armed forces. The military build-up, particularly the expansion of the number of helicopters and fixed-wing aircraft and improved intelligence on insurgent positions provided by U.S. military and intelligence agencies, was critical in confronting the FMLN strategy of concentrating its forces and attempting to defeat the ESAF militarily. Some of the U.S.-trained units, particularly the long-range reconnaissance patrols, "Hunter" battalions, and larger rapid-deployment battalions, were more effective than other units in confronting the guerrillas and helped prevent defeat.

The strategy of waging an aggressive, small-unit war was far less successful. Despite continuous pressure from the U.S. advisers, the Salvadoran High Command resisted the application of these tactics and fought a defensive war using large units, backed by artillery and air support. The U.S. advisers had some successes. They built up the reputations of Salvadoran officers who waged a more aggressive and offensive war, and helped secure changes in the ESAF High Command in 1983 to a leadership more in tune with the preferred U.S. strategy. Overall, however, no permanent change was effected in the ESAF approach to waging the war against the insurgents. Although expanded numbers and access to sophisticated equipment provided the Salvadoran military with the initiative in 1984, these advantages proved to be less significant in the future, particularly given the FMLN's shift back to a more irregular war.

Even before the war formally began, senior Salvadoran officers, under the influence of U.S. advisers, learned the language of counterinsurgency. The war, they argued, was 90 percent political and 10 percent military. In early 1981 military commanders said that they were following a political strategy of social changes to isolate the guerrillas from the population: "We have already demonstrated that we can defeat the guerrillas," said Colonel José Guillermo García, the minister of defense, "but I insist that the solution should not be military but political."[86] Later, in the words of Colonel René Emilio Ponce, "We believe we are going to end this war and solve the internal conflict by attacking the causes which are the basic needs of the population, and our entire plan is directed toward the civilian population. To win the hearts and minds of the civilian population."[87]

In practice, for most of this period, the Salvadoran military launched major sweeps that hurt the civilian population much more than the insurgents, and carried out massacres of civilians, particularly in the early years of the war. This history would hamper future attempts at civic action and, in the period 1981–1984, only one major "hearts and minds" program was launched. This was the National Plan that sought to force the FMLN from San Vicente province, restore infrastructure, win support for the government and army through social and economic improvements, and maintain security through the creation of civil-defense units.

The FMLN assigned the plan's failure to its inability to address the real needs of the people. According to Leonel González, the civic-action program failed "because it did not really seek to resolve the problems, that is the main factor. And that is what allowed us to link up with the people and push them into struggle, because the people want land, they want drinkable water, and they are offered much and are given nothing."[88]

The Salvadoran armed forces viewed the program as a "gringo plan" (reflecting U.S. interests and priorities) and tried to distance themselves from it.[89] When military pressure from the FMLN increased in the fall of 1983, the army moved troops out of San

Vicente, allowing the guerrillas to move back into the area and dooming the plan.

THE AGRARIAN REFORM.   The land reform was a politically and economically ambitious program, and when first implemented in March 1980 it was hailed as the most far-reaching in the history of Latin America. Its prime objective was to take away the banners of revolution and change from the revolutionary opposition. The transfer of a substantial proportion of the country's land to land-poor and landless peasants was designed to undercut the appeal of the insurgents and deal a crushing blow to the revolution. At the same time, the reform was intended to alter the highly unequal distribution of land and wealth that was seen as the prime cause of the insurgency. This would break the power of the oligarchy and inaugurate a new era in socioeconomic and political relations in El Salvador, promoting a political center against the extremes of left and right.

The change effected by the land reform was substantial. The reform transferred about 22 percent of the country's land to 87,547 small farmers,[90] thus affecting about half a million people including family members, some 25 percent of the rural population. But its real political and economic impact was decidedly limited. The fundamental limitation was the failure to carry out Phase 2, the core of the program. An FMLN leader, Ramón Suarez, commented on the reform's impact:

> Agrarian reform had some impact in taking away some of the banners of struggle of the FMLN. It didn't do more because land reform had so many contradictions; if Phase 2 and 3 had been implemented it would have been more difficult; peasants wanted land reform but the class struggle was so heightened they were not willing to accept *this* land reform.[91]

Phase 2 of the reform was put off indefinitely because its implementation would have exacerbated the already very tense relations between the government and the landowners linked to the far right. Because it would have affected the majority of the coffee land, implementation of the reform also threatened to disrupt an economic situation that was already desperate. The decision was thus made by the military–PDC junta, in close collaboration with the U.S. Embassy, not to implement Phase 2 and thus to trade off the possibility of undercutting the revolution for immediate political security. The result was that the appeal of the revolutionaries was not significantly affected by the land reform, as demonstrated by their ability to win popular support in the countryside during this period. Failure to implement Phase

2 also meant that the economic power of the traditional landowning class was affected but not broken by the reform, and the right wing was able to regroup and move back to the center of power, albeit under new conditions.

The success of the land reform did not lie in winning peasant support from the insurgents. There is no evidence that the reform had any significant impact in pacifying the countryside and, with the exception of the western departments of Sonsonate and Ahuachapán, the rural areas were the most volatile part of the country during the period 1981–1984. The reform had a limited impact on the economic power of the landed oligarchy. Phase 1 of the reform expropriated only 14 percent of the coffee land, 31 percent of the cotton, and 24 percent of the sugar cane. (Sixty percent of Phase 1 lands were used for cattle grazing or lay fallow.)[92] Phase 3 largely affected owners of small plots that did not form the heart of the export-crop economy. The reform actually succeeded in providing a rallying point for the far right while the most significant part of the program, Phase 2, was never put into effect.

The reform had mixed results economically. In 1982 the U.S. Embassy concluded that of 328 peasant cooperatives, about 95 were holding their own, 95 had serious problems that might be resolved, 95 were beyond hope, and 40 were closed because they were in rebel areas.[93] According to a later study by a joint team from AID, the State Department, and the Office of Management and Budget: "The agrarian reform appears to be generally accepted as permanent and irreversible, but also as an economic failure."[94] The major contribution of the land reform was political rather than economic. The *New York Times* reported in mid-1981:

> Asked whether the [land reform] program had been a success so far, a conservative Salvadoran businessman replied, "Economically no, politically, yes." . . .
> Peter Askin, the director of the office here of the United States Agency for International Development . . . said, "It has not been a total economic success. But," he added, "up to this point it has been a political success. I'm firm on that."[95]

Even the political impact was limited, operating more on the level of public relations than as a vehicle for winning popular support. Ultimately, the main contribution of the land reform appears to have been to convince the U.S. Congress that El Salvador was set on a course of reforms that justified continuing economic and military aid. The land reform came to be a critical symbol of the Salvadoran government's commitment to socioeconomic and political change, and as long as the program remained substantially intact, aid could continue even though the results of the program bore little resemblance to the original promise.

THE ELECTIONS STRATEGY. Irrespective of what major U.S. and Salvadoran participants believed about the importance of elections and their role in consolidating and maintaining democracy, the primary goal of the elections of 1982 and 1984 was a political-military one: to isolate the insurgents, project them as without popular support and hence interested only in winning power by force, and in the process legitimate the government that resulted from the elections. Elections viewed as free and fair and with an acceptable result could then help justify increased aid for the war effort. Elections also provided a framework for the political parties supporting the counterinsurgency effort to strengthen their popular base of support, and for the right-wing forces in the country to seek change through electoral contests rather than destabilizing actions such as coups.

The strategy of seeking to isolate the left and legitimate the government through elections required certain key elements to achieve its objective. First, the elections had to be seen nationally and internationally as involving a *process* that was relatively free and fair and that reflected the will of the Salvadoran people. In spite of significant doubts about the potential for the elections of 1982 to be free and fair under the prevailing conditions in El Salvador, which was reflected in the low number of official monitors sent even by U.S. allies, the campaign to project the elections favorably in international public opinion was effective. The television images of long lines of eager voters carried more weight than arguments about the conditions of war and violence in the country, the absence of the left from the process, or compulsory voting. Although the 1982 elections were not conclusive in isolating the insurgents or legitimating the government, due to the nature of the result, they were an important step in the process of legitimating the counterrevolutionary strategy in the country. The 1984 elections that resulted in Duarte's presidency further consolidated this process.

The second important element in a successful strategy of elections was to ensure an *outcome* that would be favorable in El Salvador and internationally to the effective prosecution of the war. The 1982 elections achieved an outcome that did not contribute to the effort to defeat the insurgents. The 1984 elections, by contrast, were successful in terms of both process and outcome. The Duarte victory was heralded internationally as a vote for peace and democracy and as a defeat for the insurgents. Most important, it convinced a large majority in the U.S. Congress to "give Duarte a chance" and vote substantial amounts of aid for the war.

The elections of 1982 and 1984 were of great importance in helping to turn around a very unfavorable political-military situation. The 1984 elections led to the symbolically important thawing of diplomatic relations with Mexico, the restoration of economic aid by West Germany, and the commitment by many in the U.S. Congress to increased aid levels. This improved the conditions for waging the war and made the political-military situation more difficult for the FMLN and its allies. But there were limits to the extent to which an electoral strategy could contribute to the war effort if it did not unify the bloc of counterrevolutionary forces or build a strong base of popular support for the new government. The weakness of the outcome of the 1984 elections was that the forces opposing the FMLN were still internally divided and hostile to each other and, though Duarte and the PDC were able to win a bloc of worker and peasant support on the basis of promises of peace and economic improvements, it was not clear how they could satisfy these demands under the prevailing conditions.

The "Grand Strategy" of the Two Sides

Certain strategies of the parties in the Salvadoran conflict were effective in helping to move each side toward the objective of defeating its adversary and being in a position to implement its political program. For the United States and its Salvadoran allies the strategy of guaranteeing elections that could gain international support and legitimacy for the resulting government was important in creating favorable conditions to win the political-military conflict. The military strategy of expanding, arming, and training the Salvadoran armed forces to confront the insurgency helped stave off defeat at the height of the FMLN's military offensive in 1983. Other strategies, such as the agrarian reform and the shift of the ESAF to wage a more aggressive war, were unsuccessful because they were gutted of the core elements or never implemented. For the FMLN and its allies, the ability to rebound quickly from the failure of the 1981 offensive and then build a rearguard, with a firm social base; arm, train, and provision a guerrilla army; and bring the Salvadoran military to the brink of defeat in a period of less than three years testified to the determination of the FMLN and the strength of the roots it had put down in the 1970s. But the limitations of the predominantly military strategy of the FMLN during this period were the basis for a profound shift in strategy to an approach that elevated the importance of the political dimension of the war.

Did either of the two sides succeed in integrating political, military, economic, and diplomatic strategies into a grand strategy to defeat the adversary? The overall answer is negative.

The FMLN had a coherent and effective approach to diplomacy, public relations, international solidarity, and negotiations. But its primary strategy was military, and it did not succeed in this period in parlaying its growing military strength into diplomatic initiatives to end the war on favorable terms or even to force meaningful negotiations. The de facto division of the country—with the cities dominated by the government and armed forces and large areas of the countryside under guerrilla control—and the FMLN's focus on breaking the armed forces militarily, left much of the population subject to government control and influence. The FMLN was not able in this period to integrate closely its political-military efforts, largely in the rural areas, with activities to generate political support for the insurgency in the cities. Clearly this would have been a difficult task given the campaign of terror carried out in 1980–1982. But this was precisely the task that the FMLN set itself with its change to a "people's war" strategy in 1984.

Overall the FMLN advanced during the period 1981–1984 and laid the basis for a prolonged war. But its predominantly military focus in the last part of this period prevented it from reaping political advantages from the advances it had made, played to some of the military strengths of the armed forces (particularly, their growing numbers and advanced technology), and failed to contend with the government for a large proportion of the urban population. At the same time, despite the weakness of this militaristic orientation, the FMLN had the strength of flexibility: the readiness to alter strategies based on changing situations and evaluation of their effectiveness. This allowed the insurgents to make a 180-degree turn from large-scale, quasi-conventional war to a more political struggle that would incorporate "all the people" after evaluating the strengths and weaknesses of the earlier period. Thus, the FMLN went into a new period apparently weakened and, in the view of U.S. and Salvadoran military officers, on the road to defeat, but with a strategy that could play to the strengths of the rebels and the weaknesses of its adversaries, if executed well.

The United States and the Salvadoran government and armed forces did not have an integrated or overarching strategy in the period 1981–1984. Rather, there were piecemeal efforts in the political, military, and economic areas to prevent defeat at the hands of the FMLN and to move toward military victory over the guerrillas. A great strength of these efforts was that they were generally backed up by sufficient resources to enhance their effectiveness. The buildup of the Salvadoran armed forces that helped prevent a rebel victory during this period was supported by $400 million in military aid between 1981 and 1984.[96] Similarly, the effort to stabilize the Salvadoran economy and prevent the guerrillas from taking political advantage of a deteriorating economic situation was backed by $800 million in U.S. aid during these years.[97] Thus, two of the major strategic efforts to turn the war around were largely a function of resources, the will to use them, and the ability to win sufficient congressional support to appropriate them. The major efforts involved in gaining access to the resources were to prevail upon the military and the right wing to limit human-rights violations, to pressure the right to keep the land-reform program alive, and to guarantee electoral processes and outcomes conducive to a continuation of aid. In these areas the U.S. Embassy worked consistently and effectively to ensure the necessary conditions to keep the aid flowing.

During this first period of the war, the strategies of each side succeeded in preventing the other from winning a military victory and imposing its vision upon the society. The FMLN was able to capitalize upon the organizing work it had done in the 1970s to create a guerrilla army, to build on the momentum generated in the period of popular upsurge of 1979–1980, and to bring the Salvadoran armed forces close to defeat in 1982–1983. The commitment of the United States to provide enough resources to build the capacity of the Salvadoran armed forces and to ensure that the country was not "lost" helped prevent a guerrilla victory but was not enough to defeat the rebels. The war was stalemated with no end in sight and little evidence of compromise on either side. Meanwhile, the costs of the war mounted daily.

In a mid-1984 study, Segundo Montes estimated that more than 5,000 combatants had been killed on both sides, 50,000 civilians had been murdered ("almost all by the armed forces and the death squads"), and there were more than 2,000 political prisoners and disappeared persons. Within El Salvador there were 468,000 displaced people (9.75 percent of the population), 244,000 in Mexico and elsewhere in Central America, and 500,000 more in the United States, for a total of more than 1.2 million displaced and refugees (25 percent of the population). Hundreds of schools had been closed, affecting 110,000 students in basic education in 1983 alone.[98] Much of the countryside was becoming a "free-fire zone," with grave effects on the environment and on suspected civilian supporters of the rebels (*masas*), who were viewed as legitimate targets. With real wages continuing to decline, unemployment rising, and funds for education and social programs shifted to military spending, the suffering caused by the war was building a growing constituency for peace even as the two conflicting sides sought to resolve the conflict militarily.

Notes

1. United Nations, ECLA, *Economic Survey of Latin America, 1980* (Santiago, Chile: United Nations, 1982), 251, 253, 257–259.

2. U.S. Department of State, "Annual Integrated Assessment of Security

Assistance for El Salvador," telegram from U.S. Embassy, San Salvador, to Secretary of State, Washington, D.C., 12 June 1981, sect. 1, pp. 1–2, in *The Making of U.S. Policy: El Salvador 1977–1984*, National Security Archive, doc. #01805.

3. "Plataforma programática para un Gobierno Democrático Revolucionario de la Coordinadora Revolucionaria de Masas," in *Estudios Centroamericanos* 377/378 (March/April 1980), 343.

4. Ibid., 343–345.

5. Joaquín Villalobos, *The War in El Salvador: Current Situation and Outlook for the Future* (San Francisco: Solidarity Publications, 1986), 29–30. Estimates from declassified U.S. intelligence documents put annual insurgent expenses (for the FMLN and its five constituent parties) at about $25–30 million. FMLN leaders in interviews found these estimates excessive. One FPL commander estimated the annual budget of the largest of the five FMLN parties at about $1 million a year and that what the army spent in a day would last the FMLN a month. Gerson Martínez, author interview, 11 July 1995. By comparison, U.S. economic and military aid to El Salvador during the 1980s (irrespective of the government's own revenues) averaged more than $400 million a year.

6. Examples of such actions were the killing of four U.S. marines and nine civilians in cold blood in San Salvador's Zona Rosa in 1985; and the forced recruitment of people into the FMLN.

7. Colonel John Cash, interview by Max G. Manwaring, 20 March 1987, 14.

8. Ramón Suarez, author interview, tape recording, San Salvador, 20 February 1993; Miguel Saenz, author interview, 11 July 1995.

9. See Colonel John D. Waghelstein, interview by Colonel Charles A. Carlton, Jr., U.S. Army Military History Institute, Senior Officers Oral History Program, Project 85-7, El Salvador, 1985, 8, 17, 39, 141.

10. U.S. Department of State, "Preparation of the Congressional Presentation Document (CPD) for FY 1983 Security Assistance Program," telegram #08803 from U.S. Embassy, San Salvador, to Secretary of State, 16 November 1981, sect. 1, p. 3, in *The Making of U.S. Policy: El Salvador 1977–1984*, National Security Archive, doc. #02221.

11. Loren Jenkins, "Salvadoran Rebels Down First 'Huey,'" *Washington Post*, 13 May 1981, A1.

12. In the early years of the war some of the major military massacres were carried out, including those at the Río Sumpul and El Mozote. See, for example, Warren Hoge, "Slaughter in Salvador: 200 Lost in Border Massacre," *New York Times*, 8 June 1981, 8; and UN Truth Commission Report, *From Madness to Hope*, 26–31 and 114–126.

13. See Waghelstein, interview by Colonel Charles A. Carlton, Jr., 37.

14. See Bacevich, et al., *American Military Policy in Small Wars: The Case of El Salvador* (Washington, D.C.: Pergamon-Brassey's International Defense Publishers, 1988), 5.

15. Raymond Bonner, "Salvadoran Rebels Still Predict an Offensive," *New York Times*, 3 January 1981, 5.

16. "Salvador Declares Nationwide Curfew," *New York Times*, 12 January 1981, 1.

17. Alma Guillermoprieto, "Central America at Boiling Point," *Manchester Guardian Weekly*, 1 February 1981; and General Guillermo García, interview by Max G. Manwaring, 2 July 1987, 29.

18. Ignacio Martín-Baró, "La guerra civil en El Salvador," *Estudios Centroamericanos* 387/388 (January/February 1981), 20.

19. Raúl Benítez Manaut, *La teoría militar y la guerra civil en El Salvador* (San Salvador: UCA Editores, 1989), 259.

20. *U.S. Declassified Documents II*, CIA, "Near-term Military Prospects in El Salvador," interagency intelligence memorandum, May 1981.

21. See Harnecker, *Con la mirada en alto*, interview with Leonel González, 237; Harnecker, *Pueblos en armas*, interview with Joaquín Villalobos, 140–143.

22. Luigi R. Einaudi, interview by Max G. Manwaring, 8.

23. Raymond Bonner, "The Agony of El Salvador," *New York Times*, 22 February 1981, VI, 26.

24. Benítez Manaut, *La teoría militar*, 259.

25. U.S. Department of State, "Annual Integrated Assessment of Security Assistance for El Salvador," 12 June 1981, sect. 1, p. 4, in *The Making of U.S. Policy: El Salvador 1977–1984*, National Security Archive, doc. #01805.

26. See Benítez Manaut, *La teoría militar*, 264.

27. Ibid., 270.

28. Fred F. Woerner (Brigadier General), *Report of the El Salvador Military Strategy Assistance Team (Draft)*, photocopy of classified report released with excisions under the Freedom of Information Act, San Salvador, El Salvador, 12 September–8 November 1981, 180. (Hereafter, *Woerner Report*.)

29. Harnecker, *Con la mirada en alto*, interview with Leonel González, 239.

30. See U.S. Department of State, "Preparation of the Congressional Presentation Document (CPD) for FY 1983."

31. Harnecker, *Pueblos en armas*, interview with Joaquín Villalobos, 159.

32. Loren Jenkins, "Rebel Rallies Preempted Vote in 'Other El Salvador,'" *Washington Post*, 5 April 1982, A1.

33. U.S. Department of State, "Annual Integrated Assessment of Security Assistance for El Salvador," telegram #04411 from U.S. Embassy, San Salvador, to Secretary of State, Washington, D.C., 26 May 1982, sect. 1, pp. 2–3, in *The Making of U.S. Policy: El Salvador 1977–1984*, National Security Archive, doc. #03070.

34. Harnecker, *Pueblos en armas*, interview with Joaquín Villalobos, 162.

35. Harnecker, *Con la mirada en alto*, interview with Leonel González, 244.

36. Christopher Dickey, "Salvadoran Army Tries New Tactics in Offensive," *Washington Post*, 6 June 1982, A25; Christopher Dickey, "Salvadoran Guerrillas Take Village," *Washington Post*, 9 June 1982, A24.

37. Dial Torgerson, "Salvadoran Army, Tactics Change with U.S. Training," *Los Angeles Times*, 15 July 1982, 1; Benítez Manaut, *La teoría militar*, 271.

38. Lydia Chavez, "Fighting Heavy as Rebels Attack El Salvador's Third Largest City," *New York Times*, 5 September 1983, I, 1.

39. Lydia Chavez, "Salvador Rebels Make Gains and U.S. Advisers Are Glum," *New York Times*, 4 November 1983, I, 1.

40. Sam Dillon, "Salvadoran Rebels Carve Enclave," *Miami Herald*, 27 November 1983, 1A.

41. Colonel Robert M. Herrick, interview by Max G. Manwaring, 18 December 1986, 1–2; and "Salvadoran Rebels Cut Vital Span," *Washington Post*, 2 January 1984, A1.

42. U.S. Department of State, "El Salvador: The Military Situation," briefing paper, 2 December 1983, in *The Making of U.S. Policy: El Salvador 1977–1984*, National Security Archive, doc. #04378.

43. James McCartney, "El Salvador Losing the War, Brass at Pentagon Contend," *Miami Herald*, 20 May 1983, 19A.

44. See *Woerner Report*, 179; and U.S. Department of State, "El Salvador Military Assessment," telegram #06485 from U.S. Embassy, San Salvador, to Secretary of State, Washington, D.C., 4 August 1982, sect. 5, p. 3, in *The Making of U.S. Policy: El Salvador 1977–1984*, National Security Archive, doc. #03334.

45. See Department of State, "Combined Political, Economic, Military Plan," n.d., p. 1, in *The Making of U.S. Policy: El Salvador 1977–1984*, National Security Archive, doc. #03680.

46. See Benítez Manaut, *La teoría militar*, 290–291; and Michael Getler, "Salvadoran Troops Have Seized the Initiative, Reagan Is Told," *Washington Post*, 27 August 1983, A1.

47. Lydia Chavez, "U.S. Pilot Program in Salvadoran Area in Danger of Failing," *New York Times*, 18 December 1983, I, 1.

48. Ambassador Thomas Pickering, interview by Max G. Manwaring, 28 August 1987, 4.

49. Farabundo Martí National Liberation Front (FMLN), *El Salvador vive una prolongada situación revolucionaria* (first of seven sections; no overall title), photocopy, Morazán, June 1985, 33. Although FMLN documents stress the political importance of the shift in strategy and this appears to have allowed the insurgents to wage a different and more political type of war, in interviews leaders of the FMLN stressed their troops' vulnerability in large-unit warfare and the damage that was caused by ESAF aircraft and artillery as major factors in precipitating the change in strategy.

50. Ibid., 6.

51. Ibid., 68–71.

52. Robert J. McCartney, "Rebels Use Harsher Methods: Guerrillas Recruit Youths by Force in Salvadoran Towns," *Washington Post*, 18 June 1984, A1.

53. *U.S. Declassified Documents II*, State Department, Part 24D, "Paper for the NSC Meeting on El Salvador," memorandum for Richard V. Allen, 17 February 1981.

54. Jonathan Kwitny, "Apparent Errors Cloud U.S. 'White Paper' on El Salvador," *Wall Street Journal*, 8 June 1981.

55. Max G. Manwaring and Court Prisk, eds., *El Salvador at War: An Oral History of Conflict from the 1979 Insurrection to the Present* (Washington, D.C.: National Defense University Press, 1988), 96; Christopher Dickey, "9 Nations Condemn French-Mexican Support of Salvadoran Left," *Washington Post*, 3 September 1981, A38.

56. U.S. Department of State, "Demarche to Junta re Elections," telegram #183975 from Secretary of State, Washington, D.C., to U.S. Embassy, San Salvador, 12 August 1980, pp. 1–2, in *The Making of U.S. Policy: El Salvador 1977–1984*, National Security Archive, doc. #00738.

57. Christopher Dickey, "Left Expected to Ignore Salvador Vote," *Washington Post*, 31 August 1981, A1.

58. Marlise Simons, "Negotiations Remain Elusive as Salvadoran War Continues," *Washington Post*, 4 June 1981, A1.

59. Ambassador Deane Hinton, interview by Max G. Manwaring, 10 September 1987, 7.

60. Christopher Dickey, "Salvadoran Prelate Warns of Return to Violence," *Washington Post*, 5 April 1982, A27.

61. Joanne Omang, "Salvadorans Pick Key Officials," *Washington Post*, 23 April 1982, A1.

62. Leslie H. Gelb, "U.S. Aides See Need for Big Effort to Avert Rebel Victory in Salvador," *New York Times*, 22 April 1983, I, 1.

63. Edward Cody, "Death Squads Step Up Killings in El Salvador," *Washington Post*, 3 October 1983, A1.

64. Edward Cody, "Kirkpatrick Says U.S. Opposes Negotiations on El Salvador," *Washington Post*, 12 February 1983, A7.

65. Leslie H. Gelb, "U.S. Aides See Need for Big Effort to Avert Rebel Victory in Salvador," *New York Times*, 22 April 1983, I, 1.

66. Philip Taubman, "C.I.A. Said to Have Given Money to 2 Salvador Parties," *New York Times*, 12 May 1984, 6.

67. Robert J. McCartney, "Duarte Tries Again in El Salvador," *Washington Post*, 15 March 1984, A1.

68. *U.S. Declassified Documents II*, National Security Council, "Central America Review," n.d. (1983).

69. Facundo Guardado, a leader of the peasant movement who went on to become secretary-general of the BPR and later was a leading FMLN commander, pointed to San Vicente, Morazán, the northeast of Chalatenango, Santa Ana, Cabañas, Aguilares, the San Salvador Volcano, La Libertad, La Unión, and central Usulután as major zones of FMLN influence or control during the war that had been important areas of organizing for the BPR, FAPU, and the LP-28 movement during the 1970s. Author interview, 15 July 1995.

70. Villalobos, *The War in El Salvador*, 17.

71. FMLN, *Situación revolucionaria y escalada intervencionista en la guerra salvadoreña* (Morazán, El Salvador: Ediciones Sistema Radio Venceremos, January 1984), 45.

72. Edward Schumacher, "From Washington and Salvador, Differing Views on Fighting Rebels," *New York Times*, 21 February 1981, 1.

73. United Nations, ECLA, *Economic Survey of Latin America, 1981* (Santiago, Chile: United Nations, 1983), 391–393, 397–398, 402.

74. CRS Report for Congress, *El Salvador, 1979–1989: A Briefing Book on U.S. Aid and the Situation in El Salvador*, The Library of Congress, Congressional Research Service, Foreign Affairs and National Defense Division, 28 April 1989, 26.

75. Hugh O'Shaughnessy, "IMF Refusal to Aid El Salvador Worries U.S.," *Financial Times* (London), 5 May 1983, 4G.

76. CRS Report for Congress, *El Salvador, 1979–1989*, 6–7.

77. United Nations, ECLA, *Economic Survey of Latin America, 1983* (Santiago, Chile: United Nations, 1985), 346; and United Nations, ECLA, *Economic Survey of Latin America, 1984* (Santiago, Chile: United Nations, 1986), 317, 319, 321–322.

78. CRS Report for Congress, *El Salvador, 1979–1989*, 50, 59.

79. United Nations, ECLA, *Economic Survey of Latin America, 1985* (Santiago, Chile: United Nations, 1987), 330.

80. Harnecker, *Pueblos en armas*, interview with Joaquín Villalobos, 180.

81. CRS Report for Congress, *El Salvador, 1979–1989*, 7, 50.

82. Villalobos, *The War in El Salvador*, 24–25.

83. William D. Montalbano, "Strategy of Destruction by Rebels in El Salvador Risky," *Los Angeles Times*, 26 May 1983, 1.

84. The issue of the supply of arms to the FMLN is dealt with in Chapter 5.

85. Edward Cody, "Army's Toll Doubles in El Salvador," *Washington Post*, 12 August 1983, A1.

86. Edward Schumacher, "El Salvador Says It Can Defeat Rebels," *New York Times*, 25 February 1981.

87. Colonel René Emilio Ponce, interview by Max G. Manwaring, 22 January 1987, 16.

88. Harnecker, *Con la mirada en alto*, interview with Leonel González, 256.

89. Colonel John Cash, interview by Max G. Manwaring, 20 March 1987, 33.

90. CRS Report for Congress, *El Salvador, 1979–1989*, 10.

91. Ramón Suarez, author interview, 23 July 1992.

92. Laurence R. Simon and James C. Stephens, Jr., *El Salvador Land Reform 1980–1981: Impact Audit*, with 1982 Supplement by Martin Diskin (Boston: Oxfam America, 1982), 9, 13.

93. Lynda Schuster, "'Land Reform' Proves Costly to El Salvador, Mixed Blessing to Poor," *Wall Street Journal*, 1 September 1982, 1.

94. CRS Report for Congress, *El Salvador, 1979–1989*, 10, citing "Economic Assistance to Central America—Conclusions of an AID–State–OMB Team," 1988, 1.

95. Raymond Bonner, "Salvador Land Program Aids Few," *New York Times*, 3 August 1981, 1.

96. CRS Report for Congress, *El Salvador, 1979–1989*, 26.

97. Ibid.

98. Segundo Montes, "Hambre a causa del armamentismo," *Estudios Centroamericanos* 429/430 (July/August 1984), 491–502.

5

The Primacy of the Political: Strategies of Insurgency and Counterinsurgency, 1984–1989

By mid-1984 the initiative in the war had shifted dramatically from a year earlier. The major military advance of the FMLN during 1983 had been weathered and the military initiative moved toward the Salvadoran armed forces as their expansion of personnel and new equipment allowed them to confront more effectively an insurgency that was waging almost a regular war. The FMLN's change of strategy toward a "people's war" that emphasized more conventional guerrilla strategy and tactics and a focus on political work also had initial costs that perhaps exaggerated the advantage of the Salvadoran military. Most important, however, the United States and its Salvadoran allies had made a major political advance with the 1984 elections that resulted in the victory of José Napoleón Duarte and created a significantly more favorable climate in the U.S. Congress and in international opinion for the program and objectives of the counterrevolution.

But whereas the political-military initiative was in the hands of the Salvadoran government and armed forces, the FMLN was far from being defeated and had made major advances in the first period of the war. The insurgents had built a guerrilla army that had come close to defeating the ESAF. They had consolidated a strong base of popular support and established rearguard zones that, though not areas of permanent control, could only be temporarily occupied by the Salvadoran military and were effectively political, logistical, and support bases from which the rebels could expand the war. Continued economic stagnation, the effects of the FMLN's sabotage campaign, and the huge decline in real wages in the previous four years offered prospects for the rebels to build popular support and posed a major challenge for the incoming Duarte government.

The election victory of Duarte of the PDC over former Major Roberto d'Aubuisson of the right-wing ARENA Party in May 1984 was a watershed event in the strategic conflict between the insurgent FMLN and its allies and the United States and its Salvadoran allies. Duarte's election helped further legitimate a process of "democratization" in El Salvador and inaugurated a period that was viewed by U.S. policymakers and the Salvadoran government and military as favorable to winning the war.

The election of Duarte placed at the head of the government a man with the reputation of a democrat who had been tortured and exiled by the military twelve years earlier. He led the party that was closely associated with the social and economic reforms of the early 1980s. International support for the government increased significantly and, most important for the prosecution of the war, aid to El Salvador ceased to be a contentious issue in the U.S. Congress throughout Duarte's five-year term.

Other factors helped convince U.S. and Salvadoran leaders that the corner had been turned in the war against the FMLN. The Salvadoran military had survived the FMLN's military blitz of late 1983 and, with the aid of a greatly enlarged force structure and new materiel, in particular sophisticated airplanes and helicopters, had shifted the military balance in the war. The FMLN during 1984 and 1985 reverted to a traditional guerrilla strategy with far fewer major attacks. This shift, as well as the increase in FMLN desertions and reports of lower guerrilla morale resulting from it, convinced the Salvadoran armed forces and the U.S. advisers that they had the guerrillas on the run and that achievement of a military victory was only a matter of time.

The Salvadoran economy, which had declined in the early 1980s, began to stabilize in 1984, supported by $400 million in U.S. aid, though still at levels one-fifth lower than in the late 1970s. With Duarte in office it was anticipated that U.S. aid would flow freely and that appropriate economic policies and a rapprochement between the PDC and the private sector could help create the conditions for economic stabilization and growth. An expanding economy would further improve the conditions for isolating and ultimately defeating the FMLN.

Human-rights violations had declined from the levels of 1980–1982, when an estimated 30,000 people were murdered, and high-level warnings from U.S. leaders had achieved results in moving some notorious violators from their positions in the military, thus defusing a highly contentious issue between the Reagan administration and Congress. The report in early 1984 of the Kissinger Commission[1] also helped cement bipartisan support in Congress for U.S. policy in El Salvador, and was influential in guaranteeing aid levels close to those requested by the administration in the subsequent years.

But though these factors gave rise to optimism on the part of the U.S. and Salvadoran actors in the war against the FMLN, there were counterindicators warning against excessive faith in a speedy victory. Salaries had been frozen since 1981, and real incomes had fallen by a third since 1980. A wave of strikes in 1984, the first significant labor activity since 1980, pointed to the potential political and economic difficulties of satisfying the basic needs of the population while waging the counterguerrilla war. Though viewed by the United States as essential to the effort to defeat the FMLN, the potential for consolidating private-sector support for the Duarte government was beset with difficulties. Many representatives of the business sector and leaders of the ARENA Party viewed the PDC as no more than a front for communism, and as the party responsible for the economic reforms of the early 1980s that had unseated the landowning class from its position of unchallenged political and economic dominance in the country.

Militarily, though the FMLN's shift in strategy placed it on the defensive in the initial period and resulted in a higher number of desertions and fewer spectacular actions, a continued war of attrition, mainly via ambushes, smaller-scale encounters, and the extensive use of mines, along with sabotage of the economy and the expansion of the war to new areas of the country, provided indications that the war was far from over.

In the first period of the war, 1981 to 1984, the two sides fought largely separate wars. While the FMLN consolidated its base in the countryside and moved closer to defeating the Salvadoran armed forces militarily, the United States and its Salvadoran allies focused on legitimating the Salvadoran system and government through a series of elections, and working to prevent the insurgents from winning a military victory.

In the period 1984 to 1989 both sides fought essentially the same war. Each acknowledged that the key to victory lay in the support of people rather than in the control of territory, and both accepted that politics rather than military might per se would be decisive in the outcome of the war. It was in this period that the ultimate resolution of the conflict was largely defined.

Counterinsurgency Strategies

The Context of the Strategies

In 1983–1984 the wars in Central America took on a new character as U.S. strategies in the region became more comprehensive, integrated, political, and regional in focus. This new approach was founded on the vision of the world of President Reagan and his advisers. In this view, two social systems and worldviews, one democratic and based on free enterprise, the other totalitarian and communist, were locked in a mortal struggle in which any advance for one was a setback for the other. The post–World War II order had been built on a "balance of terror" that ruled out direct confrontation between the superpowers as a strategic option, and on "containment" of communism. For the Reagan administration, however, though direct military conflict with the Soviet Union was only an option in extreme circumstances, there was no reason to accept "communist expansion," as in Afghanistan or Nicaragua, and every reason to roll back such advances. Democracy and free enterprise could be expanded at relatively low cost, with little direct involvement of U.S. forces and at low risk of escalating into a superpower confrontation. The political-military strategy that was developed to give effect to this vision and objective from the early 1980s was "low-intensity conflict."

Low-Intensity Conflict

On the spectrum of conflict in warfare, conventional wars between nations represent a midlevel intensity, while major wars and nuclear confrontations represent high-intensity conflicts. The emphasis in situations of low-intensity conflict is on addressing the political dimensions of the conflict (e.g., in a revolutionary conflict, addressing the root causes of the revolution in order to undercut support for the insurgents) rather than on the military threat. The main situations in which low-intensity conflict would be employed were revolutions and counterrevolutions. All the available assets of the United States would be brought to bear in a coordinated strategy to win, though U.S. troops would only be used as a last resort.

None of the major elements associated with low-intensity conflict—civic-action programs, psychological warfare, civil defense, counterterrorism, the integration of civilian and military agencies and programs, or the use of surrogate forces—were radical or new. All had been employed by the United States in Vietnam and lessons had been drawn from their success or failure. New in the conflicts in Central America was the level of integration and coordination among programs and agencies, and the increased regionalization of U.S. strategies to defeat the Sandinista government in Nicaragua and the FMLN in El Salvador. Interagency coordination between the Defense Department, the CIA, the National Security Agency, the State Department, AID, the National Security Council, and others became the norm in Washington and on the ground in Central America. Civilian and military efforts were meshed within an overall counterinsurgency strategy, as exemplified by the role of AID in supporting the counterrevolutionary effort in El Salvador. The increased regionalization of the wars was demonstrated in the use of Honduras as a base for training Nicaraguan counterrevolutionaries, or contras, and Salvadoran troops; the use of Honduran bases for intelligence gathering on Salvadoran guerrillas; the employment of the Ilopango airbase in El Salvador to fly supplies to the contras; and the continual military maneuvers by the United States and its allies in Central America.

Low-intensity conflict was described by one of its main proponents as "total war at the grassroots level."[2] In a situation of counterinsurgency it requires the eradication of the causes of the war to undercut the insurgents and build "viable political, economic, military and social institutions that respond to the needs of society."[3] In attempts to overthrow a government, low-intensity conflict encompasses the use of a variety of economic, social, political, psychological, and military measures to weaken and delegitimize it. Thus, to overthrow the Sandinista government in Nicaragua, the United States armed and trained a surrogate army, mined Nicaraguan ports, imposed an economic embargo on the country, and worked with other nations and international institutions to isolate Nicaragua politically and diplomatically.

Within civilian and military counterinsurgency circles, low-intensity wars were seen as the most likely conflicts for the United States to become involved in, given the potential costs of a direct confrontation with the Soviet Union. They were wars that could be fought without the direct involvement of U.S. combat forces—and such involvement would be tantamount to failure. Central America was viewed as a laboratory for this approach to fighting wars, with a major U.S.-backed counterinsurgency in El Salvador, a smaller-scale guerrilla war in Guatemala, and an insurgency against a revolutionary regime in Nicaragua in a region in which the stakes in the East-West conflict were seen to be high.

Whereas low-intensity conflict provided the political-military framework for achieving U.S. objectives in Central America, the report of the National Bipartisan Commission on Central America, better known as the Kissinger Commission, provided the policy prescriptions and strategy statement that guided U.S. actions, particularly in El Salvador, in the subsequent years.

The Report of the National Bipartisan Commission on Central America

As its official name suggests, the Kissinger Commission was formed to help develop and articulate a policy toward Central America that could get beyond the partisan divisions that beset U.S. policy in the region in the early 1980s. Created in July 1983 and including respected members identified with both major parties and important U.S. institutions, the commission issued its report in January 1984.

On the central, contentious question of the origins of the revolutions in Central America—were they the outcome of indigenous processes or the result of external interference from the Soviet bloc?—the commission took a nuanced position: The upheavals in the region had their origin in unjust and oppressive structures and arrangements, but the ensuing opposition had been taken advantage of by outside communist forces. A strategy to deal with upheaval in those countries threatened by insurgent forces would therefore need to address both the roots of the conflict, through reform and development to undercut the claims of the insurgents, and measures of security and defense to respond to the military threat posed by revolutionaries.

For El Salvador the commission recommended a combination of representative democracy, redistributive economic development, and civil-military security measures as the means to defeat the FMLN. As Schwarz states:

> The report insisted that defeating the rebels in El Salvador depended upon building a legitimate social and political order there, based on social reform, respect for human rights, and the advancement of democracy through elections and the strengthening of basic institutions necessary for political development: specifically, labor unions, the judicial system, and the press.[4]

The goals established for El Salvador by the commission were comprehensive: economic stabilization, growth of the economy, broadening of the benefits of economic growth, promotion of democracy and respect for human rights, guaranteeing security through coordinated military and civil actions, and achievement of a diplomatic settlement to the conflict.

Counterrevolutionary Strategies

In keeping with the recommendations of the Kissinger Commission, the strategies developed in this period to defeat the insurgent movement combined political, economic, and political-military elements in a more coordinated approach than was achieved in the first years of the war.

POLITICAL STRATEGIES.   For the United States in this period the key to defeating the FMLN lay in building a legitimate political system result-

ing from free elections and supported by the Salvadoran people, rein-
forced by a growing economy and backed by sophisticated political-
military efforts to undercut the appeal of the insurgents and to marginalize them. These ingredients could ensure the political defeat of
the revolutionaries in a short period (estimated by U.S. and
Salvadoran strategists at anywhere from two to five years).

Politically the objective of the United States in El Salvador was to
consolidate and institutionalize the process of "democratization" and
reforms that had begun with the socioeconomic reforms of 1980 and
continued with the elections of 1982 and 1984. A democratic system
could continue to accumulate popular support and undercut the
claims of the guerrillas to speak for the people while ensuring the
external supply of funds to support all aspects of the war effort. This
process of consolidation required the following.

1. The creation of a workable system of justice: Public support in
El Salvador and aid from the U.S. Congress would be jeopardized if
the wealthy and members of the armed forces continued to be
immune from prosecution for even the most heinous crimes.

2. Significant improvements in human rights and the subordination of the military to civilian control: More than anything else,
human-rights violations posed a threat to the continuation of U.S. aid.
By the end of 1983 the danger of Congress cutting aid to El Salvador
because of human-rights abuses was viewed as sufficiently serious to
warrant a high-level ultimatum from Vice President Bush to the
Salvadoran military to reform their behavior.

3. Continuation of the system of elections as the key mechanism
for determining the control of government at all levels: It was essential
to guarantee that the right-wing parties and the sectors they represented vied for power through elections rather than through coups or
other extralegal means. Elections were also critical to the strategy of
strengthening popular identification with the system and thereby isolating the guerrillas, as well as to providing international legitimacy to
the government.

4. Maintenance of the socioeconomic reforms of the early 1980s:
Though there was little expectation that the reforms would be extended, their maintenance was treated by the U.S. Congress as, at least symbolically, a mark of any Salvadoran government's commitment to
democracy and reform.

Whereas the strategy of the United States was to institutionalize a
system of government that could be presented as democratic and
reformist, irrespective of the party in power, and hence serve to isolate
the insurgency, the character of the specific party in government from

1984 to 1989, the PDC, naturally played a major role in the counterinsurgency strategy of this period. The PDC had a history of opposition to the authoritarian system that existed up to 1979. It was closely identified with agrarian and other socioeconomic reforms. Its leader, José Napoleón Duarte, had an international reputation and was lionized by the U.S. Congress. The party also had strong support outside the country through its links with international Christian Democracy. Thus, at least in the years 1984–1987, Duarte and the PDC provided a solid basis on which to organize the strategy of counterinsurgency.

The strategic challenge for the United States in El Salvador from 1984 was to harmonize three major sets of institutional interests: a reform agenda of the PDC that won popular support in the 1984 presidential and 1985 legislative elections on the basis of a program of social and economic reform, human rights, and peace; the ESAF, which, though committed to the government in power and depending for its survival on U.S. military aid, had its own institutional interests that did not always correspond to those of the government; and the major business interests, which, though committed to defeating the rebels, were greatly antagonistic to the PDC and its objectives. The U.S. Embassy and other U.S. agencies involved in the war sought to (1) ensure that the Salvadoran government carried out economic, political, and military policies that would be most conducive to defeating the FMLN, using as leverage economic and military aid, which averaged about $600 million a year; (2) guarantee that the Salvadoran armed forces fought the type of war considered effective by U.S. advisers, limited human-rights violations, and supported the government in power, using the potential cutoff of military aid as pressure; and (3) encourage the major private-sector interests to support the government, using as an inducement economic-support funds, a large proportion of which went to support private enterprise.

Whereas these were the main institutional forces that the United States sought to unite around a comprehensive and integrated strategy of counterinsurgency, efforts were made to incorporate other important sectors, notably the Catholic Church and labor unions, behind support for the strategy.

ECONOMIC STRATEGIES. Just as in the earlier period of the war, the economy was viewed by each side as critical to its prospects for victory. A stagnant or declining economy would mean a further deterioration in the living standards of the majority, and would likely increase social discontent and protest that could be used by the FMLN to press its vision of a society organized for the benefit of the majority. Conversely, a vibrant and growing economy would create jobs and spending power, and allow increases in government spending on social programs that could diminish discontent, increase support for the government, and isolate the insurgents. So the FMLN continued to attack the "war economy" while the United States and its Salvadoran allies placed great importance on stabilizing the economy and restoring economic growth.

The importance of the economy to the war was emphasized by the Kissinger Commission, which stressed three economic objectives—stabilization, growth, and broadening the benefits of growth—among its six goals for El Salvador. Based on the recommendations of the commission, U.S. strategy for economic stabilization and growth focused on two main elements: U.S. economic aid would provide a cushion of support while the Salvadoran government was working to defeat the insurgency; and appropriate government policies would encourage private investment, limit government spending, and expand production, particularly for export. U.S. economic aid to El Salvador in this period was designed to achieve a variety of goals that would contribute to the strategic objective of defeating the insurgency.

Balance-of-payments aid in the form of economic-support funds helped finance specific projects, paid for imports, transferred funds to offset the imbalance between the country's imports and exports, and provided the private sector with access to foreign exchange to purchase needed imports. Concessional loans for food imports under Public Law 480 Title I also supported the country's balance of payments.

Development assistance was provided through AID's development-aid account. Aid was channeled into agriculture, particularly the agrarian-reform program, and used to restore the health and education systems, organize farm workers, create jobs for those displaced by the war, and help create small businesses. Development aid also supported the restoration of war-damaged infrastructure, efforts to improve productivity in the private sector, and the encouragement of nontraditional exports through the use of economic-support funds.[5]

The economic aid provided by the United States was designed to play a crucial role in the war against the FMLN by preventing further economic deterioration that could increase popular support for the insurgents. Economic-support funds replaced money that the Salvadoran government spent on the war. U.S. economic aid also funded the civilian component of counterinsurgency programs and provided leverage to influence the Salvadoran government's economic policies and to encourage the private sector to support the government.

Appropriate government economic policies were viewed by the United States as essential to economic stabilization and growth and hence to defeating the FMLN. The economic strategies that U.S. personnel encouraged the Salvadoran government to implement during the Duarte period focused on encouraging investment and production for export, cutting back on government spending and subsidies, devaluing the colón to make exports more competitive, and keeping wage increases low to combat inflation. The problem with these approaches lay in the potential for increased social discontent and political opposition to the PDC from poor and working people who would bear the burden of these policies, at least until such time as economic recovery was achieved.

POLITICAL-MILITARY STRATEGIES.   The political and economic strategies supported by the United States and its Salvadoran allies operated at the macro level to institute a system and a government that could win internal and international support while implementing policies to consolidate support of key sectors and isolate the guerrillas and their allies. The political-military strategies of counterinsurgency operated at a micro level to separate the FMLN from its support base, win the allegiance of the population, including potential supporters of the insurgency in disputed areas, and build popular support for the government and armed forces. The main strategies included the following.

1. Separation of the FMLN from its supporters in the insurgents' rearguard areas. Applying Mao Zedong's maxim that guerrillas are like fish swimming in a sea that consists of its civilian base of support, the Salvadoran armed forces and their U.S. advisers adopted a strategy of "draining the sea." Through intensive bombardment and artillery attacks on rebel zones, the destruction of crops, and the forced removal of guerrilla supporters in army sweeps through FMLN-dominated areas, the goal was to leave the FMLN isolated from the civilian population, and militarily and politically weakened.[6]

2. The creation of civil-defense patrols in the rural areas. Civil defense is viewed by counterinsurgency strategists as a key element in defeating an insurgency because "in committing himself to protect his village through civil defense, the individual casts his lot in favor of the existing order and rejects revolution."[7] The objective in El Salvador was to create civil-defense patrols as part of the strategy of clearing the guerrillas from key areas, consolidating government control, and rebuilding damaged or destroyed infrastructure. This strategy faced two major difficulties: the repressive history of paramilitary groups, particularly ORDEN, in El Salvador; and the high priority given by the FMLN to preventing the formation of such groups.[8]

3. The implementation of psychological operations directed at

the civilian population and toward the FMLN. Psychological operations, directed toward the population at large or targeted groups, presented the government and armed forces as the legitimate authority, supported by the vast majority of the people, and dedicated to democratic ideals, human rights, and reconstruction. The FMLN was portrayed as an isolated terrorist group, linked to external forces of subversion, and dedicated only to acts of destruction that hurt the civilian population. The campaigns also sought to convince FMLN combatants that the objectives of the armed struggle had already been attained and that they should abandon the insurgency and reincorporate into society. The methods of psychological warfare, carried out by the armed forces and the Ministry of Culture and Communications, included a sophisticated campaign portraying the civilian victims of "terrorist" mines; mass leaflet drops urging rebels to desert; and interviews with FMLN defectors and dissemination of captured documents.[9]

4. Combined civic-action programs to provide a government and military presence in conflictive areas. In these programs the military and civilian agencies provided food, clothing, medical and dental care, toys, and haircuts to the civilian population in one-day visits to improve the military's image and obtain intelligence. These efforts to win the "hearts and minds" of people in conflictive areas were carried out at the rate of two per month in each department and were isolated from other counterinsurgency programs.[10]

5. Nationwide, coordinated counterinsurgency programs to recover key areas and win the allegiance of the local population. These programs, notably the National Plan that was implemented in 1983 in San Vicente and then extended to include nine departments, and United to Reconstruct (Unidos Para Reconstruir, or UPR), which was launched in 1986, were designed to force the guerrillas out of selected areas, consolidate the territory with an ongoing military presence and the formation of civil-defense units, and reconstruct infrastructure destroyed in the war. UPR incorporated psychological operations to gain "the support and sympathy of the civilian population toward the government and armed forces,"[11] created civil-defense units, and integrated civilian and military agencies behind a campaign whose key objectives were to "win the hearts and minds of the civilian population . . . destroy the tactical terrorist forces in the selected areas and neutralize the terrorist zones of persistence and expansion in each department," and "to isolate the subversion politically, physically, and psychologically, neutralizing their influence on the civilian population."[12]

Overall, the objective of the United States and the Salvadoran government and military in this period was to wage a different type of war:

a war to win popular support and isolate the insurgency. A comprehensive program of civic action, psychological operations, and civil defense, combined with the separation of the FMLN from its rural base, aggressive small-unit tactics, and constant patrolling, was seen as the basis for defeating the FMLN in a relatively short period. In the specifically military arena, the primary needs were to continue the buildup of the Salvadoran armed forces, which grew from 40,000 in 1984 to 56,000 in 1987; the provision of more advanced equipment, particularly planes and helicopters—the number of fixed-wing aircraft increasing from thirty-eight to sixty-three, and the number of helicopters from thirty-two to seventy-two, between 1984 and 1987[13]—and the implementation of almost permanent operations that would take the war to the FMLN.

Insurgent Strategies

The outline of the FMLN's strategy during the period 1984–1989 was already traced by 1984. The Salvadoran insurgents made the decision to shift from a war that stressed large-scale military confrontations with the Salvadoran armed forces to achieve a quick military victory, to a more traditional guerrilla war that emphasized political connections with the population, small-unit attacks to wear out the armed forces, economic sabotage, and rebuilding political and military structures in the main rearguard of the enemy, the cities. In the following years the FMLN elaborated and refined its strategy without fundamentally altering it.[14]

The FMLN's strategy during this period was political-military: seeking to weaken the armed forces and the government (as well as the will of the United States to continue its support of them) while strengthening the military and political capacity of the FMLN and its allies to launch the "strategic counteroffensive" that would overthrow the regime. The decisive element in the conflict was "the masses," and the FMLN viewed its potential for victory as being closely linked to its ability to mobilize the poor majority for insurrection. A popular insurrection alongside a military offensive timed to take advantage of the weakness of the government side could bring the war to a favorable resolution. All of the activities of the insurgents in this period were designed to maximize the potential for successfully launching the counteroffensive.

The FMLN viewed President Duarte and the PDC government as the immediate enemies of the revolution because of their ability to sow confusion domestically and internationally through their "reformist facade," and the insurgents embarked on a process of "wearing out" (*desgastar*) the Duarte government. Efforts were made to reorganize the mass movement in the cities, which was decimated by the terror of 1980–1982, to put pressure on the government and reveal its inability to respond to the needs of the people. From 1986, with the revitalization of the mass movement, the FMLN believed the potential existed for the movement to become an insurrectional force and embarked on an effort to "unleash the violence of the masses."[15] In the view of FMLN leaders, the precipitous decline in living standards, the greatly increased numbers of people displaced and marginalized by the war, and a government incapable of responding to the needs of the people because it answered fundamentally to external interests, all provided the conditions for insurrection. But the insurgents also considered that the leap to revolutionary or insurrectional consciousness would only be made through the active efforts of the vanguard, the FMLN. This would be the key to winning the war, which could not be achieved by military means alone.

For the FMLN, victory required taking the war to the rearguard of the government and armed forces—to the cities, particularly San Salvador—while maintaining strength, organization, and structure in its own rearguard areas. The major strategies of the FMLN to prepare the conditions for the strategic counteroffensive were the following.

1. Organizing the masses in FMLN zones and disputed areas in simultaneously open and clandestine forms (*doble cara*) that protected the legal position of the population while building structures to challenge the government and military. The FMLN evaluated its earlier efforts to organize open structures of "dual power" identified with the insurgents as vulnerable to isolation and victimization. In this later period the organization encouraged the formation of open, legal organizations, not linked to the rebels and ostensibly nonpolitical in nature, which nonetheless contained a clandestine structure that supported the FMLN. The objective of this strategy of organizing was "to integrate and mobilize the masses of our fronts and rearguard areas to struggle for their day-to-day needs, to educate and raise their consciousness and to lay the basis for their participation in the war."[16]

2. Preventing the government from exercising political or military power in FMLN-controlled areas. The FMLN saw the recovery of political and military control of key areas as a central goal of the counterinsurgency strategy and was determined to prevent the establishment of civil-defense patrols and the exercise of authority by local officials, particularly mayors and judges, in areas in which the government did not exercise military control. Hence, some mayors and local offi-

cials were kidnapped, others were killed, and many resigned under pressure while the FMLN targeted civil-defense units to discourage their formation. The FMLN argued:

> We need to organize the masses to struggle for clinics, schools, drinking water, credits, land, but oppose decisively the installation of mayors and civil defense. The Bank of Agrarian Development is like the boss and can be confronted with economic demands . . . but the mayors and civil defense are the repressive apparatus of local control designed to prevent the masses from organizing themselves and the best way to struggle against them is to stop them from re-establishing themselves.[17]

3. Maintaining a continuous campaign of economic sabotage to prevent recovery of the war economy. Economic sabotage remained a decisive element in the strategy of the FMLN in the period 1984–1989. The economy was viewed as critical to the government's ability to "buy off" the radicalism of the people, particularly in the urban areas. The sabotage of electrical towers and posts, which cut off energy for significant periods, and the destruction of railway stock, bridges, and export crops were intended to prevent economic recovery and its consequent political potential to strengthen the counterinsurgency strategy. Transportation stoppages, which from around 1987 became particularly effective in shutting down public and business transportation, were intended to affect the economy, as well as to divert ESAF military resources and show the FMLN's power.

4. Taking advantage of the increased militancy of workers and other urban sectors to generate an insurrection to overthrow the government. For the FMLN, the key to victory lay in the masses. Without violent mass action the FMLN's military activities would be insufficient to break the power of the government and its U.S. backers. But with a mass upheaval supported by a nationwide military offensive a revolutionary triumph was possible.

> In order to move with firm steps to the cities and be capable of acting within them we must be strong in our rearguard and for the military offensive to be successful we must guarantee the insurrection. Popular organizing will be the detonator that will incorporate the masses into the strike and the insurrection, and we must make efforts to guarantee they play this role. The insurrection is the decisive factor for the victory.[18]

Whereas the masses were the decisive factor for the FMLN, the insurgents' military power and armed actions would be necessary to prevent a massacre of unarmed forces and make victory possible. The

FMLN strategy for fighting the war that would lead to the strategic counteroffensive included the following.

1. Dispersion of forces throughout the country to stretch the military thin and organize politically nationwide. Small units working to build political support among the population, expansion of the FMLN's regular forces, militia, and guerrilla units through their work of organizing and extending the war, and waging a war of attrition against the armed forces could keep the military on the defensive while the conditions were laid for the strategic counteroffensive. The tactic of dispersing forces as the regular mode of operation, and concentrating them for strategic actions, particularly at night for short periods, was seen as the method of weakening the Salvadoran armed forces while carrying out military actions that brought significant political gains.

2. Waging a war of attrition against the Salvadoran military in which combat was on terms chosen by the FMLN. A major tactic employed to kill and injure government soldiers, affect morale, and limit the mobility of the military was the laying of mines. The use of mines became an increasingly central military tactic for the FMLN from 1985 and by the late 1980s the majority of ESAF casualties were caused by mines.[19]

3. Bringing the war to the cities. For the FMLN it was important to challenge the Salvadoran government and armed forces in the opponent's rearguard, the cities, placing the military on the defensive and preventing the effective deployment of troops in the rearguard of the insurgents. It was also important to carry out military actions that could inspire and encourage the masses and dispel their fear of repression.

> Our military plans must coincide with this plan of action for the masses. So military actions in the cities . . . should be carried out in such a way that they have political repercussions among the urban masses. We must lay siege to the barracks in urban centers. . . . The important thing is that the masses perceive in the cities and the peripheries the presence, the strength and power of the FMLN.[20]

4. Building the FMLN forces and improving the capacity to confront the strategies of the military. Throughout this period the insurgents sought to expand and strengthen their forces, utilizing the expansion of popular opposition to the government to recruit new members into the armed FMLN structures, to build guerrilla and militia units, and to strengthen logistical support. At the same time they looked for ways to neutralize the advantages of the Salvadoran mili-

tary, particularly its air power, by the development of new arms and tactics.

Overall the FMLN summarized its military strategy:

> The FMLN strategy . . . combined political and military struggle. One of the political components was linked to the reactivation of the urban masses to lay the basis for the insurrection, and in the military strategy was oriented fundamentally in five fields of action: wearing out the enemy, growth of our forces, political and economic destabilization, the organization of the masses, and the expansion of the war.[21]

The two other main components of the FMLN strategy in the period 1984–1989 were the building of alliances with other social forces, and the push for negotiations to bring a political resolution to the conflict.

The FMLN had an integral vision of how different organizations and sectors of society could be incorporated into the struggle for a new society. On the political level they saw the need for three separate vehicles, varying in breadth and militancy, which would come together at the time of the counteroffensive to press in their own way the call for a new government. These fronts were a "political army of the revolution," made up of the more radical elements of the popular opposition and closely articulated with the FMLN militia and guerrilla forces; the "popular front," containing the major unions and social organizations; and the "democratic-patriotic front," made up of more centrist forces in the society. The FMLN considered it possible to radicalize the mass movement, "unleashing the violence of the masses," while at the same time broadening its support among more moderate sectors of the society. In this respect the call for a negotiated solution to the conflict played an important role.

Throughout the period 1984–1989 negotiations played a complementary rather than a central role in FMLN strategy. The rebels assessed that given the commitment of the Reagan administration and the Salvadoran armed forces to a military victory, negotiations (other than a negotiated surrender of the FMLN) would only become viable once the FMLN had changed the balance of forces decisively in its favor. Negotiations, as in Vietnam and Nicaragua, could then contribute significantly to a favorable outcome.

> It is indispensable in our case that dialogue is advanced as an accompanying or complementary factor with the intensification of military action and the radicalization of the masses . . . and that it be used as a resource to strengthen the struggle of the popular movement and the Democratic Popular Front and thus contribute to a change in the correlation of forces that favors the revolution.[22]

Major Developments and Trends in This
Period and Their Relationship to the Strategies

During the period 1984–1989 the major trends in the conflict can be summarized as follows.

The PDC government eroded as opposition from key institutions and social forces increased and the government failed to resolve the most pressing problems of the society: the war and the economy.

The institutionalization of democracy and reform showed few advances. There were numerical improvements in the human-rights situation but serious problems remained. Attempts to create a workable justice system were unsuccessful. The socioeconomic reforms of the early 1980s stagnated. Only in the area of elections was the trend favorable to the counterinsurgency strategy, with the first civilian transfer of power between political parties in 1989.

The economy continued to stagnate as economic and social policies failed to create the conditions to end the conflict, and the toll of the war and its extension throughout the country prevented economic recovery.

Popular opposition to the Duarte government grew but this opposition did not translate into support for the insurrectional strategy of the FMLN. The frequent elections of the 1980s had an impact in convincing people not strongly identified with either of the warring parties to seek reforms and peace through electoral means. Although the constituency for a peaceful solution to the war grew, the FMLN did not succeed in expanding its social base of support in the cities for a revolutionary victory.

The war was stalemated in military terms for much of this period, with neither side able to move into a position of decisive advantage. In the latter phase, however, the war expanded, intensified, and hardened, and the FMLN took the strategic and tactical offensive. The FMLN's November 1989 offensive, though failing in its maximum objective of taking power, helped convince key actors on both sides that a military victory was not possible, and set the stage for negotiations to resolve the conflict.

Deterioration of the PDC Government

With the election of Duarte to the presidency in 1984, and particularly following the victory of the PDC in the legislative elections of 1985, the party appeared in a strong position to provide the political center for the counterinsurgency strategy and to solidify its own social base of support in the population.

The party's electoral victories owed much to the "Social Pact" signed with the Popular Democratic Unity (Unidad Popular Democrática, or UPD) committing the party to the search for peace, democracy, and social justice.[23] Maintenance and expansion of this base of support would require fulfillment of these commitments.

The success of Duarte and the party in strengthening support in the U.S. Congress for military and economic aid to El Salvador fortified the respect and backing of the Salvadoran military for the government in the early period (1984–1985).[24] But the limitations of the power of Duarte and the PDC vis-à-vis the United States, the armed forces, and the economic elite soon became clear and led to an erosion of the social base of support of the party while the FMLN sought to take advantage of the PDC government's failure to address the needs of the majority.

Pressure from the United States, designed to ensure that the government carry out conservative economic policies to restore growth and bring the economic elite back into the fold, led to loss of labor and peasant support for the party. In November 1984 the U.S. Embassy refused to approve the release of $65 million in aid to El Salvador unless Duarte carried out a partial devaluation of the colón, which he did.[25] In January 1986, under U.S. threats to cut aid, Duarte introduced an economic-austerity package, aimed at boosting production and exports, that included price increases and a currency devaluation. In the following months opposition to the package and to the government increased and a new antigovernment federation was formed— the National Unity of Salvadoran Workers (Unidad Nacional de los Trabajadores Salvadoreños, or UNTS)—which included the PDC's partners in the Social Pact, the UPD.[26] By mid-1986 a public-opinion poll showed that 80 percent of those surveyed opposed the government's austerity measures and that only 24 percent would vote for the governing party if new elections were held.[27]

The PDC's economic policies were in most respects conservative and favorable to private enterprise. Yet the historic animosity between the party and the economic right wing, and some specific policies, such as a "war tax" of 1986 that attempted to make the wealthy contribute their share to the costs of the conflict, ensured continued hostility during this period. By early 1987 relations between the government and the political and economic representatives of the far right contributed to a major crisis for the government. In January the economic wing of the far right organized a business strike to protest government policies, and with 6,500 businesses participating, shut down 80 percent of companies nationwide; the right-wing parties in the assembly carried out a legislative strike protesting new taxes on the rich;[28] in February 1987 the Supreme Court nullified the war tax directed toward the wealthy.[29]

Relations between the PDC and the military began favorably due to Duarte's ability to guarantee an unimpeded flow of aid from the United States. But the relationship was soured in subsequent years by the military's perception that the government was unable to develop a project that could unify the people behind the government and armed forces, and that specific PDC policies appeared to threaten the integrity of the military institution. The way in which Duarte dealt with the kidnapping of his daughter by the FMLN in late 1985—which paralyzed the government for forty days—increased tensions with the military.[30] Later, the government attempted to prosecute military leaders for violations of human rights, established an amnesty for rebels, and granted permission to leaders of the political wing of the opposition, the FDR, to return to El Salvador; these actions worsened relations between the government and military and almost led to a coup.[31] Duarte's attempts to enter into negotiations with the FMLN continually ran up against the opposition of the military (and the United States) to anything that went beyond a demand for the rebels to accept the constitution and lay down their arms.[32]

The PDC government was restricted on three sides. The United States demanded economic policies favorable to the right wing but antithetical to the grassroots base of the party, and opposed any serious dialogue with the FMLN. At the same time, it pushed the government to make advances in human rights and achieve greater control over the military to guarantee continued aid. The military accepted the aid benefits brought by the Duarte government but resisted the government's attempts to bring military violators of human rights to justice or to interfere in the running of the war. The economic right wing, despite the conservative nature of government policies and pressure from the United States, opposed the government and sought to restore the economic order as it had existed prior to 1980. Pressures from these powerful forces restricted the options of the Duarte government and contributed to the alienation of the party's base and its loss of public support. The strategies of the FMLN, targeted to undermine the government through economic sabotage, the mobilizing of public opposition, and a war of attrition, further limited the government's possibilities. Finally, widespread corruption and incompetence put the last nails in the coffin of public credibility and support for the party.[33]

By 1988 the PDC was deeply divided internally and had lost a large proportion of its popular support. In March of that year the party lost badly to the right-wing ARENA Party in legislative and municipal elections, and party leaders assessed the reasons:

"We were a government of the right without the support of the right," said a party leader analyzing the damages. "Businessmen didn't do badly, but they never supported the [party]. The poor people were hurt by inflation . . . but we broke the social pact with the unions and peasants. And we made no advances with the left."[34]

"We had no message, no moral authority, offered no hope," said one top Christian Democrat. "We deserved to lose."[35]

A *Christian Science Monitor* article evaluated the performance of the Duarte government:

> In the end, diplomats and Salvadoran officials say, Duarte never had the power to stand up to the Army, the oligarchy, or the U.S. Embassy. He never had the courage to call a halt to corruption. And despite his good intentions, he never redressed the grave social inequities that fuel the conflict.
>
> Consequently, Duarte alienated the very people that elected him. Meanwhile his government drew fire from the Army and the private sector for being too socialist and corrupt to fight the war and manage the economy.[36]

Limited Advances in the Institutionalization of Democracy

For the Kissinger Commission and U.S. policymakers and strategists, a key to defeating the FMLN was to institutionalize a democratic system that could win the allegiance of the majority of the population, isolate the insurgents, and, through these advances, guarantee the continued flow of funds to finance the military effort. Some of the main elements in this process were (1) to limit human-rights violations by the military and paramilitary elements associated with the armed forces; (2) to create a workable justice system that would punish offenders irrespective of wealth or military rank; and (3) to consolidate the electoral system as the mechanism through which power was transferred between civilian political parties. Another important element, at least in ensuring continued funding for the policy in El Salvador, was to appear open to a negotiated solution to the conflict.

Between 1984 and 1989 sufficient advances were made in these areas to prevent a cutoff of U.S. aid to the government, but not enough to represent a real institutionalization of a democratic process nor to undercut the guerrillas. The main success of the strategy of institutionalizing democracy lay in the elections, which despite their limitations—their occurring in the midst of a civil war, the absence of a left alternative in the process, and serious accusations of fraud—managed to convince many to seek change through electoral competition rather than through violence.

In the area of human rights there was a reduction in the number of politically motivated killings each year, except for 1988, but massacres by the armed forces continued.[37] Murders by paramilitary death squads continued, though more selectively than in the early 1980s, and particularly at times when there was dialogue between the government and the FMLN,[38] and no military officers were convicted of human-rights violations.

No significant progress was made in creating a functioning justice system in El Salvador in this period and, despite intense pressure from the U.S. Embassy, even the suspected perpetrators of symbolically important killings or other human-rights violations were not prosecuted. These included military officials suspected in the kidnapping of wealthy businessmen; the military officer, Colonel Elmer González Araujo, who was believed to be responsible for the killing of more than seventy peasants in the village of Las Hojas, Sonsonate, in February 1983; those responsible for the murder of the head of the land-reform agency and two U.S. advisers in 1981; and the killers of Archbishop Romero in 1980.[39] U.S. ambassador William Walker concluded in early 1989: "If there is any area where this country has made zero progress, that's the area of judicial reform and the administration of justice. . . . There ain't no justice here."[40]

There was greater success in institutionalizing the electoral system. In 1988 the ARENA Party won control of the legislative assembly and the majority of the mayoralties, and in 1989 the ARENA candidate, Alfredo Cristiani, was elected president of El Salvador. Though the number of voters was considerably less than in 1982 and 1984, the first transfer of power between two civilian political parties helped to guarantee support for Cristiani and the ARENA government despite the party's reputed connection to death-squad violence. Just as important, the elections, though they did not cut into the core base of support of the FMLN, played an important role in solidifying identification with the system and making unaligned individuals less willing to support the insurrectional strategy of the insurgents.

Finally, no significant advances in the process of dialogue or negotiations were made in this period. Six meetings took place or were attempted: at La Palma, Chalatenango, in October 1984, followed by a meeting at Ayagualo a month later, and an attempted meeting in Sesori that was aborted after the military occupied the town; in San Salvador in October 1987 following the signing of the Central American Peace Plan, Esquipulas II; and in Mexico City and San José, Costa Rica, in September and October 1989, between Cristiani's accession to power and the FMLN's offensive.

The failure of the negotiations was rooted in the belief of each side that it was strong enough either to win militarily or to weaken the other so significantly that negotiations would be a form of surrender. For each side, negotiations were subordinated to military strategies and were mainly public-relations exercises, given that neither side wished to be portrayed as intransigent and interested only in a military solution to the conflict. The positions of the two sides were far apart: The Salvadoran government demanded that the FMLN give up its arms and attempt to win power through elections; the FMLN claimed that the government was not legitimate because it had come to power through elections conducted under conditions of war and repression, and that a coalition government that included the insurgents would be necessary to guarantee a lasting peace.

Continued Economic Stagnation

The Kissinger Commission viewed economic stabilization and recovery as crucial elements in resolving the civil conflict in El Salvador and in ensuring development and peace throughout Central America. The commission proposed an $8 billion economic-assistance program to the region over five years beginning in 1985. Ultimately, $1.848 billion in economic aid was allocated to El Salvador in the period 1985–1989, 91.5 percent of the amount requested by the Reagan administration.[41] The policies specified by the Kissinger Commission for the governments in the region included "a firm commitment . . . to economic policies, including reforms in tax systems, to encourage private enterprise and individual initiative, to create favorable investment climates, to curb corruption where it exists, and to spur balanced trade. These can lay the foundation for sustained growth."[42]

Throughout this period, encouraged strongly by the U.S. Embassy, the Duarte government carried out economic policies that broadly reflected these goals. The major economic initiative during the Duarte presidency was the Economic Stabilization and Reactivation Plan of early 1986 (commonly referred to in El Salvador as the *paquetazo,* or big package), which generated broad public opposition. The package was aimed at boosting production and exports, and included a devaluation of the colón, a tax increase on consumption and wealth, the adoption of a policy of monetary restraint, increases in interest rates, the raising of transport charges and fuel prices, and wage adjustments for rural workers and employees in industry and urban services.[43] Other measures implemented to aid economic recovery included the refinancing of debts owed by cotton and coffee growers for periods of eight and twelve years, respectively; a higher guaranteed price for coffee; and increased provision to the private sector of credit, which grew by 10.1 percent in 1984 and 26.2 percent in 1985, compared with 5.5 percent per year between 1979 and 1983.[44] At the same time, the government took a hard line against wage increases, claiming that strikes and other forms of labor protest were part of the destabilization strategy of the FMLN.

The attempts at economic recovery, however, came up against the reality of the civil war that affected the economy in numerous ways. Economic sabotage by the FMLN destroyed infrastructure directly through attacks on factories, plants, equipment, and export crops. Sabotage of the electrical grid stopped or slowed down production of goods and services. The expansion of the war dissuaded export-crop producers from planting or making improvements to their crops, and in general encouraged capital flight and discouraged investment. Large areas of the countryside were depopulated, making significant productive activity impossible. The strategy of counterinsurgency involved a large-scale transfer of funds from human development to the prosecution of the war. A 1987 AID study estimated the costs to repair and replace infrastructure damaged by guerrilla sabotage at around $600 million, and lost production resulting from the war at over $1.5 billion.[45] Natural disasters, particularly the October 1986 San Salvador earthquake that caused an estimated $1 billion in damage, also contributed to the continued economic stagnation.

The parlous state of the economy can be seen in some major economic indicators.

- El Salvador's GDP grew at an average rate of less than 1 percent per year during the period 1984–1989 and in 1988 was 6.5 percent below 1980 levels, while per capita GDP was 16 percent down from 1980.[46]
- Agricultural production fell by 32 percent between 1980 and 1989, while per capita food production in 1989 had fallen to 85 percent of the 1980 level. Coffee production declined by a third, and cotton fell to 20 percent of 1980 levels by 1988.[47]
- By 1987 real wages in industry were 51 percent of 1980 levels, and those in agriculture 44.2 percent.[48] By 1989 government spending on health and education had fallen by 23.7 percent from the beginning of the war.[49]
- Depending on methods of calculation, U.S. aid to El Salvador provided between 25 percent and 33 percent of the funds the U.S. and Salvadoran governments spent in El Salvador in 1988.[50]

At the end of Duarte's term of office in 1989 there were few indications of a reversal in the economic situation. U.S. aid and credits, which averaged $582 million per year, did enough to prevent economic collapse and impede greater social dislocation but did not succeed in generating the economic recovery that was intended to provide the conditions to win the war.

Growth of Popular Opposition to the Government

In the first two years of the Duarte government, from 1984 to 1986, popular opposition, particularly as manifested in strikes and demonstrations, increased significantly. Following a three-year period when public protest and industrial action were practically nonexistent due to harsh legal restrictions and extralegal terror, strikes calling for wage increases, and demonstrations opposing the government's economic policies and calling for an end to the war, became common features of the political landscape once more. There were 100 strikes in the first year of the Duarte government, from mid-1984 to mid-1985, and some 200 strikes in 1985.[51] The average size of the major opposition demonstrations in San Salvador increased from 5,000–10,000 in 1985 to 40,000–60,000 in 1986.[52] In early 1986, following the introduction of the Duarte government's economic-stabilization plan, a new antigovernment front, the UNTS, was formed, bringing together workers, peasants, and members of a variety of communal organizations.

This increase in popular opposition appears to have had its primary roots in the dramatic decline in real incomes suffered by workers and peasants from 1980 to 1985. The opening of political space created by the elections of 1982, 1984, and 1985 and the discourse of democracy articulated in them, accompanied by a lessening of fear as the terror of 1980–1982 receded, also helped create the conditions for a rise in public opposition. Other contributing factors were the policies of the Duarte government, which were perceived as worsening the living conditions of the majority, and the strategy of the FMLN to maximize opposition to the government in order to destroy its "reformist facade."

Although the rise of unarmed political opposition to the government was only in part a product of a specific strategy of the FMLN in this period, the insurgents possessed major influence within the leadership of the largest opposition federation, the UNTS, and many of its constituent groups. The insurgents had an interest in turning economic opposition to the government into a political challenge to the system, just as the government and its U.S. backers were disposed to treat any opposition as part of an FMLN strategy of destabilization. The FMLN saw the growth of an urban mass movement, formally independent of the armed opposition and representing broad-based opposition to the Duarte government, as a confirmation of its political-military strategy to achieve victory in the war through a combination of insurrection and military offensive and, at least from 1987, sought to radicalize the grassroots political-opposition movement.

Demonstrations became more violent, with protesters burning buses, government vehicles, and private cars and attacking riot police.[53] During this period the demonstrations also diminished in size, leading some analysts to conclude that the FMLN's strategy of radicalizing the mass movement to spur insurrectional violence was in fact alienating large numbers of potential supporters and isolating the more radical elements. The left, according to this view,

> appears to have miscalculated the mood of the country. "The guerrillas are attempting to radicalize the opposition," said Ignacio Ellacuría rector of the [Central American University in San Salvador] and a frequent critic of the Duarte administration. "Because of their strident political stance and their use of violence, the left has alienated the general populace."[54]

Between mid-1987 and the FMLN's offensive of November 1989, demonstrations, though frequent, only exceeded a range of 5,000 to 15,000 when convened by the Catholic Church–sponsored National Debate for Peace in El Salvador in support of a broad call for dialogue and a peaceful resolution to the war. At the same time, even though real wages continued to decline and some economists estimated that 65 percent of the economically active population was unemployed or underemployed, the number of strikes diminished in 1987 from 1986 levels to 100, 46 in the private and 54 in the public sector.[55]

Thus the period 1984–1989 saw a broadening of opposition in the first two years of the Duarte government as workers attempted to recover some of the economic losses suffered in the first years of the war and began to lose some of the fear created by the widespread terror of 1980–1982. The opposition became more radical but narrower as the FMLN pushed its insurrectional strategy through its cadre in the leadership of the union movement (principally the UNTS) in the years 1987–1989. Observers ranging from the Jesuit-run Central American University to the international press and the FDR saw this narrowing of the unarmed opposition movement as an indication that insurrection was not in the cards. The FMLN, however, continued to bank on the potential for a "social explosion," or popular insurrection, and organized its strategy around this vision.[56]

A Changing Political-Military Situation:
From Stalemate to FMLN Offensive

In the period 1984–1989 the Salvadoran armed forces and the FMLN focused on achieving similar objectives: Each side defined its priority as winning popular support and undercutting the support of the adversary, as opposed to purely military objectives. Each attempted to secure its own rearguard and move in to destabilize and gain support in the rearguard of the other. The pattern of the war in this period saw the initiative during 1984 and 1985 in the hands of the armed forces as the FMLN adapted to its new strategy. But from 1986 onwards the fruits of the FMLN's strategic reorientation could be seen in the expansion of the war throughout the country, the continued attrition of the military, and the insurgents' ability to prevent the exercise of government powers in much of the countryside and to continue its campaign of economic sabotage. This shift in the political-military balance of the war provided the conditions for the FMLN to prepare its strategic counteroffensive to take power. Though unsuccessful in its insurrectional objectives and in overthrowing the government, the November 1989 offensive had a dramatic impact and helped convince major actors on both sides that the possibility of a military victory in the short term was remote.

The years 1984 and 1985, particularly after the election of Duarte, were difficult ones for the FMLN as the insurgents attempted to shift to a political war—a "war of all the people"—that focused on consolidating popular support, spreading the conflict throughout the country, dispersing its forces to wage a war of attrition, and continuing to destabilize the economy and the political system. Some of the results of this shift were falling morale, particularly among less politicized members, and an increase in desertions; forced recruitment drives to increase military forces and replace losses;[57] lower rates of casualties inflicted upon the military (the ESAF reported that it had suffered less than half the casualties in the year to 1 May 1984 than in the previous year, and claimed a further decline in the year 1984–1985);[58] and fewer large-scale actions.[59] However, even in this period the FMLN was able to carry out periodic actions with a political or military impact, including the destruction of the helicopter transporting the preeminent Salvadoran field commander, Colonel Domingo Monterrosa, and much of his staff in October 1984; the kidnapping of Inés Duarte Duran, the daughter of the president, and the subsequent release of wounded FMLN combatants and political prisoners in exchange for Duarte Duran and kidnapped mayors in late 1985; and large-scale attacks on the city of Suchitoto in November 1984 on the main armed-forces training base in La Unión, causing over a hundred casualties in October 1985, and on the Fourth Brigade at El Paraíso, Chalatenango, in April 1987.

In the years 1984 and 1985 the armed forces' strategy of "draining the sea" through bombing attacks in insurgent areas and the forcible transfer of civilian supporters from FMLN zones reportedly hurt the rebels, but the civilian toll made the bombing into a human-rights issue and caused Duarte to issue rules governing the use of aerial bombardment. In 1984 Americas Watch reported that air attacks accounted for the great bulk of the civilian death toll and that the attacks were "driving thousands of Salvadorans from their homes, swelling the already enormous numbers of displaced persons and refugees living in miserable conditions."[60]

Beginning in early 1986 the Salvadoran armed forces' strategy to isolate the FMLN from its civilian support base became more discriminate, with the launching of a major campaign to clear the Guazapa Volcano (strategically located just north of the capital and almost continuously occupied by the FMLN from the beginning of the war) of guerrillas and their civilian supporters. The campaign, Operation Phoenix, succeeded in clearing the guerrillas out of the area, dislodging 1,000 civilians, and capturing 500. The operation was in practice the opening salvo of the UPR counterinsurgency campaign, and was repeated with similar impact on the civilian population in the rebel-dominated department of Chalatenango.[61]

In 1986, with the launching of UPR, a new phase in the counterinsurgency war began. The Salvadoran High Command and U.S. advisers believed that the war was close to being won and that a major effort involving civic action, psychological war, the creation of civil-defense patrols, and the restoration of civilian authority and infrastructure in the conflictive zones could deal the FMLN a death blow. UPR targeted fourteen zones, one in each department, to win the hearts and minds of the population and wrest territory from the insurgents. The UPR campaign and the counterinsurgency strategy in general in this period did not, however, live up to the claims made of them.

Between the inauguration of Duarte as president in June 1984 and the launching of the FMLN offensive in November 1989, the Salvadoran armed forces were never in any real danger of losing the war militarily. Overall, the military maintained its cohesion and morale and was able to replace the casualties lost (albeit through forced recruitment). It suffered few major military defeats, an average of two to three a year. But there are scant indications that the counterinsurgency programs during this period had any significant impact in isolating the FMLN and winning the hearts and minds of people in the rural areas.

The major counterinsurgency program in this period, UPR, was implemented in all fourteen departments, giving each commander a piece of the action, rather than being located in strategic areas to weaken FMLN influence or control. The consequent diffusion of forces prevented the military from deploying sufficient numbers of troops to guarantee exclusion of the insurgents and later reconstruction and consolidation.[62] The armed forces had very little success in creating civil-defense forces. An assessment from late 1986 discussed the problem:

> Although the army has recognized the importance of the political
> aspects of the war, its recent counterinsurgency efforts have so far
> borne little fruit among the civilian population, say analysts, includ-
> ing government supporters. . . .
>   The key element of the Army's counterinsurgency strategy—the
> establishment of civil defense patrols to expand the areas of govern-
> ment control—has failed. . . . "Civil defense is the tough thing. The
> people don't want to be in civil defense," says one Western source
> close to the program. Analysts say that civilian resistance to joining
> the patrols shows that support for the government is limited and that
> most civilians are not willing to risk their lives for the government.[63]

An evaluation of the counterinsurgency war by four U.S. military officers reported on the failure to create civil-defense forces, revealing
that in late 1987, in some of the most conflictive departments, all of
Chalatenango had only seven detachments, La Unión five, and
Morazán only one.[64]

The success of combined civic action (CCA) programs, in which
the military went into conflictive areas and provided food, entertain-
ment, and medical and other services appeared equally limited. A U.S.
government sponsored assessment of these and other counterinsurgency programs concluded:

> There is reason to doubt the effectiveness of these events:
>   a. CCA events are regularly scheduled in all departments, includ-
> ing those without heavily conflictive zones. . . .
>   d. The CCA events are isolated activities, not linked with other
> civilian or military strategies.
>   e. Since there is neither an infrastructure project output nor a
> component to strengthen local institutions in CCA programs, it is too
> much to hope that occasional visits by CCA will generate significant
> attitudinal changes in populations that for over 400 years have had
> reason to distrust and become cynical about central government
> authority.[65]

Another assessment from the same period concluded:

> The army's current hearts-and-minds campaign is designed more to
> manipulate people's behavior than to fundamentally change the mis-
> erable social conditions that perpetuate the war. With its emphasis on
> pep talks and charity, the civic-action strategy has so far failed to root
> out either poverty or mistrust.[66]

One program had some success in this period and became a
model for later counterinsurgency efforts. This program, Municipalities in Action (MEA), attempted to "emphasize development of grassroots democracy and increase municipal government responsiveness
to local needs through the funding of small to medium sized infra-

structure projects."[67] Open town meetings proposed projects of benefit to the community, the mayor and municipal council made a final
selection of projects, and local labor and materials were used in the
project construction. Local involvement was viewed as a key component of the MEA program, and FMLN attacks were seen as less likely
given the local community's involvement in the project. But local
involvement did not necessarily equate to a winning of hearts and
minds, and was compatible even with allegiance to the insurgents.
Overall the program did not appear to shift the political balance in the
countryside.

The lack of success of the government/armed-forces counterinsurgency campaign can best be seen from what the FMLN was able to
accomplish between 1986 and 1989.

By 1985 the war was moving back to the capital. In March, U.S.
officials indicated that the number of urban-based guerrillas had
increased from 50 to about 500 and urban commando actions became
more commonplace.[68] Strikes and demonstrations increased and the
government was no longer able to assume a quiescent capital and to
focus the war in the rural areas. In early 1986 the FMLN was reportedly operating in all fourteen departments for the first time since
1980.[69] The FMLN's campaign to prevent the government from exercising political control where the rebels were militarily dominant
intensified from 1985: Insurgents killed two mayors, kidnapped eight
others, and burned thirty-two mayors' offices in mid-1985, and by
October one-fourth of the country's 262 mayors had been forced
out.[70] Economic sabotage continued to be a major component of the
FMLN strategy: The rebels claimed to have destroyed 8 million pounds
of coffee and twelve coffee processing plants, blown up fifty high-ten-
sion power lines and 700 other utility posts, and carried out eight
transportation stoppages in 1985. The U.S. Embassy said damage from
economic sabotage in 1984 was valued at $263.9 million and expected
to be higher in 1985.[71]

The expansion of the war, the greater use of mines, and the continued impact of economic sabotage can be seen in the declassified
State Department data for 1985–1986 in Table 5.1.

In 1987 and 1988 large-scale FMLN attacks were infrequent; the
Salvadoran High Command and U.S. advisers interpreted this as a sign
of the weakness of the insurgents and saw their defeat as only a matter
of time. But in terms of the type of war that the rebels were trying to
fight—a politically based war of attrition—other indicators were more
salient. In this period the FMLN forced government authorities out of
a large proportion of the municipalities in the countryside. By early
1989 almost half of the mayors and dozens of lesser officials had
resigned under threat from the insurgents, bringing vital services to a

Table 5.1   Changes in Insurgent Activity, 1985–1986

FMLN Military Activities	1985	1986	Percent Change
Mine attacks	457	1,018	+123
Ambushes and small-unit attacks	752	784	+4
Major attacks	110	73	-34
Increases in Rebel Activity in Western El Salvador and San Salvador	1985	1986	Percent Change
Attacks in western zones	35	65	+86
Sabotage in western zones	70	120	+71
Attacks in San Salvador	36	54	+50
Sabotage in San Salvador	54	73	+35

Source: U.S. Declassified Documents I, Department of State, "The Shift in Rebel Tactics, 1985–1986," no date.

halt in many areas.[72] FMLN traffic stoppages became much more effective after 1987. Averaging some seven per year and seven days in length, these stoppages succeeded in halting almost all transportation for days at a time with significant economic costs.[73] The costs to the government of other forms of economic sabotage also increased: In late 1987 the Salvadoran armed forces reported that sabotage was up 75 percent in the east, and the U.S. Embassy reported that the FMLN caused $14 million in damage to the electrical grid in two weeks in November 1987, compared with $17 million in the whole of 1986. In early 1988 an attack on a cotton processing facility destroyed 21 percent of the nation's cotton harvest.[74] Army casualties showed a 24 percent increase from 1986 to 1987, with two-thirds caused by land mines. In addition, the FMLN became much more effective at countering the major advantage of the Salvadoran armed forces—their airpower—through specially constructed or imported weapons. In the first half of 1989 the FMLN destroyed or damaged fifty-four aircraft, more than the total of the preceding three years.[75] From 1988 the war in the capital intensified significantly, with FMLN attacks on the headquarters of the High Command, the National Guard, the First Brigade, the Treasury Police, the National Police, and the Air Force. Scores of buses were burned and the insurgents assassinated major political figures on the right, including the attorney general and leading right-wing intellectuals.

From the start of the conflict, the flow of war materiel to the FMLN was an issue of utmost importance to U.S. and Salvadoran strategists, as well as a potentially key weapon in the propaganda war. Stopping or cutting back the flow of arms could greatly enhance the prospect of defeating the insurgents, while interception of a major shipment from Nicaragua could help portray the FMLN as merely a chain in an international communist conspiracy to take over the region, and portray Nicaragua's Sandinistas as regional aggressors. It was the objective of interdicting arms supplies from Nicaragua to the FMLN that provided the original justification for military aid to the contras. Yet, throughout eleven years of war, the United States and its Central American allies failed to stem the arms flow, and even small interceptions were infrequent. Declassified, formerly secret intelligence documents from the mid- to late 1980s reflect U.S. frustration and the sophistication of the supply network. U.S. intelligence agencies knew much about the logistics of the arms flow: Many of the shipments of weapons came through Cuba, were transported to Nicaragua, and then shipped by land, via Honduras and sometimes Guatemala into El Salvador; or from Nicaragua to El Salvador across the Gulf of Fonseca, transferred from larger boats to canoes; or, in the case of important deliveries, by small plane. A U.S. Defense Department intelligence analysis from late 1985 described the problem of interdiction:

> FMLN logistics routes are varied and dispersed at all levels. It is even more complex than the Ho Chi Minh trail. No single significant land route or method for moving the supplies exists. At the strategic and tactical level the system is flexible and can be described best as a spider web.[76]

Another Defense Department intelligence analysis of FMLN arms supplies from mid-1987 asked, "Why can't we stop it?" and detailed the characteristics of the supply system, including:

> complex structure—multinational involvement, three nation apparatus; sophisticated employment; redundant modes of supply; interconnecting transshipment points; truncate in zones of control; limited trafficability; historical smuggling corridors; orchestrated crossings; operations security; concealment techniques—modified vehicles, blend into traffic flow, travel during low vigilance; majority of M-16's; malleable physical dimensions; manageable consumption rates; small quantities. . . . FMLN seeks 90 percent success rate.

The exploitable weaknesses of the system were seen to be: "dependent on external sources; no secure entry points; no secure depots; extensive coordination." But "we can't stop it because . . . nonresponsive ESAF; experienced infiltration teams; widespread deliveries; small individual shipments."[77]

FMLN leaders point to the secret and compartmentalized organization of the logistical system and the highly diverse modes of delivery as keys to its success. An FMLN party would be told, for example, of the arrival of a consignment of arms from Vietnam to Cuba. The arms would be divided among the FMLN groups according to capacity and need. Each party had its own structure for delivery of arms and, even within a party, all of the leaders did not need to know all the details about the shipment of arms.

> It was highly complicated. . . . We used every means imaginable— land, sea, and air; big shipments and small; on shoulders . . . on donkeys. Many people collaborated, including corrupt officials of regimes allied with the U.S. who, for a bribe of say $10,000 would let a large shipment through. There were even successful efforts to move arms from the U.S.[78]

Ultimately, the FMLN's ability to smuggle arms into El Salvador, and the U.S. and Central American allies' inability to interdict these supplies in a region dominated by the United States, were critical to the insurgents' ability to prolong the war for more than a decade, during which military strategies played a dominant role on both sides.

The FMLN's 1989 Offensive

The offensive launched by the FMLN on 11 November 1989 was the culmination of the change in strategy implemented from 1984. The dispersion of forces throughout the country to wage a more political war to win the support of the population helped create the conditions to launch the largest offensive of the war. The general plan for an offensive of this type grew from mid-1986, and plans were laid for obtaining funds, arms, and ammunition, and for developing the human resources to carry it out. From late 1988 there was a growing sense in the FMLN that a large-scale offensive would be needed, and from mid-1989 intense preparations were made for the recruitment, logistics, and mental readiness to launch an attack.[79] The event that spurred the FMLN's General Command to launch the offensive was the bombing of the FENASTRAS trade-union office on 31 October that killed eight, including the union's general secretary, Febe Elisabeth Velásquez, and wounded thirty-five.

The minimum goal of the offensive was to stay in the capital for seventy-two hours. The maximum goal was to create the conditions to overthrow the government. The FMLN brought some 2,000 guerrilla fighters into San Salvador and took over whole neighborhoods, holding them for days until government aerial bombardment forced them to retreat. They returned to attack new areas, including the wealthy Escalón district, and got into a standoff with U.S. Green Berets in the Sheraton Hotel.

The offensive lasted into December, and three weeks after it was launched the *Los Angeles Times* analyzed its accomplishments: "The intensity and duration of the offensive . . . has mocked all official predictions and sent Cristiani's elected right-wing government reeling."

Although it produced neither a decisive popular uprising nor an outright military victory, it advanced at least two rebel aims: bringing "the chaos of the deadlocked peasant war into a city that has more than one-third of El Salvador's 5.8 million people—a situation that, if prolonged, could make the country ungovernable"; and unleashing "a murderous crackdown that swiftly undermined a decade of U.S. counterinsurgency policy and $4 billion in aid aimed at building a political center." For Rubén Zamora, a political ally of the FMLN and a leader of the Democratic Convergence, "the offensive of the FMLN showed that it is a strong force that cannot be defeated militarily." But it also confirmed that "the people are not in an insurrectional stage." A senior Washington official viewed the offensive as a "disaster." "We knew we had problems in El Salvador, but it's worse than we thought."[80]

The costs of the FMLN's offensive and the military response to it were extremely high for the civilian population and for the two warring parties. The Institute of Human Rights of the Central American University estimated that 1,000 civilians were killed and many more wounded in the first phase of the offensive. At least 3,000 combatants, and possibly many more, were killed or injured: the Salvadoran military acknowledged that 457 of its soldiers had been killed and 1,395 wounded while claiming to have killed 1,853 FMLN combatants and wounded 1,183; the FMLN acknowledged 401 deaths in its ranks. Seventy thousand people were displaced from their homes at the height of the fighting, 3,048 houses were damaged in aerial bombardment by the Salvadoran air force, and direct and indirect damage to the economy amounted to 597 million colones (about $120 million).[81]

On 15 November 1989, according to the investigations of the United Nations Truth Commission, at the height of the FMLN's offensive the chief of staff of the armed forces, Colonel René Emilio Ponce, in collusion with other members of the High Command, gave orders for the murder of the rector of the Jesuit-run Central American University, Father Ignacio Ellacuría. In the early hours of 16 November the rector, five other Jesuit priests, and two coworkers were killed by members of the Atlacatl Brigade.[82] This action, more than any other atrocity during the war, helped generate momentum to end aid to El Salvador and helped create the conditions for a negotiated solution to the conflict.

Assessment of the Strategies

The conditions at the beginning of this period, in June 1984, appeared to be eminently favorable for the Salvadoran government and armed forces to win the war. There was an elected government, which was viewed internationally as reformist and democratic, and had a base of popular support in El Salvador. The insurgents were on the defensive, having embarked upon their major shift in strategy during the war. Funding for the war and to stabilize the economy appeared guaranteed, as long as human-rights abuses remained relatively in check and the reforms of the early 1980s continued.

Yet the FMLN finished this period stronger than when it started, and it forced the United States and major Salvadoran forces to reconsider their commitment to a military victory and to examine the costs and benefits of a negotiated solution to the conflict. How, if at all, did the strategies of counterinsurgency and insurgency contribute to this outcome?

Counterinsurgency Strategies

The political strategy of uniting the Salvadoran counterrevolutionary forces—government, armed forces, private enterprise, and the right-wing political opposition—around a single political-military approach to the war failed. Despite high levels of economic aid channeled by the United States, and political pressure from the embassy, the private sector remained opposed to the policies of the PDC government and sought continuously to reverse the agrarian and other economic reforms and to weaken the government. U.S. efforts to generate economic recovery by ensuring conservative government economic policies that could placate the private sector and stimulate growth helped erode the PDC's base of political support. Ultimately the combination of right-wing economic and political opposition, the erosion of public support, the PDC's own inexperience and corruption, accompanied by the FMLN's strategies of building popular opposition to the government, its economic sabotage, and its ability to prolong the war left the PDC as a government in name only in the last two years of Duarte's presidency (mid-1987 to mid-1989). The most that can be said for this strategy was that the United States was able to prevent a coup and, seeing the writing on the wall, was able to prepare conditions for a likely ARENA Party victory in elections in 1988 and 1989.

The strategy of institutionalizing a democratic political system was only marginally more successful. The United States and its Salvadoran allies could point to the transfer of power from the PDC to ARENA in legislative and presidential elections in 1988 and 1989 as proof that the system was democratic and that therefore the insurgents should lay down their arms and incorporate into it. This argument had resonance but its persuasiveness was limited by the well-known connections between ARENA and death-squad and other extralegal activities. The problem was compounded by continued atrocities committed by the armed forces and paramilitary units, and the complete inability of the justice system to prosecute military violators of human rights, even in cases in which the U.S. Embassy exercised extreme pressure and U.S. aid appeared to be in jeopardy.

This strategy of institutionalizing democracy succeeded in the limited sense that the forms of democratic participation—periodic elections—continued; a substantial proportion of the population remained engaged in the electoral process and hence was more likely to seek change through the ballot rather than by supporting an insurrection; and the distortions or imperfections of the system did not lead to a cutoff of U.S. aid to El Salvador.

The strategy of generating economic recovery and growth through a combination of U.S. aid and economically sound government policies to stimulate production and exports, enforce austerity policies, and limit public spending also was unsuccessful. The economy continued to stagnate, living standards declined further, government spending on social programs fell while funding for the war increased, and public opposition to the government grew. A key element in the failure to generate economic recovery was the FMLN's ability to target the economy through sabotage, traffic stoppages, and the general prolongation of the war. The insurgents were able to restrict productive activities, discourage investment, and ensure that government funds were spent to replace damaged or destroyed infrastructure and on the armed forces. The ineffectiveness and ambivalence of government policies that attempted to win business support while maintaining a populist image, PDC corruption, and the opposition of the business sector to government policies also contributed to the failure of economic recovery.

The one success of the U.S. economic strategy of stabilizing the economy and generating growth was, with the aid of over $2 billion in economic assistance between 1984 and 1989, to prevent economic collapse, which would in all likelihood have had dramatic political and military repercussions.

The centerpiece of the strategies to defeat the FMLN in this period was the counterinsurgency campaign to isolate the rebels and win the loyalty of the civilian population for the government and military. Despite the great hopes placed in low-intensity conflict and "seizing the revolution from the revolutionaries," the political-military strategies also failed. The lack of success of the Salvadoran government and armed forces in winning hearts and minds is best demonstrated in the ability of the FMLN to expand the war to all fourteen departments, to bring the war politically and militarily to San Salvador, to continue to target the economy, and to launch the largest offensive of the war in November 1989.

The central problem of the strategy of counterinsurgency in this period appears to be that it never addressed or attempted to redress the root causes of the war, but rather dealt with the problem as one of perceptions or image. Schwarz argues:

> Civic action programs have thus far failed to persuade the mass of people freely to choose the existing order in preference to those who would destroy it. . . .
>
> Many analysts argue that the hearts-and-minds campaigns in El Salvador are better designed to manipulate people's behavior than to change fundamentally the miserable conditions that perpetuate the war. . . . Failure to recognize the real issues at the root of the insurgency is a failure to follow one of counterinsurgency's principal maxims: Apply revolutionary strategies and principles in reverse. Civic action in El Salvador has thus far failed to uproot either poverty or mistrust.[83]

The combined civic-action programs appear to have had little long-term impact in winning allegiance or gaining intelligence from the local population, given the lack of continuity, the focus on public relations, and the history of relations between the military and the rural population.[84] The creation of civil-defense units, viewed by U.S. military advisers as critical to winning the war, did not take hold sufficiently to affect the balance of power in the countryside.[85] The unwillingness of peasants to form and join the patrols suggests that even those who did not actively support the guerrillas were not willing to put their lives on the line for the government and military. This in turn may reflect a reading by the peasants of the relative strengths of the military and the FMLN in the countryside, and the potential costs of joining the civil defense, as well as memories of the bitter conflict between the guerrilla groups and right-wing paramilitaries from the 1970s. An FMLN commander discussed this history:

> We attacked the base of ORDEN head on. The majority of them disappeared as a result of the aggressive approach we imparted to the militias and the masses. Others disappeared as a military counter-revolutionary force. . . . Others simply handed over their arms or became militia members. . . . Thus we reduced their paramilitary movement to impotence and the defensive in the countryside. Since that time of campaigns against the ORDEN squads, the enemy has been incapable of raising a significant para-military force of any strategic importance in the countryside.[86]

The major campaigns to force the FMLN out of strategic areas, consolidate control, and rebuild infrastructure were equally unsuccessful. UPR focused on one area in each of fourteen provinces to give each military commander a piece of the action despite the fact that each department was not equally conflictive or of equal priority. The FMLN was able to retreat initially in the face of superior force, take advantage of the military's focus to attack in other areas, and return to the scene of the counterinsurgency effort at a later time.

A classic example of this was the case of Guazapa, which was a stronghold of the FMLN from 1981 to 1986 and a strategic area due to its closeness to the capital. The major counterinsurgency action, Operation Phoenix, launched in January 1986, hurt the insurgents and the military declared victory over a year later. The FMLN, however, was able to return to the Guazapa area; this played a crucial role in the guerrillas' offensive of 1989.

Overall, a central problem of the U.S./El Salvador counterinsurgency strategy in this period was its failure to address the problems that gave rise to the war. FMLN commander Joaquín Villalobos pointed to the problem;

> It has to be said clearly: if the reforms had functioned, the base of the FMLN would have been weakened and we would have lost the war. If there had been a real agrarian reform, the FMLN would not have been able to sustain a war whose theater of operations is fundamentally the countryside.[87]

Given the choices that the United States had made, as early as 1980, to work with the military despite its reputation, and to attempt to bring the traditional economic interests into a unified strategy to defeat the primary enemy, the FMLN, there was little space for radical initiatives to address the causes of the war and thereby weaken the guerrillas. The focus, in practice, was on trying to change the image that the rural population had of the government and the armed forces through propaganda and psychological operations.

In the military sphere the counterinsurgency strategy paid lip service to waging an unconventional, small-unit war. In practice, however, it did not succeed either in combating the insurgents in an irregular war or in bringing the advantages of the Salvadoran military—particularly its air capacity, vastly superior numbers, and U.S.-generated intelligence on guerrilla positions—to bear decisively in the conflict. The four U.S. colonels who examined the war in 1988 addressed this problem:

> Despite professed American intentions, the Salvadorans today are using a conventional army and conventional tactics to fight an unconventional war. Predilections that American officers carried to El Salvador and the quasi-conventional nature of the fighting during

the early 1980s combined to create a Salvadoran army that is most comfortable operating in battalion-size formations, that relies on helicopters and trucks for mobility, and that has become dependent upon heavy firepower: close air support, attack helicopters, indirect fire, and antitank weapons.[88]

As with the other major strategies, the main success of the military strategy of counterinsurgency appears to have been preventing the Salvadoran armed forces from losing the war.

Insurgent Strategies

A major strength of the FMLN in the period from the inauguration of President Duarte to the rebel offensive of November 1989 was in implementing a unified political-military strategy. Viewing the Duarte government as the principal, immediate enemy—as the reformist face of a repressive system of counterinsurgency—and the main long-term enemy as U.S. imperialism, the FMLN sought to "unmask" Duarte, wear down the armed forces in a prolonged war of attrition, and erode the will of the U.S. Congress to continue supporting and funding the war. Drawing the lesson from the earlier period, particularly 1982–1983, that it had focused too much on building military strength and seeking a military victory, and not enough on political contestation with the government, the FMLN saw the key to victory in the period 1984–1989 lying in the reactivation of the masses. All of the strategies of the insurgents in this period were organized around building toward the "strategic counteroffensive"—a broad-based and violent popular uprising supported by a major military offensive that would lead to the overthrow of the government under conditions that would make it difficult for the United States to intervene.

The majority of the elements of this strategy were effectively calibrated to contribute to the counteroffensive: economic sabotage, expansion of the war throughout the country, bringing the political and military dimensions of the war to the capital, waging a war of attrition against the armed forces, and preventing the establishment of the government's political authority in much of the countryside. One key element was missing in the implementation of the FMLN strategy: a popular insurrection. Yet even with this failure the insurgents were able to convince key policymakers (particularly in the United States) that the main objective of the counterinsurgency policy—the defeat of the FMLN—had failed and that it might be time to seek another form of resolution to the conflict.

The FMLN's ability to neutralize the attempt to isolate and defeat them can be seen in an examination of their major strategies in this period.

Economic sabotage was a consistent strategy of the FMLN throughout the war. It was never effectively countered by the armed forces; it caused over $2 billion in damage to infrastructure, production, and investment; and it helped prevent the Salvadoran and U.S. governments from regenerating the economy and laying the foundations for broader popular support.[89]

Expansion of the war throughout the country was a means of reaching out for new bases of popular support and stretching the capacity of the armed forces. By 1987 the FMLN was able to carry out traffic stoppages that were 90–100 percent effective nationwide, to employ military and sabotage actions in areas hitherto relatively unaffected by the war, and to conduct military activities in all fourteen departments by 1986.[90]

The FMLN's ability to bring the war to the capital is evidenced by the increase in the number of urban commandos active in San Salvador; in the quantity of actions carried out against military installations, especially in 1988 and 1989; in the assassinations and acts of economic sabotage; and, politically, in the growth of organized opposition to the government, though not all opposition was rebel generated.[91]

The effectiveness of the FMLN's war of attrition against the armed forces in this period can be seen in its ability to cause a high level of casualties even during the difficult period of changing to the new strategy. Subsequently, casualty levels to the military grew even higher and the FMLN destroyed greater numbers of aircraft and helicopters.

The FMLN's ability to prevent the establishment of government authority in rural areas undercut the counterinsurgency strategy. Its effectiveness was demonstrated by the absence of local authorities in almost half of the country's municipalities by 1989.

These strategies and others designed to broaden the insurgents' alliances and to use negotiations as a supplement within the strategic counteroffensive were organized around a strategy that was fundamentally insurrectional in nature. The FMLN believed that a purely military victory was not possible; that only through a reactivation of the masses would they be able to achieve power; that the objective conditions were favorable for a reactivation of the mass movement (deteriorating living standards and government inability or unwillingness to address the needs of the majority); and that with sufficient efforts by the rebels, the masses could be radicalized to carry out acts of insurrectional violence that would precipitate a popular victory, in conjunction with military activities. This view was not shared by others, even those close to the FMLN, and the insurrection did not come to pass.

Jesuit leaders at the Central American University, particularly

Father Ignacio Ellacuría, argued that there had been a dramatic change in the reality of the country between 1980 and 1984 that had affected the perceptions of the majority:

> It is four years since the FMLN has been present politically in San Salvador and in much of the republic; almost 40,000 people who were at least sympathizers, if not organized, have disappeared; about 700,000 have fled the country, many of whom were connected to the revolutionary movements; the best activists who worked with the masses either were killed or claimed for military tasks. This impoverishment of the mass revolutionary movement that began in 1981 has continued in the subsequent years. Today the memory is distant and there is a great tiredness; the illusion of a rapid change in the situation has faded. . . .
>
> It must be said that in El Salvador there are two realities: the reality of the war which is lived by very few and the everyday reality that is lived by the vast majority.[92]

Four years later, in 1988, the Jesuit editors of *Estudios Centroamericanos* argued that the FMLN leadership's inability to appreciate that the situation of the masses had changed and its continued belief that a popular insurrection was imminent and feasible was due to the leadership's "being situated in geographical, sociological and mental positions that are very distinct from those to whom they are directing their proclamations and projects."[93]

Based on their perceptions of the potential for generating a popular insurrection, the FMLN leadership advanced the line and the practice of radicalizing the urban political-opposition movement: encouraging confrontation with the security forces to raise the level of enthusiasm of the movement, and to force the government and armed forces to give in and suffer a defeat or repress the workers and generate higher levels of protest. The reality was, however, that while the demonstrations and protests became more violent they also diminished in size. In a later editorial the Jesuit leaders argued:

> Opinion polls and behavior demonstrate today a great support of the masses for a process of negotiations and show that the support for insurrectional violence is very small. . . .
>
> The acceleration and radicalization have brought and will continue to bring the majority of the population, not only to step back from collective actions, but to oppose them as a way of action, that appears more dangerous than useful.[94]

The essential problem, as seen by the Jesuits at the Central American University, was that though there was great popular discontent this did not translate into support for the FMLN:

> The growing misery is attributed more today to the war than to struc-
> tural injustice, and the war is attributed more to the FMLN than to
> the armed forces or to the United States. Rational analysis of the war,
> of its causes and effects, shows the enormous responsibility of the
> business class, the international economic order, U.S. interests, etc.
> But the emotional impact, orchestrated by the major media, shows
> sabotage, social disorder and other actions attributed to the FMLN as
> the principal causes of the growing misery.[95]

The FMLN maintained its belief in the potential for insurrection
and organized the November 1989 offensive around the possibility of
generating a popular uprising that could link up with major military
actions to overthrow the government. Though there was sympathy for
the insurgents, especially in poorer communities in and around San
Salvador, the failure to precipitate an uprising was not merely due to
the aerial and artillery bombardment of FMLN positions in San
Salvador from 15 November. The strategy of insurrection appeared to
have been based on a misreading of the state of mind of the majority
living outside FMLN zones. Some leaders of the FMLN later acknowledged the problem:

> In '89 we had as an objective the insurrection. . . . The problems in
> the offensive of '81 had been due to setbacks in unity; by contrast, the
> problems of the '89 offensive were errors of analysis, and therefore,
> of expectations. We started from the position that there existed in El
> Salvador a form of insurrection. . . .
>   There was in the masses an attitude of struggle, of belligerence,
> but not necessarily of insurrection, and that situation gave us the pos-
> sibility of making a political and military push but not of launching
> an insurrection.[96]

The Grand Strategy of the Two Sides

The period from the inauguration of José Napoleón Duarte in June
1984 to the FMLN offensive of November 1989 was the decisive period
in determining the parameters for the ultimate resolution of the civil
war. It was in this period that the FMLN, particularly through the
November 1989 offensive, was able to convince important elements
within the Salvadoran armed forces, among the political and economic elite, and in the U.S. administration and Congress, that the insurgents could not be defeated militarily in the short to medium term;
and that the search for a victory in the long term might require more
will and treasure than these forces were willing to expend. But this
period also demonstrated to the insurgents that although they could
continue the war into the distant future and prevent any genuine
recovery, their political and military strength was unlikely to increase,

and their potential for generating the conditions for a popular insurrection was remote. The realization by each side that it could not win the war without drastic and unforeseeable changes in the material conditions in the country and internationally strengthened the tendencies within each side that argued that a negotiated solution might provide the best mechanism to guarantee its long-term vision and objectives.

The grand strategies of the two sides during the period 1984–1989 appear to have played an important role in this outcome. Each side had a grand strategy: a strategic vision of what it wanted to achieve, the major approaches to guaranteeing its objective, and the intention of unifying all of the major elements to achieve its strategic goal. The major differences lay in implementation.

The United States had a "global" and coherent vision of what it wanted to achieve in El Salvador and the Central American region. It sought in El Salvador the military isolation and political defeat of the FMLN through a unified strategy that incorporated the creation of a legitimate government, economic recovery and growth, and the isolation of the insurgents through sophisticated political-military strategies of counterinsurgency. The war was viewed as a "total war," a low-intensity conflict using the gamut of political, military, economic, psychological, social, and diplomatic measures to defeat the enemy. A major policy document, the Kissinger Commission report, provided authority for this strategic approach; the political strategies from the earlier period, particularly those focused on elections, provided conditions for a favorable resolution to the conflict.

But whereas the grand strategic vision existed, flaws in its implementation went to the root of what the United States was attempting to accomplish in El Salvador, its methods, and its ability to achieve its objectives in the face of a determined adversary. Among the failures of U.S. strategy in El Salvador in this period were the following.

1. The inability to unify the forces within the counterrevolutionary coalition. For example, the economic elite and the political representatives of the far right were not willing to subordinate their antipathy and opposition to the PDC in order to achieve what the United States saw as the primary objective—the defeat of the FMLN.

2. The inability to bring about a transformation of the Salvadoran armed forces so that it would internalize the importance of ending human-rights violations against the civilian population, accept a role in society subordinate to elected civilian officials, and fight the type of low-intensity war viewed as essential to defeating the insurgents. The Jesuit murders and the subsequent coverup were proof to many that,

despite the rhetoric, the military institution had not changed fundamentally in ten years.

3. The related failure to isolate the insurgents in the countryside and win their social base of support for the government and armed forces, or at least their neutrality. The failure of the hearts-and-minds campaigns appears to have been rooted in the decision to limit social and economic reforms in order to maintain the support of the traditional economic elite. Hence the focus of rural counterinsurgency programs was on changing the perceptions of the population, stressing image and public relations, rather than on addressing the root causes of the conflict.

4. The underestimation of the military and political strength of the FMLN. Though the United States and the ESAF had extensive intelligence on the insurgents, they appear to have been victims of their own propaganda and triumphalism. Although U.S. and Salvadoran intelligence agencies obtained copies of many strategic documents that laid out the rebels' plans in much detail, and human and electronic intelligence provided information on insurgent strength and locations, the United States and its allies were caught by surprise by the November 1989 offensive and suffered a major political defeat that helped set the stage for the resolution of the conflict.[97]

In contrast, the grand strategy of the FMLN was not only coherent and unified but also largely carried out in practice. Once the decision was made in 1984 to shift from a predominantly military focus on defeating the ESAF in large-scale combat to a politically based strategy that emphasized laying the groundwork for a strategic counteroffensive, the strategies, tactics, and plans maintained a singular focus on the main objective. The majority of the elements of the strategy—attacks on the local powers of the government, breaking down into small units to wage a war of attrition, shifting cadre to the cities to intensify actions there, maintaining a high level of economic sabotage, rebuilding popular opposition to the government in urban areas—were decided upon in 1984 or earlier. Other tactics, for example the increasing use of mines, reflected technical advances or changes in tactics within the overall strategic framework. The objective of all of the varied tactics and actions of the insurgents was to create the conditions for the strategic counteroffensive, and when assessed, these activities can be seen to form a strategic whole that laid the basis for the 1989 offensive and helped create the conditions for the resolution of the conflict.

The central weakness of the FMLN strategy lay in its misreading of the willingness of a large part of the population to risk everything and engage in insurrectional activities to overthrow the government. This misreading may have come, as the Jesuits at the Central American University argued, from the failure of insurgent leaders to appreciate the changes that had taken place in Salvadoran society between 1980 and the latter part of the decade, or it may have resulted from a mixing of analysis and desire, and a belief that with sufficient will favorable material conditions could be created.

In this period the FMLN was able to develop increasingly sophisticated political-military strategies that helped create a relative equilibrium in the armed conflict and prevented the Salvadoran armed forces and their U.S. backers from moving toward the military victory they expected. The insurgents had built up a committed cadre that could keep the war going for years more and prevent economic recovery and social peace. But although they possessed a form of veto over future political and economic development, they had not broadened their base: The quality and commitment of core supporters was not in doubt, but general support in the population appears to have shrunk during this period due to growing weariness of the war, the belief or hope (particularly among the less committed) that elections could bring about reforms, and alienation from the increasingly violent tactics of the FMLN and its opponents.

Ultimately, the more focused and unified strategies of the FMLN culminating in the November 1989 offensive offset the major advantages possessed by the Salvadoran government and military, and, at great cost to the civilian population and the warring parties, gradually convinced leading actors on both sides that no military victory was to be won.

Notes

1. National Bipartisan Commission on Central America, *Report of the President's National Bipartisan Commission on Central America* (New York: Macmillan, 1984) (hereafter *Kissinger Commission Report*).

2. Col. John Waghelstein, "Post-Vietnam Counterinsurgency Doctrine," *Military Review* (January 1985), 42.

3. Headquarters, Department of the Army, Department of the Air Force, *Military Operations in Low Intensity Conflict*, FM 100-20/AFM 2-X4, Final Draft, 24 June 1988, 2-14–2-15, quoted in Benjamin C. Schwarz, *American Counterinsurgency Doctrine: The Frustrations of Reform and the Illusions of Nation Building* (Santa Monica, Calif.: Rand, 1991), 7.

4. Schwarz, *American Counterinsurgency Doctrine*, 11.

5. See CRS Report for Congress, *El Salvador, 1979–1989: A Briefing Book on U.S. Aid and the Situation in El Salvador* (The Library of Congress, Congressional Research Service, Foreign Affairs and National Defense Division, 28 April 1989), 31–42; and Francisco Alvarez Solis and Roberto Codas Friedmann, *La asistencia de Estados Unidos a El Salvador en los ochenta:*

Una revisión preliminar, Programa Regional de Investigación sobre El Salvador (PREIS), Cuaderno de Trabajo No. 6, San Salvador, September 1990.

6. See James LeMoyne, "Salvador Air Role in War Increases," *New York Times,* 18 July 1985, 1; Chris Norton, "Salvador's Army Moves Civilians in Effort to Oust Rebels," *Christian Science Monitor,* 6 February 1986, 11; Tim Golden, "Salvador Evicting Peasants from Guerrilla Stronghold," *Miami Herald,* 19 February 1986, 8A.

7. Lt. Col. A. J. Bacevich et al., *American Military Policy in Small Wars: The Case of El Salvador* (Washington, D.C.: Pergamon-Brassey's International Defense Publishers, 1988), 40.

8. See James LeMoyne, "Just Miles from Ruined Base, Salvador Rebels Defy Army," *New York Times,* 7 April 1987, 1; Chris Norton, "Salvador: Peace Is Distant," *Christian Science Monitor,* 24 November 1986, 1.

9. See Tim Golden, "Former Rebel Now a Recruiter," *Miami Herald,* 14 July 1985; Marjorie Miller, "Salvador Aims Psychological Fire at Rebels," *Los Angeles Times,* 9 September 1985, 1; Marjorie Miller, "Land Mines Inflict Rising Toll on Salvador Peasants," *Los Angeles Times,* 10 August 1986, 1.

10. See Allan Austin, Luis Flores, and Donald Stout, *CONARA Impact Evaluation,* Research Triangle Institute, Contract No. PDC-0000-I-00-6169-00 (North Carolina, September 20, 1988), 14–15.

11. Government of El Salvador, *Campaña de contrainsurgencia "Unidos para reconstruir,"* March 1986, anexo 'C,' 1.

12. Ibid., 16–17.

13. Bacevich et al., *American Military Policy,* 5.

14. See Farabundo Martí National Liberation Front (FMLN), *El Salvador vive una prolongada situación revolucionaria* (photocopy, Morazán, June 1985).

15. FMLN, *Apreciación de la situación,* document prepared for the November 1986 meeting of the General Command of the FMLN entitled "Preparatory Phase of the Strategic Counteroffensive," 17.

16. FMLN, *El poder popular de doble cara: Lineamientos de organización,* (Publicaciones FMLN, January 1987), 26.

17. Ibid., 60.

18. Ibid., 21.

19. *U.S. Declassified Documents I,* CIA, "El Salvador: Guerrilla Use of Mine Warfare [excised]," Latin America Review, 5 June 1987. Nearly two-thirds of all Salvadoran military casualties were caused by mines in 1986, compared to one-third in 1985, and less than 3 percent in 1984.

20. FMLN, *Apreciación de la situación,* 19.

21. FMLN, *El poder popular de doble cara,* 16.

22. FMLN, *Organizar el 'Fuego': Una necesidad imperativa para avanzar hacía la victoria* (Synthesis of the conception for implementation, based on the interchange of opinions of members of the General Command of the FMLN), proposal, Morazán meeting, January 1988, 13, 14.

23. "PDC-UPD en el pacto social," *Estudios Centroamericanos* 426/427 (April/May 1984), 349.

24. See Steven V. Roberts, "Congress Passes Extra $70 Million in Aid to Salvador," *New York Times,* 11 August 1984, 1; Tim Golden, "Duarte's Support Is Solid," *Miami Herald,* 21 June 1985, 1A.

25. James LeMoyne, "Duarte's Power Seems Eroded as Voting Nears," *New York Times,* 17 February 1985, 12.

26. Marjorie Miller, "Thousands of Salvadorans March to Protest Duarte's Economic Austerity Plan," *Los Angeles Times,* 22 February 1986, 3.

27. Marjorie Miller, "Duarte Calls for Revival of Talks with Guerrillas," *Washington Post*, 2 June 1986, 5.

28. Chris Hedges, "Duarte Regime Facing Challenges," *Dallas Morning News*, 25 January 1987, 20A; Julia Preston, "Salvadoran Left, Right Attack Duarte's Policies," *Washington Post*, 3 February 1987, A15.

29. "Top Salvador Court Rules 'War Tax' Unconstitutional," *Los Angeles Times*, 20 February 1987, 13.

30. Marlise Simons, "Duarte, Under Criticism, Leaves to Visit U.S.," *New York Times*, 31 October 1985, 8: The military and others viewed Duarte's response to his daughter's kidnapping as overpersonalized—allowing the conduct of government business and the war to be put on hold while the issue of the kidnapping was dealt with.

31. Lindsey Gruson, "Salvador Divided Over Aid to Police," *New York Times*, 22 October 1987, 1.

32. Chris Norton, "Duarte's Call for Peace Talks Sparks Some Skepticism," *Christian Science Monitor*, 3 June 1986, 11.

33. Chris Norton, "Salvador Ruling Party Battered by Mounting Charges of Corruption," *Christian Science Monitor*, 10 August 1987, 7; Philip Bennett, "Discontent Growing in San Salvador," *Boston Globe*, 10 August 1987, 1; Clifford Krauss and Robert S. Greenberger, "Peril to Democracy: Corruption Threatens Political Gains Made by U.S. in El Salvador . . ." *Wall Street Journal*, 14 September 1987, 1.

34. Marjorie Miller, "Salvador Moves to Right as War, Money Woes Continue," *Los Angeles Times*, 28 March 1988, 1.

35. Douglas Farah, "Salvadoran Party Dogged by Failures," *Washington Post*, 24 May 1988, 1.

36. Brook Larmer, "Backsliding to the Bad Old Days," *Christian Science Monitor*, 19 October 1988, 14.

37. See, for example, Kenneth Freed, "Salvador Rebels Step Up Pressure," *Los Angeles Times*, 11 October 1988, 6; "El Salvador Orders Arrests of 4 Soldiers in 10 Killings," *Boston Globe*, 14 October 1988, A28; Americas Watch, *El Salvador's Decade of Terror: Human Rights Since the Assassination of Archbishop Romero* (New Haven: Yale University Press, 1991), 149–157.

38. See Marcel Niedergang, "Death Squads Back on the Rampage in El Salvador," *Manchester Guardian Weekly*, 10 February 1985.

39. See Marjorie Miller, "Four High Salvador Officers Called Kidnapping Suspects," *Los Angeles Times*, 7 April 1986, 1; Americas Watch, *El Salvador's Decade of Terror*, 49–50; and *U.S. Declassified Documents I*, Department of State, "Human Rights in El Salvador," ER 4a vol. 3, telegram #08711, from U.S. Embassy, San Salvador, to Secretary of State, 29 June 1988.

40. Guy Gugliotta, "Abuses Tilt Scales of Justice in Salvador," *Miami Herald*, 16 January 1989, 1A.

41. CRS Report for Congress, *El Salvador, 1979–1989*, 4.

42. *Kissinger Commission Report*, 64.

43. United Nations, ECLA, *Economic Survey of Latin America 1986* (United Nations: Santiago, Chile, 1989), 333.

44. Fernando Sánchez, "Crisis y política económica Demócrata Cristiana," *Estudios Centroamericanos* 453 (July 1986), 542.

45. Agency for International Development, *El Salvador: Economic Cost of the War*, Memorandum 1020K, 2 March 1987, 1, quoted in CRS Report for Congress, *El Salvador, 1979–1989*, 6.

46. United Nations, *ECLA, Economic Survey of Latin America 1988* (United Nations: Santiago, Chile, 1989), 346.

47. Ibid., 349.
48. United Nations, ECLA, *Economic Survey of Latin America 1987* (United Nations: Santiago, Chile, 1989), 340, 342, 352.
49. CRS Report for Congress, *El Salvador, 1979–1989*, 11.
50. Ibid., 43–57.
51. Tim Golden, "Salvador Unions Challenge Duarte with New Activism," *Miami Herald*, 5 June 1985, 10A; Clifford Krauss, "Radical Unions Revive in Salvador as Duarte Opens Political System," *Wall Street Journal*, 24 September 1985, 1.
52. See, for example, *Estudios Centroamericanos* 447/448 (January/February 1986), 112; and 451/452 (May/June 1986), 375–387.
53. James LeMoyne, "Salvador's Rebels Push Hard in Capital," *New York Times*, 17 July 1987, 3.
54. Chris Hedges, "Salvadorans Reported Angry at Leftists' Push," *Dallas Morning News*, 23 August 1987, 1.
55. Ignacio Martín-Baró, "El Salvador 1987," *Estudios Centroamericanos* 471/472 (January/February 1988), 30.
56. See Douglas Farah, "El Salvador's Rebels Vow to Escalate Their Attacks," *Washington Post*, 30 March 1988, A1.
57. Lydia Chavez, "1,500 Abandon Guerrilla Area in El Salvador," *New York Times*, 7 June 1984, 1.
58. "Salvador Casualties Decline, Army Says," *Miami Herald*, 26 July 1984, 5A; Tim Golden, "U.S.-Backed Salvadorans Haunt Rebels: Minister Reports Doubling of Raids," *Miami Herald*, 10 July 1985, 6A.
59. James LeMoyne, "Salvador Puts Guerrillas on the Defensive," *New York Times*, 19 May 1985, IV, 1.
60. Robert S. Greenberger and Clifford Krauss, "Reagan Plan to Revive Intelligence Flights Used by El Salvador Prompts Concerns," *Wall Street Journal*, 8 August 1984, 35.
61. "Comentarios: La guerra en el primer trimestre de 1986," *Estudios Centroamericanos* 449 (March 1986), 231.
62. Austin, Flores, and Stout, *CONARA Impact Evaluation*, 8–10.
63. Chris Norton, "Salvador: Peace is Distant," *Christian Science Monitor*, 24 November 1986, 1.
64. Bacevich et al., *American Military Policy*, 41.
65. Austin, Flores, and Stout, *CONARA Impact Evaluation*, 14–15.
66. Brook Larmer, "The Shifting Battle-Front," *Christian Science Monitor*, 20 October 1988, 16.
67. Austin, Flores, and Stout, *CONARA Impact Evaluation*, 11–13.
68. Sam Dillon, "Guerrillas: We Killed ex-General," *Miami Herald*, 25 March 1985, 1A.
69. Ernesto Cruz Alfaro, "Crónica del mes: enero–febrero," *Estudios Centroamericanos* 447/448 (January/February 1986), 108.
70. James LeMoyne, "Rebels Reported to Seize and Kill Salvador Mayors in a New Tactic," *New York Times*, 12 May 1985, 1A; Marlise Simons, "Uprooted Salvador Mayors Carry On," *New York Times*, 9 October 1985, 2.
71. Marjorie Miller, "El Salvador: No End in Sight to War," *Los Angeles Times*, 14 January 1986, 1.
72. Lindsey Gruson, "Salvador's War Gets Dirtier; Civilians Forced to Take Sides," *New York Times*, 5 March 1989, 12.
73. Guillermo Espinosa, "Sabotage Has Cost $1.6 Billion Since 1979," *Excelsior* (Mexico City), 3 June 1989, 2A, translated by and published in *Central America Newspak* (Austin, Texas: Central American Resource Center).

74. Marjorie Miller, "No End in Sight to El Salvador's Civil War," *Los Angeles Times*, 16 January 1988, 16; Chris Norton, "Salvador's Ruling Party in Trouble as Voters Ask: Where's the Peace?" *Christian Science Monitor*, 7 March 1988, 4.

75. Antonio Cañas, "La guerra en los primeros cien días de ARENA," *Estudios Centroamericanos* 490/491 (August/September 1989), 678.

76. *U.S. Declassified Documents II*, Department of Defense, United States Southern Command, Panama, "El Salvador: Overland Infiltration," 10 September 1985.

77. *U.S. Declassified Documents II*, Department of Defense, "Command Estimate Update (Intelligence Agenda): FMLN Logistics" (August 1987).

78. Facundo Guardado, author interview, 15 July 1995.

79. Gerson Martínez, author interview, 9 November 1992; Facundo Guardado, author interview, 19 February 1993.

80. Richard Boudreaux and Marjorie Miller, "Offensive Pushed Salvador War to New, Bloodier Level," *Los Angeles Times*, 30 November 1989, 1.

81. Instituto de Derechos Humanos de la UCA, "Los derechos humanos y la ofensiva del 11 de noviembre de 1989," *Estudios Centroamericanos* 495/496 (Janurary/February 1990), 59–72; and Aquiles Montoya and Julia Evelyn Martínez, "La ofensiva militar de noviembre y su impacto económico social," *Estudios Centroamericanos* 495/496 (Janurary/February 1990), 29–39.

82. UN Truth Commission Report, *From Madness to Hope: The 12-Year War in El Salvador* (New York: United Nations, 1993), 45–54.

83. Schwarz, *American Counterinsurgency Doctrine*, 55–56

84. See Austin, Flores, and Stout, *CONARA Impact Evaluation*, for an overall evaluation of U.S. counterinsurgency programs in El Salvador.

85. Bacevich et al., *American Military Policy*, 40–41.

86. Harnecker, *Con la mirada en alto*, interview with Facundo Guardado, 174.

87. Marta Harnecker, "La propuesta del FMLN: Un desafío a la estrategia contrainsurgente," Entrevista a Joaquín Villalobos (25 de febrero de 1989), *Estudios Centroamericanos* 485 (March 1989), 213.

88. Bacevich et al., *American Military Policy*, 37.

89. CRS Report for Congress, *El Salvador, 1979–1989*, 6.

90. See Ernesto Cruz Alfaro, "Crónica del mes: enero-febrero," *Estudios Centroamericanos* 447/448 (January/February 1986); 108.

91. *U.S. Declassified Documents I*, CIA, Director of Central Intelligence, "El Salvador: Government and Insurgent Prospects," Special National Intelligence Estimate, February 1989, 12, pointed to a tripling of FMLN actions in San Salvador between 1986 and 1988.

92. Ignacio Ellacuría, "Visión de conjunto de las elecciones de 1984," *Estudios Centroamericanos* 426/427 (April/May 1984), 315.

93. "Editorial: 1988, un año de transición para El Salvador," *Estudios Centroamericanos* 471/472 (January/February 1988), 16.

94. "Editorial: Recrudecimiento de la violencia en El Salvador," *Estudios Centroamericanos* 480 (October 1988), 874–876.

95 Ibid., 876

96. Marta Harnecker, *Con la mirada en alto*, interview with Valentín, (Gerson Martínez), 292–294.

97. See *U.S. Declassified Documents I*, CIA, "El Salvador: Government and Insurgent Prospects," February 1989: "We judge that the FMLN cannot launch a political-military offensive along the lines of its proposed strategic counteroffensive in 1989."

6

Resolving the Conflict Through Negotiations

At the end of 1989, following the FMLN's largest offensive of the war, the prospects for serious negotiations improved even as enmity between the two sides hardened. After a decade of war no end was in sight. Public pressure to resolve the conflict was becoming a factor that both sides had to take seriously. International factors pressed both sides to consider serious bargaining to end the war. From the mid- through the late 1980s the momentum for peace within Central America had grown. The Arias Plan of August 1987 laid the foundations for negotiations to end the contra war in Nicaragua and placed the quest for peace in El Salvador on the regional agenda. The prospect of an end to the Cold War, symbolized by the fall of the Berlin Wall on the weekend the FMLN launched its November 1989 offensive, had serious implications for both sides. For the FMLN the decline of the Soviet bloc removed an important political, diplomatic, and logistical rearguard.[1] For the Salvadoran government, the easing of Cold War tensions promised to make the acquisition of funds from the U.S. Congress, exacerbated now by the Jesuit case, more difficult. The defeat of the Sandinistas in Nicaragua's February 1990 elections was also a double-edged sword. Whereas it was a political blow at the leadership and combatant level and caused some logistical problems for the FMLN, it also further removed Central America from the front rank of U.S. foreign-policy concerns, with foreseeable implications for aid levels to the Salvadoran government and armed forces. In these circumstances, both sides were forced by the realities of the war and a changing world to contemplate serious negotiations. At the same time, the reality of a decade of war that had cost some 70,000 lives and had been fought with little quarter given on either side ensured that negotiations would not be easy.

Perspectives and Strategies

The Impact of the FMLN's 1989 Offensive

Prior to the FMLN's strategic counteroffensive, U.S. strategists and their Salvadoran counterparts continued to believe the insurgents were on the run and were gradually being worn down. A declassified secret CIA National Intelligence Estimate of February 1989 reflected the prevailing wisdom on the Salvadoran civil war:

> The war itself is a complex arena where shifting insurgent strategies have allowed the guerrillas to mask a weakening military capability overall with more visible and politically successful efforts in the cities. The guerrillas have lost 15 to 19 percent of their force over the last two years, their base areas are less secure, and their attacks on military targets have been less effective. To compensate, they have tripled incidents in the capital, attacked previously unaffected areas, and assassinated and forced large numbers of officials to abandon their posts. . . .
> Salvadoran military performance has improved markedly since 1984, although the armed forces' efforts are still too piecemeal and not yet tied effectively to civic action. Assuming current trends, we believe that the government is likely to grind down the insurgency as a military force over the next three to five years, perhaps reducing its personnel size by one-third.[2]

In light of this ongoing analysis of the relative strength of the FMLN and the ESAF, U.S. ambassador Corr in a secret assessment of the prospects for the 1990s had counseled patience and the need to stay the course:

> The U.S. media and some political interest groups are painting an increasingly bleak picture of El Salvador as a country adrift and about to fall apart due to a failure of U.S. policy. These prophecies do not reflect reality, as I see it. Progress continues to be satisfactory or better in four of the five key areas of U.S. interest (consolidation of democracy, defeating the Marxist-Leninist FMLN insurgency, improving the economy, obtaining Salvadoran support for U.S. Central America policy.) In the fifth area, human rights, there is hope that recent slide can be halted. . . . We [must] desist from looking for quick fixes such as pushing prematurely for a negotiated solution that cannot guarantee the future of democracy. . . . Success in El Salvador depends on our willingness to outlast our adversary.[3]

In early 1989 the CIA considered the FMLN incapable of launching the type of offensive that captured documents showed the rebels were planning:

We judge that the FMLN cannot launch a political-military offensive along the lines of its proposed strategic counteroffensive in 1989: . . . new militia units . . . would be of only marginal value. . . . The FMLN has not greatly increased the pace of its purely military operations nor has it been able to bring about a lasting strategic dispersion of government forces; FMLN front groups and penetrations of the armed forces are not able to foment a popular or military insurrection.[4]

Two months after the FMLN's offensive the CIA evaluated its impact and the implications for El Salvador and U.S. policy:

The FMLN failed to spark a popular insurrection or inflict a crippling blow on the Salvadoran armed forces . . . but it did achieve some notable political gains. The intensity and duration of the fighting probably has caused many Salvadorans—particularly the elite, who previously were more insulated from the war—to question the government's ability to provide for their most basic requirement: security. . . .

Militarily, the FMLN emerged from the offensive weakened but not defeated, and apparently has kept many of its regular forces intact. . . .

Unlike most insurgent "offensives" which generally consist of coordinated harassment of military targets and economic sabotage, the November action was noteworthy for its scope, intensity and audacity. The rebels' principal focus was the capital, but they also initiated heavy fighting throughout much of the country, including the departments of Santa Ana, San Miguel, and Usulután. . . .

The rebels' clearest victory was in the war of perceptions. They demonstrated a military prowess that has boosted their credibility and focused international attention on El Salvador. The FMLN probably believes its offensive helped depict the war as "unwinnable," bolstering the argument that US assistance to the government has been ineffective and encouraging additional international pressure on San Salvador to make concessions during future negotiations. . . .

In addition, the offensive altered domestic perceptions about the government's credibility and authority. The rebels' seeming ability to operate with impunity throughout the capital no doubt shook the faith of many Salvadorans—particularly those directly affected by the fighting—in the government's ability to provide for their security. Such a lack of confidence will not only contribute to elite emigration, capital flight, low investment, and other practical problems, but in the long run also could [excised words] undermine the democratic process and hinder efforts to build a political consensus.[5]

An assessment in the *Christian Science Monitor,* made a month after the start of the FMLN's offensive, noted:

The rebel offensive, now entering its fourth week, has shaken the political and military realities of El Salvador so profoundly that the

> country will never return to the way things were before it began Nov.
> 11, analysts here say.
> The strongest offensive of the 10-year-old war is being compared
> to the 1968 Tet offensive in Vietnam. . . .
> Among the apparent effects of the Salvador offensive:
> —The . . . FMLN has dramatically increased its military stature.
> —The Army and the government have lost credibility.
> —Capital residents, both wealthy and poor, say they feel vulner-
> able to a war that had previously affected mainly the rural areas. . . .
> The rebel offensive may be slowly convincing some of the coun-
> try's elite that concessions have to be made.[6]

The events of November and December 1989 also helped confirm
to the U.S. military that a government victory was not possible in El
Salvador. Asked if the Salvadoran government could defeat the rebels,
General Maxwell R. Thurman, the head of the U.S. Southern
Command, told the Senate Armed Services Committee, "I think they
will not be able to do that."[7]

But among U.S. institutions, the impact of the FMLN's offensive
and the Jesuit murders, which occurred during it, was perhaps felt
most strongly in the U.S. Congress.

> Intense reaction to the Jesuit murders and the FMLN offensive has
> raised profound doubts about the success of U.S. policy there in gen-
> eral, assuring, at the very least, the first major debate in five years
> over Washington's future role in El Salvador.
> "The rebel offensive shook a lot of people here" [said an aide to
> the chairman of the Senate Foreign Relations Committee]. "We'd
> been getting a pretty rosy picture of how things had been going, that
> the rebels posed no threat, that they were incapable of large-scale
> actions. All that got blown away in the space of a week or two" in
> November.[8]

But although the November 1989 offensive helped convince major
Salvadoran and U.S. actors that a military victory over the FMLN was
not achievable, the limitations of the offensive also sent a message to
the insurgents that a military victory or popular insurrection to overthrow the government was not in the cards. A rebel leader discussed
the offensive's impact:

> The army and a good part of the U.S. advisers remained convinced
> that they could win the war militarily. . . . I think they were overly
> influenced by the arrogance of the military leaders who often didn't
> tell them the truth, who lied about the number of troops they had,
> the effectiveness of their operations, the number of casualties. They
> created a false image and helped convince those who were making
> decisions in the U.S. that with the difficulties that the socialist camp
> was having it was just a question of time, to wait for the collapse of the

FMLN and offer a decorous surrender. . . . And I think that the '89 offensive changed that perception internally and internationally— including that of the high command and a sector of the ruling party. Also in our own case the offensive laid down the parameters of what we could achieve by military means and what we couldn't. We believed we had made an impressive show of force but it was not something we could do every six months, much less every month. It was a question of years. And we were presented with an opportune moment, internally and internationally, to push for a negotiated end to the conflict.[9]

The Move to Negotiations

Prior to 1990, negotiations played a subordinate or ancillary role in the strategies of insurgency and counterinsurgency. Each side believed between 1981 and 1989 that it could win the war militarily, or at least change the balance of forces substantially enough to ensure that negotiations would be little more than the coup de grace for its adversary. From mid-1989, and more strongly following the November 1989 rebel offensive, negotiations became a central strategic option for each side for bringing an end to the civil war. A number of factors contributed to this change in the dynamic of the war as it entered its tenth year, including the impact of the 1989 FMLN offensive; an increased openness on the part of the U.S. government to a negotiated solution to the conflict; a desire on the part of the ARENA government to end the war to facilitate economic recovery and expansion; growing pressure for peace within El Salvador; and an international climate of lessening superpower tension with a movement toward the peaceful settlement of regional conflicts (e.g., in Angola, Afghanistan, Cambodia, and Nicaragua).

The 1989 FMLN offensive established relative parity in the strength of the opposing forces that built momentum for a move toward genuine negotiations. It punctured the illusion of a gradual but inexorable march toward military victory by the government side, particularly in the U.S. Congress, which was responsible for funding the war. The offensive forced powerful economic and political actors in El Salvador to consider whether economic recovery and political stability would be possible if the war continued and, while not immediately building a strong constituency for negotiations, helped dampen overt opposition. Whereas the FMLN viewed the 1989 offensive as a substantial political victory, it acknowledged internally the limitations of a predominantly military/insurrectional strategy and gradually shifted its focus to exploring the possibility of a negotiated end to the war.

The shift in the U.S. government's attitude toward a negotiated solution in El Salvador predated the FMLN offensive and was observable from the accession to power of the Bush administration in January 1989. Following years of conflict between the executive and legislative branches in Washington over human rights in El Salvador, aid to the Nicaraguan contras, and Central America policy in general, which culminated in the Iran-contra scandal, the new administration desired to craft a bipartisan policy toward Central America. In March 1989 President Bush announced an extension of nonlethal aid to the contras that resulted from an agreement reached with congressional leaders in a "spirit of trust, bipartisanship, and common purpose."[10] Though the new bipartisan approach focused more on U.S. policy in the Nicaragua war, greater flexibility by the administration was also visible toward El Salvador. Whereas Ambassador Corr had warned in June 1988 against "pushing prematurely for a negotiated solution that cannot guarantee the future of democracy,"[11] Secretary of State Baker, in an internal cable in February 1989, made clear that "we are encouraging the GOES [Government of El Salvador] to carefully assess the proposal" of the FMLN to enter into the electoral process under certain conditions.[12]

The changes taking place within the Soviet Union, epitomized by President Gorbachev's policies of "glasnost" and "perestroika," and the consequent lessening of tensions between the superpowers supported a more flexible and bipartisan approach by the Bush administration toward Central America and a lessening of the emphasis on the region in the global scheme of U.S. interests. As the Soviet Union and the Eastern bloc progressively crumbled during the first three years of the Bush administration, the perception of the importance of Central America and the danger posed by a rebel victory diminished substantially. While the new administration sought to bolster the Salvadoran government and armed forces and prevent an FMLN victory, it also began to explore more seriously the possibility of a negotiated end to the war.

The economy was the major focus of the ARENA government of Alfredo Cristiani that came to power in June 1989. Cristiani and other political, economic, and military leaders on the right acknowledged that economic recovery and expansion would only be possible if the war was ended. In his inaugural address Cristiani proposed a process of negotiations, and peace talks were held in September 1989 in Mexico and the following month in San José, Costa Rica. An assessment of the prospects for negotiations was contained in the observations of a diplomat: "ARENA is largely business oriented. . . . They realize things can't continue like this. They really want to get it over with."[13] Similarly, a September 1989 cable from U.S. ambassador

Walker discussed the Cristiani government's orientation toward negotiations and the U.S. position:

> I will be meeting with President Cristiani and a full range of political
> and military leaders to reiterate our support of a peaceful settlement.
> . . . Cristiani's motives include what I firmly believe is a personal com-
> mitment to a negotiated, constitutional solution: a conviction that
> further political and economic progress requires peace; recognition
> that a purely military victory is impossible in the short to medium
> term; and (possibly) a desire within ARENA to lessen dependence on
> the US. . . . If, as I believe, the relative balance of force between the
> GOES and FMLN has moved progressively in the government's favor
> since the earlier talks . . . the FMLN or important elements therein
> may be gradually drawn into some sort of political role before the
> 1991 elections. This offers opportunities for both the GOES and the
> US: it also presents risks. I believe we must signal all involved that the
> USG will not be an obstacle to a political settlement, and expects a
> serious approach towards the negotiation process. If we don't send
> such signals, our Congress will. . . . Nor is the military necessarily
> opposed to an agreement, although their leaders understandably will
> question FMLN motives. To keep those reservations in perspective,
> we need to offer the military signs of continued support.[14]

The FMLN's offensive had the effect of reinforcing the beliefs of
some government and business leaders that economic recovery and
the maintenance of public support would require a negotiated end to
the conflict necessitating compromise and concessions on both sides.
The effect of the offensive was to strengthen the demands that the
FMLN could make, backed by the threat of a new military offensive.

At least as important as the willingness of President Cristiani to
explore the possibilities of a negotiated solution was the much greater
ability of the ARENA government to sell such a process to their supporters and powerful sectors of society than that of their predecessors
in the PDC. Although President Duarte had made various attempts to
engage in negotiations, his efforts were limited substantially by opposition from military leaders, representatives of private enterprise who
were hostile to the PDC, political representatives of the right, and the
Reagan administration. With ARENA's victory in legislative and presidential elections in 1988 and 1989, respectively, the party controlled
all major branches of government, had the confidence of the country's main economic interests, and had better relations with the armed
forces than had the PDC. Although opposition to negotiations
remained in the ruling party and its political and economic base,
Cristiani was in a much stronger position to deliver on negotiations
than Duarte had been.

Additional momentum for negotiations came from public weariness of the war and organized pressure for a negotiated end to the conflict. From at least September 1988, when the Catholic Church organized the National Debate for Peace in El Salvador, public support for negotiations had been growing. The largest demonstrations in the period 1988 through 1990, attended by 30,000 to 100,000 participants, were called by the Permanent Committee of the National Debate in support of a negotiated solution to the civil war. Public-opinion polls also indicated that the desire for peace through a negotiated end to the conflict commanded overwhelming support in Salvadoran society. A poll by the Central American University showed that for the first time in five years a majority of Salvadorans, 63 percent, supported a negotiated end to the war. Before that year the percentage had never been above 30 percent.[15]

Ultimately, it was the coming together of a series of internal and international conditions that made possible the move to genuine negotiations to end a decade-long civil war that had cost over 70,000 lives. Relative parity between the military forces, as demonstrated in the FMLN's offensive, and the growing acceptance among leaders on both sides that no short-term victory was possible contributed to the move toward negotiations. International changes were also a critical factor. David Escobar Galindo, one of the government's three main negotiators, argues that had the Cold War continued, the negotiations would have had to operate on a double level—requiring international agreements between the superpowers and domestic agreements among the main Salvadoran actors—and could not have succeeded.[16] But even with favorable domestic and international conditions a successful outcome was far from guaranteed. The negotiating process itself was an extremely complex one involving a wide variety of Salvadoran and international actors. The process interacted with and was strongly affected by the military conflict that continued until agreement was reached on all major points.

The Changing Role of the United States

An important shift took place in the counterrevolutionary coalition as the war moved closer to a negotiated resolution. From the start of the war, the United States had played a central role within the counterrevolutionary bloc, taking major responsibility for the strategic direction of the conflict. Major strategies including the social and economic reforms of the early 1980s, the buildup of the Salvadoran armed forces in the first half of the 1980s, and the main counterinsurgency programs were planned and instigated by U.S. strategists. The U.S. Embassy played a crucial role in bringing and holding together erstwhile enemies and in preventing coups that would have disrupted U.S.

interests in El Salvador. U.S. military and economic aid was the essential element in staving off both economic collapse and military defeat.

By the end of the 1980s the situation had changed sufficiently to allow the Bush administration to play a somewhat different role in El Salvador. The danger of a military victory by the FMLN had lessened with the massive buildup of the Salvadoran armed forces. Successive elections had provided greater government stability than in the early 1980s. The collapse of the Soviet bloc made Central America less critical from a strategic and ideological standpoint, and U.S. policymakers appeared to realize that a negotiated solution was the best way to resolve the Salvadoran conflict and extricate the administration from a costly and contentious policy. In these circumstances, the role demanded of the United States was a different one. If a stable resolution to the conflict were to be reached, it would have to come from the Salvadoran parties themselves: the government, business, the armed forces, the FMLN, and other sectors of society. The United States would continue to be engaged throughout the process of negotiations but would play a more back-stage role, at some times supporting the positions of the Salvadoran government and armed forces; at other times cajoling them to make concessions to advance the negotiations. Although the U.S. role in the Salvadoran conflict remained a central one, the process of negotiations and its outcome responded more specifically to the interests of internal Salvadoran actors than had the strategies undertaken in earlier periods of the war.

Strategies of the Two Sides in This Period

The strategies of the opposing sides during the period from the end of 1989 to the end of 1991 were relatively straightforward compared with the earlier periods of the war. For both sides, once the framework of UN-mediated discussions was agreed upon, negotiations became the central strategy for bringing about a favorable resolution of the conflict. The shift in the balance of forces within El Salvador between the FMLN and the Salvadoran military, and the changing international environment, strengthened the forces on each side that were disposed to a negotiated solution. But the process was a difficult and, at times, tortuous one. On the counterrevolutionary side, the different interests and positions of the Salvadoran government, the armed forces, the government's economic backers and political base, and the United States had to be reconciled within a context of increasing domestic and international pressure for peace. On the insurgent side, the views of five political parties, which at times during the negotiations were as much divided internally as among themselves,[17] had to be harmonized, and their political bases convinced that the gains made in the negotiations justified the years of sacrifice and lives lost.

The main card held by the FMLN was its ability to continue the war and prevent economic recovery and social peace. At issue was the price the rebels could make the government pay in exchange for the FMLN's demobilization and integration into the political life of the country. Would this require the dissolution of the two armies, their merging, or some more limited changes that would guarantee the security of the rebels as a political force and ensure the democratization of the country? The interest of the government of El Salvador lay in conceding the minimum amount of change in political, military, social, and economic structures and arrangements in order to win the demobilization of the FMLN and an end to the war. The issue here was the price the government would be willing to pay to end the war and whether this would be sufficient for the insurgents. The interest of the Salvadoran armed forces lay in guaranteeing its continued existence as an institution, and it appears to have been willing (or forced) to concede much so long as the institution continued and there was no merger of the two armies. The U.S. government, which held the purse strings for the continuation of the war, supported a negotiated settlement but was concerned to ensure that the negotiations not result in a victory for the FMLN that the rebels had not won on the battlefield. At the same time, the United States was willing to see changes in Salvadoran society that it had been attempting to achieve for a decade—such as judicial and other political reforms, a lessening of the political power of the armed forces, and guarantees of human rights and security—brought about through negotiations.

During the last two years of the war the strategies of both sides were directed primarily toward the negotiating table. Whereas in the previous decade negotiations had played an ancillary or supporting role within the strategies of the opposing sides, during these two years military strategies were designed primarily to change the balance of forces at the bargaining table. Thus the offensives or major maneuvers launched by the FMLN were intended to demonstrate insurgent strength and convince its opponent to make concessions in the negotiations. Similarly, the government and armed forces undertook major actions in FMLN zones in order to deny rebel claims to control large areas of the country in the leadup to a cease-fire. The shift in the relationship between military strategies and negotiations was expressed by an FMLN leader:

> We began with a political-military strategy of popular war. Throughout the seventies that was the strategy. But as the war advanced and

the possibility of a resolution appeared the strategy changed first to a military strategy and later to a strategy of war and negotiations. In 1988 the FMLN had a strategy of war and negotiations—a two-track approach. At that time the military strategy predominated and the negotiations were secondary. But as the negotiations gained strength and began to win domestic and international support the roles changed. The negotiations became the determining strategy and the military became the ancillary one. In that way the war was brought to an end.[18]

For both sides there was a growing realization that the war had to end and that negotiations would be the most likely method. The objective of each remained to defeat the adversary, though now through a combination of war and negotiations. As the bargaining process commenced, the sides were far apart, with little evidence of willingness to compromise on the essentials.

Major Developments and Their Relationship to Strategies, 1990–1991

The Jesuit Case and U.S. Aid

The murder of six Jesuit priests and two coworkers on 16 November 1989, during the FMLN's offensive, created the most important crisis for U.S. policy in El Salvador in a decade, threatened continued U.S. aid to the country, and greatly complicated U.S. strategies for bringing about a favorable, negotiated end to the Salvadoran conflict.

That the military was involved in the killings became clear early in the investigation, and tended to undercut claims by U.S. policymakers that the Salvadoran armed forces had changed fundamentally and had learned to respect human rights in their conduct of the war. Increasing evidence of high-level involvement in planning the killings and in the subsequent coverup galvanized public and congressional demands for an end to aid to the Salvadoran armed forces. This firestorm of opposition in the United States, coupled with the inability of U.S. officials to move Salvadoran military officers to help resolve the case, led the Bush administration into the difficult and contradictory situation of using U.S. aid to increase pressure on the military to bring results in the Jesuit case, while opposing cuts publicly to avoid strengthening the position of the FMLN in the negotiations and undercutting the U.S. claims of the previous decade.

In early January 1990 President Cristiani announced that Colonel Benavides, head of the Salvadoran Military Academy, two lieutenants, and six lower-ranking soldiers were suspects in the Jesuit killings. In the following months, controversy around the case increased as evidence grew that log books had been destroyed, witnesses had apparently been intimidated, and the alleged killers, members of the Atlacatl Battalion, had participated in a U.S. training exercise in El Salvador that broke off less than three days before the murders. A congressional task force set up by the House Speaker and led by Representative John Joseph Moakley (a Democrat from Massachusetts) reported in early May 1990 that the colonel charged with ordering the killing might never stand trial, that the investigation had come to a "virtual standstill," and that the government had made "almost no effort" to determine whether senior military officials had played a role in the murders.[19]

In early July 1990 a declassified secret cable from U.S. ambassador Walker expressed frustration at ESAF leaders stonewalling in the Jesuit case:

> It is abundantly clear from the public record and information from other sources that members of the armed forces have: perjured themselves in statements to the court . . . failed to present obviously relevant materials to the court. . . . It is thus clear that deliberate effort by senior members of the armed forces to cover up events surrounding the killings began within hours of the crime, involves a large number of persons, and continues today. This must be as apparent to the high command as it is to everyone else.
>
> [B]y various independent means we now have a better understanding of what happened that led to the killings, other players involved, activities that indicate broader ESAF participation than hitherto revealed.[20]

A month later a staff delegation from the House Speaker's task force received credible evidence from "one of ESAF's most senior and respected officers"[21] that the order to kill the Jesuits had come from the Salvadoran High Command. A mid-August 1990 "eyes only" cable from Ambassador Walker to Assistant Secretary of State Bernard Aronson discussed the implications of this information:

> I am not so certain [about the accuracy of the information provided], but if basic story is true or if Congress believes it to be, our policy is at peril since the difficult to dismiss implications would be that (1) the decision to kill the Jesuits was a deliberate one made at the highest levels of the ESAF; (2) Colonel Ponce later suggested that he took credit for that decision; (3) possibly hundreds of officers knew the truth at the time of the killings and have maintained a desperate silence since; and (4) President Cristiani was informed of these allegations by the Staffdel's [staff delegation's] military source but has appeared to take no action to verify and/or act on the information.[22]

Growing evidence of high-level military involvement in the Jesuit murders led the United States to increase pressure on the Salvadoran government and military to get to the bottom of the case. In August 1990 the Bush administration froze $19 million in military aid, though it made clear that the decision could be reversed if the leadership of the ESAF cooperated in the Jesuit case.[23]

Pressure in the U.S. Congress for cuts in aid intensified throughout 1990. In May the House of Representatives voted overwhelmingly to halve military aid to El Salvador. The measure did not become law because the foreign-aid bill of which it formed a part was defeated, but a strong message was sent to Salvadoran political and military leaders. In October 1990 both houses voted to halve aid to El Salvador, including in the bill provisions to restore the aid if the FMLN launched a major offensive or imported sophisticated arms, and to cut off all aid if the government did not negotiate seriously or if progress was not made in the Jesuit case. The Bush administration made the decision to restore the $42.5 million in withheld aid following large-scale insurgent military actions in November and December 1990 and the murder of two U.S. soldiers in January 1991 by FMLN combatants; nevertheless, the administration continued to pressure the ESAF, though with few results. A declassified secret cable from Ambassador Walker expressed U.S. frustrations:

> Despite advancements in other areas, on the Jesuit case the ESAF remains committed to a hermetic conspiracy to protect its own at whatever cost. USG [U.S. Government] pleas, threats, turning on and off the military assistance spigot, and appeals to institutional honor have all had the same results—zilch. We have made enough demarches and arguments—our position is clear to the ESAF. I reluctantly conclude MOD [Minister of Defense] Ponce is a fatally flawed leader. Absent immediate turn-around, and despite the downsides, I recommend that the GOES be informed that we will not move on their pending requests for Cobra helicopters, armored personnel carriers, and will support heavy conditioning of FY 92 military assistance unless and until Ponce is removed and a new leadership solves the Jesuit affair. . . .
>
> In my mind the evidence is overwhelming, consistent and profoundly disturbing. This armed force, under this leadership, is either unwilling or unable to understand the meaning, the consequences or its role in the Jesuit case.[24]

Overall, the Jesuit case weakened dramatically the position of the Salvadoran armed forces in the government's negotiations with the FMLN. The military leadership's unwillingness or inability to bring to justice the intellectual authors of the Jesuit murders convinced U.S. policymakers that reform of the military had not been successful, and that the negotiations could be a vehicle for bringing about fundamental military reform. Although they sought to ensure that the FMLN not emerge the victor from negotiations, U.S. officials acknowledged the legitimacy of some of the insurgents' positions on military reform. A mid-1990 assessment highlighted the U.S. dilemma:

> The armed forces of El Salvador, once a cornerstone of U.S.-financed counterinsurgency efforts, are now seen by U.S. officials as a major liability and an impediment to prospects for peace in this tiny Central American nation. . . .
>
> "There's been some progress in reforming the military," said one U.S. official, "but fundamentally it's not working. Our pressure on them to reform has turned to dung." . . .
>
> "Trying to reform them is like squeezing a bag of water," said one U.S. official. "Now we have to play hardball." Once vehemently opposed to the idea, the official said recently that, "we're now basically supporting the move to condition or cut military aid." . . .
>
> In off-the-record conversations, both U.S. and Salvadoran government officials said military reform is the FMLN's most potent and legitimate point.[25]

Negotiations and War

The final two years of the Salvadoran conflict were characterized by the central role played by negotiations for the first time in the history of the war. However, the polarization in the views of the two sides as to the terms they would find acceptable for a resolution of the conflict ensured that the military option remained important, both as a potential alternative to negotiations and as a method of strengthening the bargaining position of each side at the negotiating table. The radically different views of the two sides as to their relative strength and, hence, what they could win through negotiations, also increased the importance of the role of other parties—particularly the UN as mediator, but also the United States, and the four "friends of the UN Secretary-General" in the negotiating process, Mexico, Colombia, Venezuela, and Spain—in influencing the belligerent forces to compromise.

THE EARLY PERIOD OF NEGOTIATIONS.   The attempt to resume a process of negotiations began soon after the FMLN's November 1989 offensive. The United States expressed strong support for the process, and the Salvadoran government and the FMLN agreed in April 1990 to begin negotiations mediated by the UN. The initial agreements that defined the framework and objectives of the process (Geneva Agreement, 4 April 1990), the agenda and schedule of the negotiations (Caracas Agreement, 21 May 1990), and a partial accord on human-rights verification (San José, Costa Rica, 26 July 1990) created optimism and momentum for a favorable resolution to the negotiation process. But from mid-1990 to April 1991, when agreements were reached on changes to the Salvadoran constitution covering judicial and electoral reform and the role of the armed forces, the two sides were at loggerheads on the central issue of the entire process: the future role of the Salvadoran armed forces.

The FMLN argued that because neither side had defeated the other on the battlefield, the only reasonable solution would be "the phasing-out of both armies in a gradual, symmetrical and simultaneous process, with the formation of a new public security force of a civilian nature."[26] The position of the Salvadoran government was that the future existence of the armed forces was outside the bounds of discussion. Another central and related difference concerned the sequence of political agreements and a cease-fire. The Salvadoran government, supported strongly by the United States, argued that certain political agreements should be reached, followed by a cease-fire, after which the negotiations would conclude the remaining agreements. The FMLN believed equally strongly that the cease-fire should follow political agreements because the government and armed forces would have little incentive to negotiate seriously if they had already achieved their primary goal, the end of the military conflict. A State Department cable, referring to a discussion with FMLN ally Rubén Zamora, summarized the problem from the insurgent standpoint:

> Zamora said an immediate ceasefire is not agreeable to the FMLN. They perceive it would be the beginning of their end. He pointed out that the FMLN has no permanent military installations and that its troops are unpaid peasants who would be back picking coffee two months after the fighting stopped. The FMLN therefore needs some guarantee that the GOES would continue negotiating after the cease-fire.[27]

The Salvadoran government continued to press for the earliest possible cease-fire, while the FMLN resisted until fundamental political agreements were in place.

THE ROLE OF MILITARY STRATEGIES.   In this impasse, military actions played a prominent role as each side sought to create conditions on the ground to favor its negotiating stance. The FMLN launched heavy attacks in May, June, and September before unleashing in November 1990 its largest military actions since the 1989 offensive. Though more military in focus than the offensive of the previous year, these actions contained a component that threatened to shift the entire military balance of the war: the FMLN's use of sophisticated surface-to-air missiles. Following the shooting down of two war planes in an eleven-day period, the *New York Times* reported that the use of the missiles marked a shift in the military balance of power.[28] Another assessment from the same period argued:

> After 11 years of U.S. aid and counsel, the Salvadoran armed forces are incapable of defeating the guerrilla insurgency and need $25 million in advanced technology and training to restore a military balance that existed just three months ago, a senior U.S. military official concludes.
>
> The rebels' introduction of sophisticated SA-14 anti-aircraft missiles and improved ground-fire strategies have turned daytime flying into a deadly gambit, seriously undercutting the military's greatest tactical advantage, U.S. and Salvadoran officers say. . . .
>
> The military impact of the rebels' new capability has been profound. Troop performance, intelligence-gathering and combat readiness have been compromised. . . .
>
> "The FMLN can now make larger attacks" [said a Salvadoran army captain]. "Basically we would have to shift our strategy to fight this. . . . We relied on the air power to bring firepower to whatever area was attacked. Now we won't be able to do that."[29]

An internal U.S. report also acknowledged the impact of the new missiles on the course of the war:

> The introduction of state-of-the-art surface to air missiles into the conflict, however, has all but neutralized the tactical advantage of the air force, affected the morale of the ground forces, and reduced the aggressiveness of ground operations. Additionally, aircraft modifications necessary to counter the threat are extremely costly and have diverted already scarce security assistance funding from other much needed sustainment programs.[30]

The FMLN attempted to push the government forces out of areas that the insurgents had traditionally controlled. The political objective, one analyst noted, was "to create conditions on the ground that would back up negotiating demands for a cease-fire in place that would put considerable territory under FMLN control."[31] At the same time, and to counter the insurgent strategy, the Salvadoran military from mid-1990 carried out extensive operations in the traditional zones of the FMLN in the north and east of the country. This strategy continued through 1991 and was described by a Salvadoran military leader as

> designed to deny FMLN claims to territorial control. The cornerstone of the strategy is to use immediate reaction infantry battalions (BIRI's) as so-called organic (i.e. already present in the area) forces to permanently secure zones traditionally thought by the FMLN to be

territory under its control. While calling in units stationed elsewhere in case additional help is needed to counteract insurgent activity, ESAF strategy focuses on the departments of Chalatenango and Morazán. . . . The strategy was a success—the Atlacatl was not dislodged, while FMLN initiated military activity was otherwise countered.[32]

In the period 1990–1991 the continued importance of military activity can be seen from the fact that the intensity of combat, as measured in casualties and economic losses, was as high or higher than in any other year since 1985, excluding 1989. Salvadoran authorities reported that 1,000 of its soldiers were killed in 1990, and 878 in 1991, compared with 859 (1985), 742 (1986), 832 (1987), 788 (1988), and 1,356 (1989).[33] Economic sabotage also continued to take a heavy toll. The U.S. Embassy reported that

> direct and indirect damage to the economy inflicted by the FMLN in 1990 totaled $125 million. Actual production losses to industry, commerce and agriculture totaled $45 million—equivalent to 1.2 percent of GDP. These losses likely reduced real GDP growth by more than 25 percent. The FMLN executed more than 1,000 bombing attacks against primary and secondary electrical transmission lines and power stations in 1990.[34]

It appears overall that although military factors were not decisive in the period 1990–1991, the FMLN's ability to launch large-scale military actions, and its use of surface-to-air missiles to neutralize the Salvadoran military's main advantage on the battlefield, worked to strengthen the bargaining position of the insurgents and increased pressure on the Salvadoran government to compromise. The congressional halving of military aid, accompanied by administration pressure on the government and armed forces on the Jesuit case, also appear to have placed the government and military on the defensive in the negotiations, particularly on the question of the future of the armed forces. However, the pressure was not only on the government and armed forces. The Sandinista defeat in the February 1990 elections in Nicaragua and the dramatic changes taking place in the Soviet Union and Eastern Europe created logistical problems for the FMLN, and gave rise to significant soul searching within the insurgent organizations over the purposes and future direction of the Salvadoran revolutionary process. Diplomatic efforts by the United States to force the FMLN to accept a speedy cease-fire, and later efforts by the "friends of the Secretary-General" to convince the rebels to modify their demands on incorporation of FMLN members into the armed forces, also increased pressure on the insurgents to compromise.

BREAKING THE DEADLOCK IN THE NEGOTIATIONS. The continuing impasse on the issue of the future role of the armed forces from mid-1990 into early 1991 prevented any significant advances in the negotiations, and substantive discussions were put on hold until the results of the March 1991 legislative and municipal elections in El Salvador were known. At the same time, other factors pressed the parties toward serious negotiations. The FMLN's November/December 1990 offensive confirmed that the insurgents were still a powerful military force to reckon with, and this, coupled with the U.S. congressional cut in military aid, increased pressure on the Salvadoran government to reach agreements on military reform. The two parties' agreement in November 1990 on a more active role for the UN mediator in the negotiations, Alvaro de Soto, and a joint U.S.–Soviet communiqué supporting the talks, also appear to have helped build momentum for serious negotiations. But the major factor in increasing the urgency of the process was the terms of the Salvadoran Constitution, which contained a provision (Article 248) requiring any changes to the constitution to be ratified by two successive legislative assemblies. With the outgoing assembly scheduled to finish work at the end of April 1991, an objective deadline was imposed on the parties to reach agreements by that date, to change Article 248 of the constitution, or to wait until 1994 to enact the agreements.

The two sides met for three weeks in Mexico in April 1991 against a backdrop of intensive organized pressure within El Salvador. Grassroots pressure from the left and the center urged a change in Article 248 to prevent the negotiations from being held hostage by the constitution. Rightist groups protested any changes and published threats to legislators who might consider constitutional reforms. Ultimately, the negotiators reached agreement on important changes to the constitution in the areas of judicial and electoral reform, on a greatly restricted definition of the function and role of the armed forces and their subordination to civilian leadership, and on the formation of a Truth Commission to investigate major human-rights cases. The Salvadoran government did not accept the reform of Article 248; the changes made to the constitution by the outgoing assembly would need to be ratified by the new assembly that resulted from the March 1991 elections. This left the ARENA government with an important bargaining tool: It could hold back ratification of the agreements reached as a pressure on the FMLN to compromise in the talks.

The Mexico Agreement on constitutional reform was important in building confidence and momentum within the negotiations. But the key question, reform of the armed forces, had only been deferred. Throughout the spring and summer of 1991 the FMLN held to its position that to demand its demobilization while the Salvadoran army continued to exist, though smaller in size and subordinate to civilian authority, would be tantamount to demanding the FMLN's surrender. Although the FMLN refined its position, from the total demilitarization of the society by the disbanding of both armies to the inclusion of rebel cadre in the army and security forces, its proposal was still fundamentally unacceptable to the Salvadoran government and armed forces. The United States strongly supported the government position, and the UN mediator held out little hope for acceptance of the rebel position or of persuading the FMLN to modify its position significantly. A UN "aide memoire" discussed the problem:

> If indeed the idea of participation by ex-FMLN members in the army is unthinkable, then ways must be sought to persuade the FMLN not to press this point. It is hard to be optimistic on this score, since it is at the very heart of the FMLN's position and in truth it constitutes a mere vestige of what they have sought in the past.[35]

A U.S. government "talking points" on the negotiations noted:

> —We are also glad that the UN agrees with the friends of the Secretary General that the FMLN proposal to integrate some of its fighters into the Salvadoran armed forces (ESAF) was unrealistic.
> —We believe that the UN should firmly advise the FMLN that any such proposal is impractical and that the FMLN should expect no "compensation" for dropping this demand.[36]

In September 1991 a breakthrough was achieved that laid the basis for the final resolution of the conflict. In New York the two parties signed a far-reaching set of agreements that included the creation of a National Commission for the Consolidation of Peace (COPAZ) that would include representatives of the government, the FMLN, and political parties represented in the assembly, and would have wide powers to oversee the implementation of the peace agreements; the creation of an ad hoc commission to vet members of the armed forces and carry out a "purification"; agreement to reduce the size of the Salvadoran military and to reform its doctrine and training system; the creation of a National Civilian Police force, which could include former members of the FMLN; and accords on social and economic questions including the maintenance of the existing landholding situation in conflictive zones until legal solutions were found. The parties also agreed to compress the negotiating agenda with the objective of resolving all outstanding political issues prior to a cease-fire.

Following the New York Agreement the two sides moved toward a final accord to end the conflict. In mid-November 1991 the FMLN

announced that it was halting all offensive military operations indefinitely in an effort to end the war. The Salvadoran government ensured
passage of the constitutional reforms agreed to in April 1991. In an
intensive round of negotiations carried out in New York in December
1991, the two sides reached final agreement on the terms for ending
the military conflict and the transformation of the FMLN from an
insurgent force into a legal political organization. On 16 January 1992
the final agreement to end the war was signed in Mexico City.

Factors Leading to the Success of the Negotiations

Certain domestic Salvadoran and international factors—notably the
relative parity of the military forces and the transformed international environment—played an important role in making possible the first
genuine negotiations of the Salvadoran civil war, yet major barriers
remained to be overcome before a settlement was reached. The role
of particular individuals and institutions, as well as developments within or closely related to the negotiation process, helped bring about a
political solution to the war.

THE ROLE OF THE UN.   The UN played an essential role in the resolution of the conflict in mobilizing international support for the process:
conducting impartial mediation, developing potential solutions that
could break through logjams at the negotiating table, and ultimately
guaranteeing the implementation of the final accords.

Unlike the Salvadoran Catholic Church, which had mediated earlier attempts at negotiations but was perceived as a Salvadoran actor
divided into right and left wings,[37] the UN was viewed by the two sides
as an objective mediator. UN Secretary-General Javier Pérez de Cuéllar
mobilized the support of the two superpowers prior to the initiation of
formal negotiations, and further support for the process was provided
by the formation of a support group consisting of Mexico, Colombia,
Venezuela, and Spain that could exercise influence on the two sides.
In the negotiating process itself, the Secretary-General's representative, Alvaro de Soto, began by playing a traditional mediating role;
with the agreement of the two sides in November 1990 he played a
more active role in developing positions and proposals to narrow the
gap between the parties and bring agreement closer. His willingness to
search for solutions to what one government negotiator called the
"political distortions of the Salvadoran system," showed the UN position to be closer to the FMLN's than to that of the government; this
led U.S. officials to accuse the mediator of being partial in the
process.[38] The accusations reflected more than anything a frustration
on the part of the U.S. government that a speedy cease-fire was not

being reached; the ultimate assessment of the parties to the negotiation was that the UN mediator and his team played an indispensable
and impartial role in the negotiations.

THE U.S. ROLE.   Support for negotiations from the country that had
given some $6 billion in economic and military aid to the Salvadoran
government to prevent a leftist victory was clearly essential for the
process to take off and succeed. According to one FMLN negotiator,
the main initial contribution of the United States to the process was to
"permit" it to go forward.[39] The FMLN viewed the U.S. role during
1990 as unproductive and unrealistic—in resisting profound changes
and seeking an immediate cease-fire that would essentially preclude
further meaningful negotiations—but saw U.S. involvement in the
negotiations on constitutional reforms in April 1991, and those on the
armed forces that led to the final agreement, as very productive.
Salvadoran government negotiators highlighted three major contri-
butions of the United States in the process: in protecting Cristiani and
warning off potential assassination attempts against him from the
right; in providing pressure on the Salvadoran armed forces to accept
agreements that were unpalatable to them; and in giving reassurance
to the FMLN that the final agreements would indeed be carried out.
Ultimately, as the main backer of the Salvadoran government and
armed forces, the United States had the leverage to press for compromises that would move the process forward, and at key moments was
willing to exercise its influence, particularly on the Salvadoran military.

THE ROLE OF THE NEGOTIATORS.   The role of the two negotiating teams,
made up of large plenary groups and a working group of three persons
for each side that conducted much of the day-to-day negotiations, was
an important factor in reaching a negotiated settlement. The negotiating teams tended to be more supportive of the process and, under-
standably, of the specific agreements reached than the parties they
represented who were not involved in the negotiations. The negotiators had to deal with the opposing side, the UN, other international
actors involved in the process, the Salvadoran political parties and
other interest groups, and their own parties. Salvador Samayoa, one of
the FMLN's main negotiators, reported that debate within the FMLN
and its constituent parties was far more difficult than negotiating with
the government. In general, the FMLN leaders who took part in the
negotiations supported the process while those who were not directly
involved tended, particularly in the early period, to be "more opposed,
more apprehensive, more obstructive."[40] A similar process took place
on the government side, with the changes proposed to the armed

forces causing the greatest difficulty. The government's military representative on the negotiating team, Colonel Mauricio Vargas, was responsible for keeping the armed forces informed of the progress of the negotiations, and for explaining proposed changes in a series of seminars for military officials that, supported by U.S. pressure, ensured that the changes were "less traumatic than they might have been."[41]

PRESIDENT CRISTIANI AND THE FMLN'S GENERAL COMMAND.   On the government side, President Alfredo Cristiani played a central role in the negotiated settlement to the conflict. Though he never met directly with FMLN leaders until after the final agreement, Cristiani was the major supporter of a settlement and he used the power of his office to build support and minimize opposition among his political and economic base. Organized support for a negotiated solution on the government side was extremely limited, according to a key government negotiator.

> This process was not a product of groups supporting it but more of individuals. It was basically a personal effort of Cristiani. . . . His great legacy will be to have administered the extremely scarce support that existed, because in reality there were practically no individuals who supported the process, much less groups . . . and to have prevented the rejection of the process from becoming an organized action against the government. Not to have prevented rejection of the process because that always existed—in the armed forces, in the private sector, and in the ARENA Party—but to have prevented this opposition from becoming an organized phenomenon against the government and against the negotiations. . . . If you were to ask me how many people supported the process and how many opposed it, I would say that 0.2 percent supported it and 99.8 percent opposed it, for different reasons, some more openly, some with a total skepticism. The president was very much alone. But he was president of the Republic with a great capacity to keep pushing for this result. I think in the FMLN there was a similar process—little support for a solution that implied there would be no revolution. So there was a process with a great deal of publicity but with little accompaniment.[42]

On the FMLN side there was a great deal of skepticism about the negotiating process and a wide variety of opinions both within and among the five constituent parties. The human-rights agreement of July 1990 caused dissension at the base level because of its partial and limited nature. Midlevel commanders were apprehensive about the military agreements and were brought into some of the later discussions. FMLN leaders met for a month "from 8 a.m. to midnight" prior to the September 1991 meeting in New York, but boarded the plane without reaching agreement.[43] Yet the FMLN was able to hold out and win major political and military changes while also accepting compromises that fell short of the rebels' objectives. What was critical in this period of negotiations, as it had been in the first nine years of the war, was the strategic unity maintained at the leadership level that allowed the FMLN to reach agreements after much internal debate, present unified positions in the talks, and convince its base of the value of the agreements reached.

The Outcome of the Negotiations:
What the Parties Sought and What They Achieved

The Salvadoran government and military, on one side, and the FMLN-FDR, on the other, went to war to achieve basic political and socio-economic objectives that they believed could only be attained by military means. The government and military, supported by the United States, sought to defeat the insurgents through a variety of political and military strategies in order to be able to maintain a modified version of the traditional economic and political systems in El Salvador. The FMLN and its allies sought the eradication of the traditional socioeconomic and political model through a revolutionary civil war that would result in the rebels taking power and bringing about basic structural changes in the country.

After ten years of war, negotiations became the preferred option to resolve the conflict for both sides when relative military parity suggested the improbability of a swift victory for either side and international conditions became favorable to a negotiated solution. An assessment by Vickers highlights the general conditions that tend to favor negotiated solutions to military conflicts:

> Wars that end through real political negotiations are actually rather rare. They tend to occur when (1) neither side perceives a possibility of near-term victory, (2) all the combatants perceive high immediate costs to continued fighting, and (3) all the combatants are uncertain that they can maintain sufficient resources to avoid defeat in the medium and long term. Under such circumstances all the parties may settle for minimum, rather than maximum, objectives.[44]

In El Salvador these conditions appear to have been present and the two sides, supported by strong outside pressure, were able to reach agreement following a long and complex process of negotiations. Both sides came out of the negotiations able to claim certain victories that related to the outcomes they sought through the war and through the negotiations.

It is clear, however, that neither side achieved its basic objective, the political-military defeat of its enemy, which would have left the space open for the victor to implement its overall political and socioeconomic vision. Each side had to compromise and accept substantially less than its maximum program. For the FMLN the most unfavorable outcome of the negotiations was the continued existence of the Salvadoran military after the FMLN had demobilized and ceased to be a military force. (The continuation in power of the Salvadoran government was not even an issue in the peace talks, although in earlier negotiations in the 1980s the call for a power-sharing government had been a central insurgent demand.) This was the hardest thing for the FMLN to accept and the Salvadoran government had to pay a substantial price to gain the demobilization of the insurgents while maintaining its own armed forces in existence.

Part of the price paid by the government was the acceptance of FMLN participation (up to 20 percent) in the new security force, the National Civilian Police (PNC), which provided some reassurance to the rebels on the security front. Other changes in the armed forces that provided confidence to the FMLN that military domination of the society was coming to an end were the dissolution of the National Guard, the Treasury Police, and the Customs Police, and the replacement of the National Police with the PNC; the establishment of a process for the reduction of the armed forces; dissolving the National Intelligence Directorate; dissolving the elite infantry battalions, all paramilitary groups, the civil defense, and village patrols; and reforming the doctrine and training methods for the military.

The formation of an ad hoc commission to rid the armed forces of human-rights violators and others unsuited to the new form of military provided reassurance that though the armed forces would continue to exist, it would be different from that which existed prior to and during the war (provided the agreements were faithfully carried out). The creation of a Truth Commission to investigate major violations of human rights carried out during the war provided some satisfaction that the truth would be told about some of the most egregious violations, and that a measure of justice might be done (through dismissal of armed-forces personnel and banning from political activity violators on both sides).

The formation of COPAZ, which had exceptional powers to ensure the implementation of the agreements, provided the FMLN with a high level of participation in the major mechanism created to carry out the accords. Other key elements of the agreement guaranteed basic human rights and provided mechanisms to ensure compliance; provided limited socioeconomic reforms; and ensured UN oversight and verification of the cease-fire and the implementation of the accords.

These agreements promised to bring about substantial changes in Salvadoran society. Two of the major changes—the democratization of the political system and its opening to the entire spectrum of political forces for the first time; and the ending of the military's dominant role in society and the impunity of the armed forces—went a substantial way toward addressing the root cause of the war. These changes were significant enough to lead the UN mediator, Alvaro de Soto, to term the final agreement a "negotiated revolution."

In reality, however, despite the breadth of the changes agreed to by the parties, the agreement fell short of a revolution in two main respects: Political power and a monopoly of the legal means of coercion remained in the hands of the Salvadoran government; and the agreement did not effect a fundamental social and economic transformation of the society.

The war began as a conflict between two exclusive, competing visions of society: one an authoritarian model modified through U.S. pressure toward a restricted democracy; the other a model of socialist transformation modified over the war years by the FMLN's willingness to accept change in stages. Neither of these visions triumphed. The outcome, reflecting the inability of either side to win a political or military victory in eleven years of war, was an agreement that, if implemented effectively, would lead to a genuine democratization of the society, creating the conditions for the Salvadoran people to choose freely among competing visions of the future political and socioeconomic order. The settlement was ultimately an agreement to reverse Clausewitz's maxim and continue the eleven-year conflict by other—political—means. After eleven years of military conflict that had cost over 70,000 lives, military strategies had brought a stalemate: Each side had developed effective means of prolonging the conflict and avoiding defeat, but not of winning the war. Under these conditions a compromise that each side could claim protected or achieved its central objectives appeared better than an uncertain future.

During this period the strategies of the two sides did not play a decisive role in the outcome of the conflict. The potential for a negotiated solution resulted from the inability of either side to win a military victory, and to a changed international environment that was more favorable to a political solution. But political, diplomatic, and military strategies were important in determining the specific terms of the agreement. The FMLN's ability to continue the war and to affect the potential for economic recovery appears to have been a factor in making the Salvadoran government more willing to compromise. At the same time, the Salvadoran military was able to prevent further rebel advances that might have strengthened the FMLN's argument for a dissolution of both forces or the integration of the rebels into the armed forces. Diplomatic strategies also played an important role in the specific outcome of the negotiations, though neither side appears to have made gains at the bargaining table that were not commensurate with the political and military balance of forces of the two sides.

Overall, the terms of the peace agreement reflected the reality of a long, bloody, and stalemated war. The gains made by the rebels through negotiations were very significant, but arguably only reflected the strength of a guerrilla force that was able to fight to a draw a government and military that was backed by the major (and by the end of the war, only) superpower, with some $6 billion in military and economic aid. At the same time, the Salvadoran government had not been overthrown and the military had not been defeated. Given this reality, there was little potential (or incentive) for the government to agree to dissolve itself or to accept a dissolution of the armed forces. Some form of integration of the two forces was not beyond the bounds of possibility; such had been agreed to in other negotiations, for example in agreements to end the civil wars in Angola and Mozambique, and might have reflected the reality of a military stalemate. This, however, was the major issue that the Salvadoran government and armed forces were unwilling to accept and on which they were supported by the United States and international "friends" of the negotiations. Military, political, and diplomatic pressure from the FMLN could not shift their opponents' position on this issue.

On balance, the terms of the negotiations appear to reflect closely the relative strengths of the two sides after eleven years of war. The FMLN had demonstrated that it had the power to continue the war almost indefinitely and to "veto" any major socioeconomic developments or advances. But it was not strong enough to defeat a Salvadoran government and military in which the U.S. government had invested heavily, in terms of economic and military aid and credibility, and that it was determined should not fall to a leftist insurgency.

Notes

1. Salvador Samayoa, author interview, tape recording, San Salvador, 14 July 1995.
2. *U.S. Declassified Documents I*, CIA, "El Salvador: Government and Insurgent Prospects," February 1989, iii–iv.
3. *U.S. Declassified Documents I*, Department of State, ER5n vol. 2, "El Salvador: An Increasingly Brighter Future in 1990's—Provided US Stays the Course," telegram #08638, from U.S. Embassy, San Salvador, to Secretary of State, 28 June 1988.
4. *U.S. Declassified Documents I*, CIA, "El Salvador: Government and Insurgent Prospects," February 1989, 11.

5. *U.S. Declassified Documents I*, CIA, Directorate of Intelligence, "El Salvador: The FMLN After the November 1989 Offensive," 26 January 1990.

6. Chris Norton, "After Salvador's Rebel Offensive," *Christian Science Monitor*, 8 December 1989, 4.

7. Michael R. Gordon, "U.S. General Says Salvador Cannot Defeat the Guerrillas," *New York Times*, 9 February 1990, 9.

8. Phil Bronstein, "No Cuts Likely in U.S. Aid to Salvador," *San Francisco Examiner*, 29 January 1990, A14.

9. Facundo Guardado, author interview, 19 February 1993.

10. Cynthia J. Arnson, *Crossroads: Congress, the Reagan Administration, and Central America* (New York: Pantheon Books, 1989), 223.

11. *U.S. Declassified Documents I*, "El Salvador: An Increasingly Brighter Future," 28 June 1988.

12. *U.S. Declassified Documents I*, Department of State, ER5n vol. 2, "FMLN Peace Proposal," telegram #036272, from Secretary of State, Washington, D.C., to All American Republic Diplomatic Posts, 6 February 1989.

13. Chris Norton, "Salvador Peace: Hard Work Ahead," *Christian Science Monitor*, 22 September 1989, 6.

14. *U.S. Declassified Documents I*, Department of State, ER5n vol. 3, "GOES–FMLN Negotiations: Where Do We Go from Here?" telegram #12271, from U.S. Embassy, San Salvador, to Secretary of State, 22 September 1989.

15. Christopher Marquis, "Key Issues Block Salvador Peace," *Miami Herald*, 6 November 1990, 15A.

16. David Escobar Galindo, author interview, tape recording, San Salvador, 10 July 1995.

17. Rebeca Palacios, author interview, tape recording, San Salvador, 11 July 1992.

18. Gerson Martínez, author interview, 9 November 1992.

19. Martin McReynolds, "Probe at a 'Standstill' in Murder of Jesuit Priests in San Salvador," *Miami Herald*, 1 May 1990, 1.

20. *U.S. Declassified Documents I*, Department of State, ER1h vol. 8, "Demarche to the Armed Forces," telegram #08839, from U.S. Embassy, San Salvador, to Secretary of State, 2 July 1990.

21. *U.S. Declassified Documents I*, Department of State, ER1h vol. 8, "The Jesuit Case: Another Big Jolt," telegram #10791, from U.S. Embassy, San Salvador, to Secretary of State, 13 August 1990, 1.

22. Ibid., 2.

23. *U.S. Declassified Documents I*, Department of State, ER1h, "Ambassador's Demarche to ESAF High Command on Jesuit Case," telegram #11226, from U.S. Embassy, San Salvador, to Secretary of State, 21 August 1990.

24. *U.S. Declassified Documents I*, Department of State, ER1h, "The ESAF and the Jesuit Case: Reaching the End of the Rope," telegram #02156, from U.S. Embassy, San Salvador, to Secretary of State, 19 February 1991.

25. Phil Bronstein, "U.S. Officials Reverse View on Salvador Army," *San Francisco Examiner*, 6 May 1990, 1A.

26. Farabundo Martí National Liberation Front, General Command, "The FMLN's Rationale for Ending Militarism, Reaching a Cease-fire and Advancing to an Unarmed Democracy," communiqué, El Salvador, 17 August 1990.

27. *U.S. Declassified Documents I*, Department of State, ER1h, "Aronson-

Zamora Meeting on 15 November," telegram #395387, from Secretary of State to U.S. Embassy, San Salvador, 22 November 1990.

28. Lindsey Gruson, "Missiles Give Salvador Rebels a New Advantage," *New York Times,* 10 December 1990, 4.

29. Christopher Marquis, "U.S. Advisors: Salvadorans Need High-Tech Arms," *Miami Herald,* 15 January 1991, 7A.

30. *U.S. Declassified Documents I,* Department of State, "Security Assistance Report," telegram #07072, from U.S. Embassy, San Salvador, to Secretary of State, 7 June 1991.

31. George R. Vickers, "The Political Reality After Eleven Years of War," in Joseph S. Tulchin, ed., with Gary Bland, *Is There a Transition to Democracy in El Salvador?* Woodrow Wilson Center Current Studies on Latin America (Boulder, Colo., and London: Lynne Rienner Publishers, 1992), 41.

32. *U.S. Declassified Documents I,* Department of State, ER5n vol. 9, "ESAF Seeks to Deny FMLN Territorial Claims," telegram #13603, from U.S. Embassy, San Salvador, to Secretary of State, 28 October 1991.

33. UN Truth Commission, *From Madness to Hope,* Appendix to Spanish-language edition, Anexos, Tomo 8, "Lista de caídos de la Fuerza Armada en el conflicto armado."

34. *U.S. Declassified Documents I,* Department of State, "Report on El Salvador Required Under the Foreign Assistance Appropriations Act of 1991," January 1992.

35. United Nations, aide memoire, 22-point document, untitled, August 1991, point 15, in Salvadoran government–FMLN negotiations documents in author's possession.

36. United States, "El Salvador: Talking Points," 26 August 1991, in Salvadoran government–FMLN negotiations documents in author's possession.

37. Escobar Galindo, author interview, 10 July 1995.

38. Ibid.

39. Samayoa, author interview, 14 July 1995.

40. Ibid.

41. Gen. Mauricio Vargas, author interview, tape recording, San Salvador, 13 July 1995.

42. Escobar Galindo, author interview, 10 July 1995.

43. Samayoa, author interview, 14 July 1995.

44. Vickers, "The Political Reality After Eleven Years of War," 47–48.

7

Conclusion

Recent social-scientific and historical approaches to revolution provide useful insights into the conditions that are most likely to give rise to revolutionary crises and outcomes in predominantly agrarian societies. Socioeconomic analyses have pointed to the importance of the relationship between landowning classes and the peasantry, the impact of capitalist market relations on peasant society, and the role of outside forces and events in contributing to peasant mobilization and revolution. Other more politically focused approaches stress the role of political crises, often brought on by international events, or the isolation of the incumbent regime from key sectors of society in explaining social revolutions. However, these approaches provide only part of the explanation for revolutionary upheavals and outcomes. What is missing is the role of people in these processes—particularly the part that the strategies of revolutionaries and incumbent regimes play in helping generate revolutionary crises. When structural economic and political factors are overemphasized, the role of human agency and the responsibility of individuals in these large historical processes is diminished.

An examination of major twentieth-century social revolutions demonstrates the importance of socioeconomic and political factors in generating revolutionary outcomes in Russia, China, Vietnam, Cuba, and Nicaragua, while at the same time illustrating the essential role that strategic choices of revolutionaries and regimes played within these processes. A more complete understanding of twentieth-century revolution requires a deeper analysis of the role of strategy and the way it relates to the underlying socioeconomic and political realities of a given society.

The Role of Strategy in
El Salvador's Crisis of 1979–1980

A study of the origins of a profound revolutionary crisis in El Salvador in the late 1970s highlights the essential role played by the strategies

197

of revolutionary groups and the incumbent regime in precipitating this upheaval. At least five key elements were necessary to the development of this crisis. Economic factors—particularly a dramatic deterioration in the living conditions of the peasant majority (as well as other marginal sectors) caused by the expansion of the export-crop economy at the expense of subsistence peasant production—laid the groundwork for a revolutionary opposition to form and mobilize support. Political factors, including the repressive and exclusive nature of a regime that linked the landed oligarchy with military rulers and closed down the limited political spaces that were opened in the 1960s, were also indispensable to the later crisis. Repression and authoritarian military rule convinced many educated, middle-class youth who had been influenced by Marxism or the social teachings of the Catholic Church to form or join guerrilla groups to effect change through force of arms. The combination of a harsh and deteriorating economic situation for the majority and a response of violence and repression to any attempts to change this reality became explosive when the peasantry, which had been subdued and quiescent for forty years, was awakened to its own potential power through pastoral work carried out by Catholic clergy and lay activists in barrios and villages in many parts of El Salvador.

Revolutionary groups that combined political and military strategies to challenge the regime were formed from 1970 and focused organizing efforts in the countryside from 1973. These activities intersected with and (in many cases) built upon the Catholic pastoral work. The "religious awakening" among peasants to the reality of their condition and the potential for leading more dignified lives spurred many to build or reactivate grassroots peasant organizations. The political-military groups were able to provide links to other social sectors, a vision of a new society organized for the benefit of the majority, the political vehicles to help effect change, and limited forms of self-defense from attacks by the state or landowners.

The strategies of the political-military groups were an essential element in creating the revolutionary crisis of the late 1970s. These strategies included focusing major efforts on organizing the peasantry at a time when conditions were deteriorating in the countryside and many peasants were becoming willing to organize for change, despite the risks. The effort to build broad popular organizations that incorporated peasants and workers alongside teachers, students, and marginalized sectors of Salvadoran society was a major factor in increasing the potency of the challenge to the Molina and Romero regimes in the 1970s. The creation of groups that combined political organizing with military attacks also built pressure on the regime. The political strategies in this period were most effective in isolating the regime and, in the main, the revolutionary groups put their resources into this area. The military component served to intensify pressure on the regime, provided some self-defense in the face of massacres that were carried out from the mid-1970s in the cities and the countryside, and provided military experience and structures that would be built on when the conflict evolved into a civil war.

Just as the strategies of the revolutionary groups helped generate the crisis of the late 1970s, so the strategies of the regime ensured that opportunities to avert a crisis were missed. The choices made by military rulers (under pressure from right-wing landowners) not to permit even a limited land reform ensured that an opportunity was missed to try to channel peasant radicalism in a reformist direction. The overturning of apparent election victories won by a reform coalition in 1972 and 1977 marginalized democratic parties and convinced many that revolution was the only method of bringing about change. A strategy of increased repression launched by the Romero regime in the late 1970s only galvanized the opposition to further action rather than subduing it.

It was the danger of a revolutionary overthrow of the government, graphically illustrated by the Sandinista victory in Nicaragua, that caused progressive military officers to ally with civilian reformers to try to bring about democratic change before it was too late. The 15 October 1979 reformist military coup launched an effort to bring an end to the traditional military-landowner domination of the society and to effect serious reforms. It also began a period of major U.S. involvement in the country. When reformist civilians resigned from the first junta in January 1980 because they felt powerless to end the repression, the stage was set for civil war. Over the next twelve months the major actors prepared for war or to win a political-military victory that would make war unnecessary.

The strategies of the revolutionaries and the regime in El Salvador in the 1970s played a crucial role in the generation of a revolutionary crisis in 1979–1980. The left, however, was not able to take advantage of the most favorable moment (when the open, popular opposition was at its height) to seize power by force of arms. This failure was due to military weakness, the time it took to unify the left parties, massive repression from the military and right-wing death squads, the U.S. role in cementing a military–Christian Democrat coalition, and the solidarity maintained by the traditional dominant class and its willingness to unleash extreme violence to maintain its position. But although the left was kept from power, it was not defeated, and it was able to lay the foundations for a prolonged war to achieve its revolutionary goals. Once the left failed in its attempt to effect a revolutionary seizure of power and the conflict evolved into a prolonged civil war, the strategies of two competing coalitions took on an even more central role. The political and economic causes of the crisis were to some extent frozen in place, and the strategies adopted became critical to each side's attempt to win a political-military victory.

The Role of Strategy in the Civil War

Dividing El Salvador's civil war in three periods allows one to see the role that strategy played in creating provisional advantages to one side and forcing the other to readjust, as well as to observe the relationship between strategy and the ultimate outcome of the conflict.

In the first period, from the FMLN's January 1981 offensive to the inauguration of José Napoleón Duarte in June 1984, the political-military strategies of the FMLN brought the Salvadoran armed forces to the brink of defeat in late 1983 and consolidated a base of support for a prolonged war. However, the major investment of resources by the United States was enough to prevent military defeat; it allowed the armed forces to take advantage of the military strength of the FMLN, which had permitted the insurgents to fight in large units but made them increasingly vulnerable to ESAF airpower. This vulnerability and the attendant losses suffered caused the FMLN to carry out a major strategic shift toward a more political conflict, using small units and waging a war of attrition while contesting the government's support, particularly in the urban areas. During this first period, the United States focused on political strategies of consolidating a regime that could win domestic and international support through elections and the development of democratic institutions. With the elections of 1982, and particularly of 1984, that brought Duarte to power, the United States and its Salvadoran allies moved into a very strong position while the FMLN hunkered down to a prolonged war of resistance.

In the second period, from mid-1984 to the FMLN's offensive of November 1989, the United States and its allies sought to build upon their advantages by consolidating a democratic system, ensuring economic stabilization and growth, and winning the hearts and minds of the rural population through a strategy of low-intensity conflict: contesting with the FMLN for the allegiance of the population with civic-action programs, psychological warfare, separating the rebels from their civilian base, and civil-defense programs. The FMLN waged a war of resistance—consolidating its own zones of influence and control and moving into the government's main rearguard, the cities, and focusing on killing and maiming government forces at low cost to the insurgents—in preparation for launching a strategic counteroffensive, combining a popular insurrection and military offensive, to overthrow the government. The counterrevolutionary side, despite its advantages, had scant success. The Duarte government eroded; there was very limited progress in the consolidation of a democratic system, and little economic growth, while the FMLN succeeded in spreading the war throughout the country. The United States and its allies believed they had the insurgents on the run by the late 1980s and were shocked at the strength of the FMLN's November 1989 offensive, which called into question the advances U.S. and Salvadoran strategists had claimed in previous years. The FMLN failed to spark a popular insurrection and the offensive was very costly to them, as well as to their opponents and the civilian population, but they won what was viewed as a political victory that set the stage for the first genuine negotiations of the war.

The third period, from the end of 1989 to the end of 1991, when agreement was reached on a settlement to the conflict, was characterized by the centrality of negotiations as the main strategy to end the war. Domestic and international conditions—notably the relative parity that had been reached between the two sides in military terms, and the end of the Cold War—helped convince both sides that the benefits of negotiations might outweigh their costs, and provided a favorable international environment for bargaining. For two years military strategies supplemented and interacted with negotiating strategies, and external factors—particularly the Jesuit case—helped create conditions that permitted agreements that would bring about important social and political changes.

The outcome of the conflict was largely defined in the previous period, when the insurgent strategies succeeded in neutralizing their adversary's attempts to isolate and defeat them. The peace accords were a compromise that left both sides well short of their maximum objectives but opened the possibility of a genuine democratization of Salvadoran society. The result was not a revolutionary outcome. But the strategies of the war period did contribute to an outcome that was markedly different from that which could have been predicted from the resources available to the two sides.

Contrasting the Competing Strategies

Strategy was an important factor in the outcome of the eleven-year Salvadoran civil war, but in a negative more than a positive sense. The insurgents were able to *neutralize* all efforts by the counterrevolutionary coalition to marginalize and defeat them, but were not able to expand their base of support and generate a violent insurrection to overthrow the government. The Salvadoran government and military and their U.S. backers were able to *contain* the FMLN militarily and politically so as to ensure that a military offensive and popular insurrection did not succeed but were unable to isolate and defeat the rebels as their strategies had promised. The ultimate political outcome reflected this mutual veto.

The FMLN brought to the conflict a single-minded commitment to winning power through a political-military strategy of revolutionary war. This involved unifying political, military, economic, diplomatic, and other initiatives to defeat the Salvadoran government and armed forces. This grand strategy took different forms in different periods. From 1981 to 1984, military objectives predominated. Thus, while the groundwork was laid for a prolonged guerrilla war, the efforts to win a speedy military victory played to some of the strengths of the government side and limited the reach and effectiveness of the FMLN as a political force.

In the next period, a major shift in rebel grand strategy caused some short-term weaknesses but helped create the conditions for a prolonged war leading to a strategic counteroffensive to overthrow the government. During this period, rebel efforts on a variety of levels were articulated to contribute to the goal of weakening the government politically, and wearing out the military in a war of attrition in preparation for the counteroffensive. This strategy culminated in the November 1989 offensive that demonstrated to major Salvadoran and U.S. actors the failure of their ambitious political and military strategies to defeat the insurgents.

In the final period of the war, late 1989 to late 1991, the FMLN's grand strategy focused on political negotiations as the optimal and most probable means of resolving the conflict. There were differences within and among the parties in the FMLN as to the possibility of winning a favorable solution through negotiations, and on the relative importance of military and negotiating strategies. Moreover, military actions continued to play an important role in increasing pressure to win concessions at the bargaining table. Nevertheless, throughout this period the impact of the FMLN's earlier strategies and the changed international and Salvadoran environments placed negotiations at the center of the insurgents' grand strategy.

For most of the eleven years of the civil war the United States and its Salvadoran allies either lacked a grand strategy for defeating the insurgents or held the strategy in theory but failed to implement it in practice. Between 1981 and 1984 the counterrevolutionary coalition effected major strategic initiatives to stabilize the economy, legitimate the government domestically and internationally through elections, and turn around the military situation through extensive military aid and advice. But these efforts were largely piecemeal and uncoordinated.

In the next period, from mid-1984 to the 1989 FMLN offensive, the United States and its allies developed a grand strategy to defeat the insurgents through waging a low-intensity war to win political support for the government and armed forces, and to isolate and erode the guerrillas as a political-military force. This strategy involved a sophisticated counterinsurgency effort to win the sympathy of the population through civic-action programs, psychological-warfare campaigns, and the creation of civil-defense units. These efforts were to be supported by a quantitative and qualitative improvement of the military, institutional changes to increase the legitimacy of the government, and major efforts to rebuild the economy. In practice, however, they fell victim to divisions among the major components of the counterinsurgency coalition, PDC government incompetence and corruption, the military's unwillingness to change, and FMLN strategies designed to weaken the government politically and the armed forces militarily. In the final years of the war, 1989 to 1991, the United States and its allies came closest to implementing a unified strategy to achieve their objectives. But by this stage, the effort was largely defensive in nature and intended to ensure that the government and armed forces remained intact and did not have to concede too much in the process of negotiations.

The problem of strategy for the counterrevolutionary coalition lay in the nature of the coalition itself and can be traced to the U.S. decision to become deeply involved in the Salvadoran conflict in late 1979 and early 1980. At that stage, key decisions were made that would have implications throughout the war. The primary objective was defined as defeating the armed insurgency. To undercut the appeal of the revolutionaries, actions were taken to weaken the domination of the traditional oligarchy, particularly through the agrarian reform and nationalization of the banks and foreign trade. But, for fear of weakening the opposition to the insurgency, the most important part of the land reform was shelved indefinitely, and the oligarchy, though dislocated, was not broken as an economic or political force. This ensured that the traditional landowning class and its political representatives remained a potent political force that worked continuously to undermine the reforms and win back political power. It also guaranteed that the reforms, which might have had a greater impact in weakening the insurgency if they had been fully implemented, were more significant on a level of public relations than in "taking the revolution from the revolutionaries."

Similarly, the U.S. government cast its lot with conservative military officers who were known by U.S. intelligence agencies to be involved in massacres and death-squad activities and who, by late 1980, had wrested control of the institution from progressive officers. This decision was made to ensure that the primary objective of defeating the insurgents was not compromised; the result was a constant struggle on the part of U.S. political and military officials to change the attitudes and practices of military leaders while claiming to Congress and the American people that the armed forces had been transformed decisively.[1] Throughout the 1980s the Salvadoran military paid lip service to human rights and civilian control while continuing to violate human rights and prevent the punishment of its members for murders and other serious crimes. Having made the decision to work with and through the leadership of the Salvadoran armed forces and to attempt to bring the Salvadoran oligarchy to participate constructively in the counterinsurgency war against the FMLN, the United States was in the position of trying to square the circle. It sought to win the hearts and minds of actual or potential rebel supporters through radical measures that would transform social relations, particularly in the Salvadoran countryside. However, it balked at taking the measures that might in practice have won support away from the insurgents, for fear of further dividing the counterrevolutionary coalition. Thus, symbolic actions and public-relations measures replaced the truly radical measures that counterinsurgency strategists have argued are necessary to defeat an entrenched insurgency. A military force that was notorious for carrying out massacres in the early 1980s was presenting itself a few years later as the defender of democracy and the protector of the people. Not surprisingly, there is scant evidence of this change winning many hearts and minds among the rural population.

Another major difference between the two sides lay in their levels of unity, which had a major impact on the effectiveness of the strategies implemented. The FMLN was made up of five political parties that each maintained its own structure, organization, finances, and leadership. The parties often had deep disagreements over strategy (e.g., the approach to negotiations in the early 1980s) and tactics (e.g., the appropriateness of kidnapping and killing mayors and local officials). But throughout the eleven years of war they maintained a central leadership that was responsible for the conduct of the war, and a unified approach to strategy that obliged all five parties to implement directives of the General Command (even if, at times, the level of enthusiasm varied). By contrast, the counterrevolutionary coalition never achieved strategic unity, and different political, economic, and institutional interests among the economic elite, the PDC, the military, and the United States prevented the implementation of a unified political-military strategy to win the war. The far right worked to undermine the political and economic initiatives of the PDC government in the mid-to-late 1980s. The armed forces sought to protect their own interests and to take the leading role in counterinsurgency to distance themselves from an unpopular government in the same period. The United States worked covertly to prevent right-wing electoral victories in 1982 and 1984, and sought to advance its own geostrategic interests in the country and the region. The contrasting levels of unity of the two sides made a difference to the effectiveness of each, and particularly to their ability to conceive and implement strategies that would advance their overall objectives.

Ultimately, the large disparity in access to political, military, and economic resources between the two sides was equalized by the advantages possessed by the FMLN in maintaining a unified front with an overall strategic vision. This was implemented in practice over a counterrevolutionary coalition that was deeply divided and unable to implement a shared vision of how to defeat the insurgency. In the terms of insurgency and counterinsurgency theory, the FMLN "won by not losing": By avoiding defeat, and having the potential to sustain the war into the future and prevent economic and social recovery, the insurgents ensured that peace would not be attained until many of their demands were achieved at the bargaining table. By the same token, however, the FMLN "lost by not winning": By failing to achieve the overthrow of the government through their political-military strategies, the insurgents had to accept at the culmination of negotiations the continued existence of the government and military that they had tried hard to oust. Instead of winning power, which was the rebels' central objective, they won the right to compete for power in a democratic setting. Because this had traditionally been denied to opposition elements and was a major cause of the war, it could be claimed as a victory. The price paid by the people and the society to reach this stalemate after eleven years of war was enormous.

The Importance of Specific Strategies

No specific strategies were decisive in ensuring the ultimate outcome of the Salvadoran conflict. What was more significant was the difference in the ability of the two sides to unify different approaches within a grand strategy to achieve their overall objectives. Certain strategies, however, were effective in strengthening the position of one side and weakening its opponent. For the FMLN the most effective strategies were those that prevented the government from implementing its own strategies for winning the sympathy of the civilian population, isolating the insurgents, and generating economic recovery. But the most effective strategies were also double-edged swords that carried with them political as well as human costs.

Sabotage helped prevent economic stabilization and recovery but also affected the lives and living standards of many, including the poor to whom the FMLN looked for support. The continuous destruction of electrical towers and posts, bridges, buses, and other forms of transportation undoubtedly had political costs, particularly among those not clearly aligned with either protagonist, and allowed the government to portray the rebels as a purely destructive force.

The war of attrition—particularly the use of land mines to kill and wound the maximum number of Salvadoran soldiers from the second half of the 1980s—lessened the speed and determination of Salvadoran military offensives, wore down military morale, and made the implementation of the war more difficult for the government. But it also killed and maimed many civilians (as well as soldiers) and allowed the government and the United States to present the FMLN as terrorists who were indifferent to the suffering they were causing.

The expansion of the war throughout the country and particularly to the capital, San Salvador, allowed the FMLN to present itself as a ubiquitous force that the government could not defeat, and helped convince U.S. policymakers responsible for funding the war that the decade-long counterinsurgency was not a success. But the actions carried out or encouraged by the FMLN in attempting to "unleash the violence of the masses"—car bombings, assassinations, and violent demonstrations—appear to have alienated many of those targeted by the rebels to support an insurrection.

The strategies of the U.S. and Salvadoran governments had immense human costs and were largely ineffective in weakening or defeating the insurgents. Military massacres and death-squad killings, organized by military officers and right-wing civilian allies, were not successful in defeating the FMLN but had great political costs that placed major constraints on the ability of the two governments to win financial and political support for the war. The major counterinsurgency campaigns sought to clear civilian supporters of the rebels from insurgent-dominated areas by aerial bombardment, army sweeps, or forced displacement, but they were not effective in undercutting the FMLN and had serious political costs because of the human-rights violations involved.

For the United States and its Salvadoran allies the most effective strategy adopted was the use of elections to legitimate the government and isolate the insurgents. The electoral strategy helped move the government from a position of domestic and international isolation to one in which it enjoyed greater domestic support (for a period) along with greater international legitimacy and recognition. The elections helped bring about a change in Salvadoran politics and society whereby sectors of the population not strongly identified with either the government or the FMLN held out some hope that voting in elections would help resolve their fundamental problems. However limited was this change, it appears to have been sufficient to persuade a proportion of the population to work within the electoral system rather than pin their hopes on a successful insurrection. The failure of the FMLN to spark a popular insurrection in November 1989 appears to be related to these changes that had taken place in Salvadoran society through the 1980s.

At the same time, there were limitations to the success of the electoral strategy in the absence of electoral outcomes that could help consolidate the disparate counterrevolutionary forces behind a unified strategy for defeating the FMLN. In practice, the electoral strategy did not succeed in weakening the FMLN substantially and, in spite of the institutionalization of a limited process of democratization, the rebels were able to maintain their core of popular support and wage a political-military campaign to weaken the government and military.

The Role of Strategy in Revolutionary Processes

Chapter 1 highlighted a number of characteristics of strategy and its role within revolutionary processes. The study of strategy in El Salvador's conflict reinforces these elements.

1. The choices made by the revolutionary and counterrevolutionary coalitions operated within the context of given socioeconomic and political realities but were not the inexorable result of these factors. Some of the major choices had enormous costs and tragic consequences. Notable among these choices were the strategy of El Salvador's economic and military elite not to permit any meaningful changes in the country's political or socioeconomic structures; the decision by the revolutionary groups to embark on a strategy of armed conflict as the primary means of effecting change; and the decision by the U.S. government in mid-1979 to enter the Salvadoran conflict in a major way, defining the defeat of the insurgents as the central objective and justifying alliances with the very sectors that had been responsible for bringing El Salvador to a situation of revolutionary upheaval.

2. The dynamic and interactive nature of strategy is seen clearly in the Salvadoran conflict in the ways in which one side's strategy led to shifts in the other's, which in turn brought changes in the strategy of the first. For example, the expansion of the FMLN's military buildup in the first years of the war led to a strategy on the part of the armed forces that focused on taking advantage of the military's airpower, which in turn brought a shift in rebel strategy to a prolonged war of attrition. This process of action and reaction, and the external support for it, escalated the war in El Salvador—one of the smallest

countries in the hemisphere, with no major natural resources and little strategic significance—into one of the major battlegrounds of the Cold War.

3. In the Salvadoran conflict there were clearly alternative strategies that could have been adopted and, in many cases, might have made a difference for better or worse. Although history cannot be repeated to compare alternatives, one may draw on comparative historical situations to assess whether, for example, the implementation of the originally planned land reform, or even a more radical version, might not have favored the counterinsurgency strategy; or the likely outcome if a strategy of negotiations had been seriously developed and implemented, particularly by the United States, in the early years of the war.

4. The importance of the relationship of strategy to organization is illustrated by the contrasting ability of the two sides to implement specific strategies. Though it consisted of five parties, the FMLN was able to develop strategies at the highest level that would then be implemented by each of the groups. This did not work perfectly and there were times when strategies were more honored in the breach, but the practice still compared favorably with the counterrevolutionary coalition, which was much more internally divided and, hence, unable at key points to unite behind a common political-military approach.

5. Both sides were able to formulate strategies well and the U.S. and its Salvadoran allies developed very effective political and military strategies to defeat the insurgents. The weakness of the counterrevolutionary side lay in implementation. The conflicting groups with competing interests undercut the effectiveness of the counterinsurgency effort. In the military field the Salvadoran armed forces could never be convinced to fight the sort of war that U.S. strategists believed was necessary to overcome the FMLN.

6. The relationship of strategy to objectives can be seen in El Salvador in the clarity of objectives of the two sides. There was never any doubt about the objectives of the insurgents' revolutionary war. By contrast, in the early 1980s the U.S. ambassador and the Commander in Chief of Southern Command clashed over U.S. objectives in El Salvador: Was the objective to hold the line or to win a military victory over the insurgents? Where the objective is unclear it is very difficult to carry out effective strategies.

7. The importance of the relationship between revolutionary strategies and socioeconomic realities can be seen in the success of the left-wing groups in El Salvador in the 1970s. The revolutionary groups were able to calibrate their strategies effectively to take advantage of the deteriorating economic and social conditions and their impact on the majority.

8. The way in which strategy can overcome major obstacles can be seen in El Salvador in the way a united approach and effective strategies by the left compensated for a huge imbalance in resources and largely unfavorable international developments.

9. The development and implementation of a grand strategy by the insurgents, particularly from the mid-1980s, was more important than any specific strategies in the achievement of a settlement that brought substantial changes to Salvadoran society.

10. The FMLN's flexibility allowed the rebels to make a dramatic shift in strategy in 1983–1984 that over time transformed a highly unfavorable situation into one in which parity, at least, was achieved and the stage set for a political solution to the conflict.

11. Among the strengths of the FMLN during the period of the war were strategic unity, a long-term political vision that kept its members and supporters motivated through extremely difficult times, the will to do whatever was necessary to achieve the objective, a mode of organizing that strengthened identification with the cause and maintained a high level of security from outside attack, and strategies that were linked to an overall political objective. The strengths of the counterinsurgency coalition lay in the commitment of successive U.S. administrations not to allow the FMLN to prevail and a willingness to mobilize the resources necessary to win the war, high levels of financial support that brought significant changes in the way the war could be fought and in the general society, and effective political strategies to legitimate the Salvadoran government and isolate the rebels. Successive U.S. administrations were able to effectively market the idea of democratization in El Salvador and so to mobilize resources to win the war or, at a minimum, prevent the FMLN from winning. The FMLN was able to convince the U.S. and Salvadoran governments that it could keep the war going ad infinitum, and that even if it were not able to take power it could prevent the government from achieving what most governments aspire to: economic growth, social peace, and political stability. The strengths and resources of each side were enough to prevent the other from winning, but not enough to guarantee victory. The war ended in a stalemate that helped create the conditions for a political settlement.

The Tragedy of El Salvador and the Hope for the Future

At the end of the war both sides could claim victory to their core supporters while presenting a public position that there were "no winners and losers." Each side could claim to have protected or advanced its central interests: The ARENA government remained in power, the army continued to exist, the United States had helped prevent a leftist revolution, and the FMLN could compete politically for power in a democratic (or democratizing) and largely demilitarized society. But in the process 75,000 Salvadorans had died violent deaths; a quarter of the population had been forced from their homes; much of the country had been devastated; and a generation of children had grown up knowing only war and civil strife. It was El Salvador's tragedy that such a huge price had to be paid to reach the point at which the major issues of the society could be resolved in nonviolent political debate. Important elements of this tragedy included the country's social, economic, and political arrangements; the choices and actions of the main protagonists; and the particular moment at which El Salvador found its central place in the international arena.

An unjust and elitist social and economic system supported by an exclusive political order helped generate a ruling landowner–military alliance that was unwilling to compromise on the nature of the political and economic orders and shut down all avenues to peaceful change. These conditions helped create an opposition that, not unnaturally, viewed the questions of economic and political power in equally absolutist terms. They saw change as only being possible through a complete defeat of the traditional order and believed that violent conflict would need to play a central role. Those who sought change through compromise and democratic methods were forced to take sides or to step aside as the social polarization and violence intensified and the system reached a point of revolutionary crisis in the late 1970s.

Throughout the 1970s the conflict remained largely internal. But with the victory of the Sandinistas in Nicaragua, along with events in Iran and Afghanistan, El Salvador's struggle was sucked into the vortex of the superpower conflict. The U.S. government, believing it could superimpose a rational external solution on the Salvadoran crisis, attempted to defeat the left by moulding a coalition of former enemies, including many of those responsible for causing the crisis. Rightwing military and civilian elites, encouraged by U.S. intervention in the conflict, carried out an orgy of violence against suspected opponents, murdering tens of thousands of civilians between 1980 and 1982. The Soviet Union, though not involved to the level of the United States, was happy to take advantage of problems in the U.S. government's own "backyard" and provided arms, funds, and political and moral support to the insurgents.

The internationalization of El Salvador's crisis, which polarized the conflict even more by framing it within the East-West ideological struggle, made compromise even more difficult. For a decade the contending coalitions saw their objectives as being attainable only through the complete defeat of their enemy, and they developed political, military, and economic strategies to achieve their goals. Though varying in effectiveness, the strategies succeeded mainly in neutralizing or containing the efforts of the adversary and prolonging the war, but not in bringing victory to either side. A resolution of the conflict came when international developments, particularly the decline of the Soviet bloc, pulled El Salvador's war out of the East-West conflict at a time when both sides began to see that they could not win and domestic pressure for peace increased.

But whereas El Salvador's conflict, and particularly its internationalization, brought only suffering to the majority of the people, its mode of resolution points to the hope for a peaceful and better future for the country; it is an example that even the most bitter conflicts may be resolved through peaceful negotiations. Ultimately, although both sides may not share equally in the responsibility for the conflict, each was indispensable to its peaceful resolution. After two decades of war and social strife, during which each side saw its vision for the country as requiring the destruction of the other, the two main protagonists were willing to imagine living side by side in the same society and testing the viability of their visions through democratic and peaceful means. That it took so many years and lives is El Salvador's tragedy. That it could happen at all is the country's hope for the future.

Note

1. See, for example, Thomas W. Lippmann, "1989 Salvadoran Atrocity Posed Agonizing Choice for U.S.," *Washington Post*, 5 April 1994, A13.

Epilogue

In the first four years after the signing of the peace accords in January 1992, Salvadoran politics and society changed dramatically. The civil war that had lasted eleven years and cost 75,000 lives appeared to have definitively ended. By mid-1995 the majority of the agreements signed between the government and the FMLN had been carried out, although the process involved a great deal of struggle and, at times, required outside intervention to move the process forward. The FMLN was successfully reincorporated into the political life of the country and became a major electoral force. With the end of the war, delinquency and common crime became major problems and a revival of death-squad activity raised concerns of a return to the right-wing terror of the early 1980s. A new civilian police force was created as mandated by the peace accords, but the wholesale incorporation of members of the old security forces, and scandals concerning high police officials, raised questions as to how much had been changed by the peace agreement.

Salvadoran politics took a major step forward with the elections in 1994 for the presidency, legislature, municipalities, and the Central American Parliament. Despite serious problems with registration and election-day irregularities, the elections were viewed domestically and internationally as generally free and fair. The elections were won by the ARENA Party, which gained a plurality of the legislative seats and retained the presidency when Armando Calderón Sol defeated Rubén Zamora, the candidate of the Democratic Convergence and the FMLN, in a runoff by a ratio of two to one. However, the FMLN performed creditably in the elections, winning a quarter of the seats in the legislative assembly and becoming the second-largest political party, eclipsing the PDC.

The FMLN's relative success in the elections, however, belied serious internal problems. Divisions arose over who should be the FMLN's presidential candidate and which sectors of the society the former rebels should reach out to. The ERP (whose name was changed from the People's Revolutionary Army to the Renewed Expression of the People), led by Joaquín Villalobos and the FARN, headed by Eduardo

Sancho, wanted to reach out to sectors that had not supported either side in the war. These groups preferred a candidate not identified with the left. The FPL, the PCS, and the PRTC wanted to consolidate their base as the left and to have a candidate identified with the historic goals of the FMLN. The struggle was won by the latter grouping; Rubén Zamora, a longtime ally of the FMLN, was chosen as the candidate. Internal divisions and a focus on the interests of the particular group within the FMLN contributed to a lackluster campaign that did not seriously challenge ARENA's political domination. In the aftermath of the elections, divisions grew deeper.

The ERP-RN felt that the historic goals of the FMLN had been achieved with the signing and implementation of the peace accords that created a democratic society. Deputies from these groups broke ranks with the rest of the FMLN and took leadership positions within the legislative assembly. These two groups left the FMLN and entered into a formal agreement with ARENA in which ERP-RN leaders saw their role as ensuring that the government's "neoliberal" economic policies contained a social component.[1] The three remaining FMLN groups saw the peace accords as a major step, but only a step, toward the implementation of the FMLN's program, and from which to struggle for the socioeconomic and political changes that were still required to transform a society they viewed as elitist and highly unequal. They sought to organize and mobilize the classes and sectors that had been the FMLN's traditional base to push for a more just and equal society.

The alliance that had successfully held together during eleven years of war reverted in the mid-1990s to the ideological divisions of the 1970s. The ERP-RN, which formed the Democratic Party, distanced itself from any identification with Marxism and defined itself as a social-democratic party looking to the middle class as a key sector within which to win support. The FPL, the PCS, and the PRTC, while accepting the reality of capitalism and the market, sought to mobilize popular support for an economic model that would prioritize the interests of the poor and working people and maintain an important role for the state. With the left on the defensive throughout Latin America and no compelling alternative to neoliberal economic policies, the proof of the pudding in El Salvador between these competing visions will, once again, likely be the effectiveness of the strategies employed by these coalitions to mobilize their bases, build alliances, and articulate a broad social vision, as much as on the correctness of their theoretical formulations.

Note

1. Juan Ramón Medrano, author interview, San Salvador, 14 July 1995.

Acronyms

AID	U.S. Agency for International Development
AIFLD	American Institute for Free Labor Development
ANDES	Asociación Nacional de Educadores Salvadoreños/National Association of Salvadoran Education Workers
ANEP	Asociación Nacional de la Empresa Privada/National Association of Private Enterprise
ANSESAL	Agencia Nacional de Seguridad Salvadoreña/Salvadoran National Security Agency
ARENA	Alianza Republicana Nacionalista/Nationalist Republican Alliance
BIRI	Batallón de Infantería de Reacción Inmediata/Rapid Deployment Infantry Battalion
BPR	Bloque Popular Revolucionario/Popular Revolutionary Bloc
CIA	U.S. Central Intelligence Agency
CONARA	Comisión Nacional de Restauración de Areas/National Commission for Restoration of Areas
COPAZ	Comisión Nacional para la Consolidación de la Paz/National Commission for the Consolidation of Peace
CRM	Coordinadora Revolucionaria de Masas/Revolutionary Coordination of the Masses
DIA	U.S. Defense Intelligence Agency
ERP	Ejército Revolucionario del Pueblo/People's Revolutionary Army
ESAF	El Salvador's Armed Forces
FAN	Frente Amplio Nacional/Broad National Front
FAPU	Frente de Acción Popular Unificada/United Popular Action Front

FARN	Fuerzas Armadas de Resistencia Nacional/Armed Forces of National Resistance
FARO	Frente de Agricultores de la Región Oriental/Eastern Farmers Front
FDR	Frente Democrático Revolucionario/Democratic Revolutionary Front
FECCAS	Federación Cristiana de Campesinos Salvadoreños/Christian Federation of Salvadoran Peasants
FENASTRAS	Federación Nacional Sindical de Trabajadores Salvadoreños/National Trade Union Federation of Salvadoran Workers
FMLN	Frente Farabundo Martí para la Liberación Nacional/Farabundo Martí National Liberation Front
FPL	Fuerzas Populares de Liberación–Farabundo Martí/Popular Liberation Forces–Farabundo Martí
GOES	Government of El Salvador
JRG	Junta Revolucionaria de Gobierno/Revolutionary Governing Junta
LP-28	Ligas Populares–28 de Febrero/Popular Leagues–28 February
MNR	Movimiento Nacional Revolucionario/National Revolutionary Movement
MPSC	Movimiento Popular Social Cristiano/Popular Social Christian Movement
ORDEN	Organización Democrática Nacionalista/Democratic Nationalist Organization
PCN	Partido de Conciliación Nacional/National Conciliation Party
PCS	Partido Comunista Salvadoreño/Salvadoran Communist Party
PDC	Partido Demócrata Cristiano/Christian Democratic Party
PRTC	Partido Revolucionario de Trabajadores Centroamericanos/Central American Revolutionary Workers' Party
SOUTHCOM	U.S. Southern Command in Panama
UCA	Universidad Centroamericana "José Simeón Cañas"/Central American University "José Simeón Cañas"
UDN	Unión Democrática Nacionalista/Democratic Nationalist Union

UGB	Unión Guerrera Blanca/White Warriors' Union
UNO	Unión Nacional Opositora/National Opposition Union
UNTS	Unidad Nacional de los Trabajadores Salvadoreños/National Unity of Salvadoran Workers
UPD	Unidad Popular Democrática/Popular Democratic Unity
UPR	Unidos Para Reconstruir/United to Reconstruct
UTC	Unión de Trabajadores del Campo/Union of Rural Workers

Bibliography

Note on U.S. Declassified Documents

In November 1993, in response to a directive from President Clinton to "Search for and Conduct a Declassification Review of 32 Human Rights Cases Investigated by the [United Nations] El Salvador Truth Commission," the U.S. State Department, Department of Defense, Central Intelligence Agency, and other executive agencies released some 40,000 pages of declassified documents on El Salvador. This collection of declassified documents is referred to in this book as *U.S. Declassified Documents I.*

In August 1994 a second set of declassified documents was released in response to a request from members of Congress for documents related to twenty-three questions regarding events or issues concerning El Salvador and U.S. policy from the period of the Carter administration, and two questions related to sources of support for the FMLN and relations between the FMLN and government officials, individuals or groups in the United States between 1 July 1979 and 31 December 1991. This collection of declassified documents is referred to in this book as *U.S. Declassified Documents II.*

The State Department documents from both collections can be found in the department's Office of Freedom of Information, Privacy and Classification Review. The first set of documents is organized according to the thirty-two human rights cases and is entitled "El Salvador: Human Rights 1980–1993." The second set of State Department documents is entitled "El Salvador II Document Collection" and is organized according to the twenty-five questions raised by members of Congress. Documents from the Defense Department, the CIA, and other government agencies from both collections can be found in the Hispanic Division of the Library of Congress.

An earlier set of declassified U.S. documents from 1977–1984 was published in 1989 by the National Security Archive. (See National Security Archive).

Alvarez Solis, Francisco, and Roberto Codas Friedmann. *La asistencia de Estados Unidos a El Salvador en los ochenta: Una revisión preliminar.* Programa Regional de Investigación sobre El Salvador. Cuaderno de Trabajo No. 6. San Salvador: PREIS, September 1990.

Americas Watch. *Draining the Sea: Sixth Supplement to the Report on Human Rights in El Salvador, March 1985.* New York: Americas Watch, 1985.

———. *Land Mines in El Salvador and Nicaragua: The Civilian Victims, December 1986.* New York: Americas Watch, 1986.

———. *El Salvador's Decade of Terror: Human Rights Since the Assassination of Archbishop Romero.* New Haven, Conn.: Yale University Press, 1991.

Amnesty International. *Amnesty International Annual Report, 1980.* London: Amnesty International, 1980. (See also yearly reports 1979–1991.)

———. El Salvador. *"Death Squads": A Government Strategy.* London: Amnesty International, 1988.

Anderson, Thomas P. *Matanza: El Salvador's Communist Revolt of 1932.* Lincoln: University of Nebraska Press, 1971.

Arias Gómez, Jorge. *Farabundo Martí.* Esbozo biográfico. San José, Costa Rica: EDUCA, 1972.

Armstrong, Robert, and Janet Shenk. *El Salvador: The Face of Revolution.* Boston: South End Press, 1982.

Arnson, Cynthia J. *Crossroads: Congress, the Reagan Administration, and Central America.* New York: Pantheon Books, 1989.

Austin, Allan, Luis Flores, and Donald Stout. *CONARA Impact Evaluation.* Research Triangle Institute. Ref: Contract No. PDC-0000-1-00-6169-00. September 20, 1988. North Carolina, Research Triangle Park: Research Triangle Institute, 1988.

Bacevich, Lt. Col. A. J., Lt. Col. James D. Hallums, Lt. Col. Richard H. White, and Lt. Col. Thomas F. Young. *American Military Policy in Small Wars: The Case of El Salvador.* Washington, D.C.: Pergamon-Brassey's International Defense Publishers, 1988.

Baloyra, Enrique A. *El Salvador in Transition.* Chapel Hill: University of North Carolina Press, 1982.

Barry, Tom. *El Salvador: A Country Guide.* Albuquerque, N.M.: Inter-Hemispheric Education Resource Center, 1990.

Benítez Manaut, Raúl. *La teoría militar y la guerra civil en El Salvador.* San Salvador: UCA Editores, 1989.

Blachman, Morris J., William M. Leo Grande, and Kenneth Sharpe, eds. *Confronting Revolution: Security Through Diplomacy in Central America.* New York: Pantheon Books, 1986.

Black, George. "Central America: Crisis in the Backyard." *New Left Review* no. 135 (September/October 1982): 5–34.

Bonner, Raymond. *Weakness and Deceit: U.S. Policy and El Salvador.* New York: Times Books, 1984.

Browning, David. *El Salvador: Landscape and Society.* London: Clarendon Press, 1971.

Byrne, Hugh G. *The Problem of Revolution: A Study of Strategies of Insurgency and Counter-Insurgency in El Salvador's Civil War, 1981–1991.* Ph.D. diss., University of California, Los Angeles, 1994.

Cabarrús P., Carlos Rafael. *Génesis de una revolución: Análisis del surgimiento y desarrollo de la organización campesina en El Salvador.* México: La Casa Chata, 1983.

Cañas, Antonio. "La guerra en los primeros días de ARENA." *Estudios Centroamericanos* 490/491 (August/September 1989): 669–682.

Cardenal, Rodolfo. *Historia de una esperanza: Vida de Rutilio Grande.* San Salvador: UCA Editores, 1985.

Cash, John (Colonel). Interview by Max G. Manwaring, 20 March 1987, for use in the Oral History of the Conflict in El Salvador, prepared by the BDM Management Services Co. for the Small Wars Operational Requirements Division (SWORD), USSOUTHCOM, Republic of Panama.

Castro Morán, Mariano. *Función política del ejército salvadoreño en el presente siglo.* San Salvador: UCA Editores, 1984.

Clements, Charles. *Witness to War: An American Doctor in El Salvador.* New York: Bantam Books, 1984.

Colburn, Forrest D. *The Vogue of Revolution in Poor Countries.* Princeton, N.J.: Princeton University Press, 1994.

Colindres, Eduardo. "La tenencia de la tierra en El Salvador." *Estudios Centroamericanos* 335/336 (September/October 1976): 463–472.

———. *Fundamentos económicos de la burguesía salvadoreña.* San José, Costa Rica: EDUCA, 1977.

Congressional Research Service. CRS Report for Congress, *El Salvador, 1979–1989: A Briefing Book on U.S. Aid and the Situation in El Salvador.* The Library of Congress, Congressional Research Service, Foreign Affairs and National Defense Division, 28 April 1989.

———. Report to Congress. *Central America: Major Trends in U.S. Foreign Assistance Fiscal 1978 to Fiscal 1990.* The Library of Congress, Congressional Research Service, 19 June 1989.

Coordinadora Regional de Investigaciones Económicas y Sociales (CRIES). *Proceso de paz en El Salvador: La solución política negociada.* CRIES/IDESES, Cuadernos, Serie Documentos 6, Managua, Nicaragua: 1992.

Cruz Alfaro, Ernesto. "Crónica del mes: enero–febrero." *Estudios Centroamericanos* 447/448 (January/February 1986): 105–117.

Danner, Mark. "A Reporter at Large: The Truth of El Mozote." *The New Yorker* (6 December 1993): 50.

DeNardo, James. *Power in Numbers: The Political Strategy of Protest and Rebellion.* Princeton: Princeton University Press, 1985.

Dickey, Christopher. "Behind the Death Squads: Who They Are, Why They Work, and Why No One Can Stop Them." *New Republic* (26 December 1983).

Didion, Joan. *Salvador.* Toronto: Lester and Orphen Dennys, 1983.

Diskin, Martin, and Kenneth Sharpe. *The Impact of U.S. Policy in El Salvador, 1979–1985.* Berkeley: University of California Institute of International Studies, 1985.

Downing, T. J. *Agricultural Modernization in El Salvador.* Cambridge University: Centre of Latin American Studies, 1978.

Duarte, José Napoleón, with Diana Page. *Duarte: My Story.* New York: Putnam, 1986.

Dunkerley, James. *The Long War: Dictatorship and Revolution in El Salvador.* London: Verso Editions, 1983.

———. *Power in the Isthmus: A Political History of Modern Central America.* London: Verso, 1988.

"Editorial: 1988, un año de transición para El Salvador." *Estudios Centroamericanos* 471/472 (January/February 1988): 5–20.

"Editorial: Recrudecimiento de la violencia en El Salvador." *Estudios Centroamericanos* 480 (October 1988): 861–881.

Einaudi, Luigi R. Interview by Max G. Manwaring (Washington, D.C., 10 September 1987), edited by W. R. Christensen, for use in the Oral History of the Conflict in El Salvador, prepared by the BDM Management Services Co. for the Small Wars Operational Requirements Division (SWORD), USSOUTHCOM, Republic of Panama.

Ellacuría, Ignacio. "Visión de conjunto de las elecciones de 1984." *Estudios Centroamericanos* 426/427 (April/May 1984): 301–324.

Farabundo Martí National Liberation Front (FMLN). General Command. *Situación revolucionaria y escalada intervencionista en la guerra salvadoreña.* Morazán, El Salvador: Ediciones Sistema Radio Venceremos, January 1984.

———. *El Salvador vive una prolongada situación revolucionaria.* Photocopy. 75 pp. Morazán, June 1985.

———. *Apreciación de la situación.* Document prepared for the November 1986 meeting of the General Command of the FMLN entitled "Preparatory Phase of the Strategic Counteroffensive." Photocopy. 34 pp. January 1987.

———. *Línea militar FMLN: Fase preparatoria de la contraofensiva estratégica.* (Reunión Comandancia General, El Salvador, noviembre 1986). Photocopy. 34 pp. January 1987.

———. *El poder popular de doble cara: Lineamientos de organización.* Photocopy. 83 pp. Publicaciones FMLN. January 1987.

———. *Organizar el "Fuego": Una necesidad imperativa para avanzar hacia la victoria.* Proposal for Morazan meeting of FMLN General Command. Photocopy. 32 pp. January 1988.

———. *Apreciación estratégica.* Photocopy. 18 pp. 1988.

———. "The FMLN's Rationale for Ending Militarism, Reaching a Cease-fire and Advancing to an Unarmed Democracy." Communiqué. El Salvador. 17 August 1990.

Fuerza Armada de El Salvador. Estado Mayor Conjunto. 1986. *Campaña de contrainsurgencia "Unidos para reconstruir."* San Salvador: 1986.

Fuerzas Populares de Liberación (FPL). *Revolutionary Strategy in El Salvador.* London: Tricontinental Society, 1980.

García, (José) Guillermo (General). Interview by Max G. Manwaring (San Salvador, 2 July 1987), translated by A. E. Letzer, both of BDM Management Services Co. for the Small Wars Operational Requirements Division (SWORD), J-5, USSOUTHCOM, Republic of Panama.

Gettleman, Marvin E., et al., eds. *El Salvador: Central America in the New Cold War.* New York: Grove Press, 1986.

Giap, Vo Nguyen (General). *People's War, People's Army.* Hanoi: Foreign Languages Publishing House, 1961.

Goodwin, Jeff, and Theda Skocpol. "Explaining Revolutions in the Contemporary Third World." *Politics and Society* 17, no. 4 (December 1989): 489–509.

Gott, Richard. *Guerrilla Movements in Latin America.* New York: Anchor Books, 1972.

Guevara, Che. *Guerrilla Warfare.* With an introduction and case studies by Brian Loveman and Thomas M. Davies, Jr. Lincoln: University of Nebraska Press, 1985.

Guidos Vejar, Rafael. *El ascenso del militarismo en El Salvador.* San Salvador: UCA, 1980.

———. "La crisis política en El Salvador, 1976–1979," *Estudios Centroamericanos* 369/370 (July/August 1979): 507–526.

Handal, Shafick Jorge. "Consideraciones acerca del viraje del partido comunista de El Salvador hacia la lucha armada." *Fundamentos y perspectivas* no. 5, San Salvador (April 1983).

Harnecker, Marta. *Pueblos en armas.* Managua, Nicaragua: Editorial Nueva Nicaragua, 1985.

————. *Los desafíos de un partido que se integra a la guerra.* Interview with Schafik Jorge Handal. Photocopy. 55 pp. February 1985–February 1988.

————. "La propuesta del FMLN: Un desafío a la estrategia contrainsurgente." Entrevista a Joaquín Villalobos (25 de febrero de 1989). *Estudios Centroamericanos* 485 (March 1989): 211–228.

————. *Con la mirada en alto: Historia de las Fuerzas Populares de Liberación Farabundo Martí a través de entrevistas con sus dirigentes.* San Salvador: UCA Editores, 1993.

Herman, Edward, and Frank Brodhead. *Demonstration Elections: U.S. Staged Elections in the Dominican Republic, Vietnam and El Salvador.* Boston: South End Press, 1984.

Herrick, Robert M. (Colonel). Interview by Max G. Manwaring, edited by Wendy R. Christensen, 18 December 1986, for use in the Oral History of the Conflict in El Salvador, prepared by the BDM Management Services Co. for the Small Wars Operational Requirements Division (SWORD), USSOUTHCOM, Republic of Panama.

Hinton, Deane (Ambassador). Interview by Max G. Manwaring, edited by W. R. Christensen, 10 September 1987, for use in the Oral History of the Conflict in El Salvador, prepared by the BDM Management Services Co. for the Small Wars Operational Requirements Division (SWORD), USSOUTHCOM, Republic of Panama.

Huizer, Gerrit. *Peasant Rebellion in Latin America.* London: Penguin, 1973.

Huntington, Samuel P. *Political Order in Changing Societies.* New Haven, Conn.: Yale University Press, 1968.

Joint Low-Intensity Conflict Project. *Analytical Review of Low-Intensity Conflict.* Vol. 1. Fort Monroe, Virginia: United States Army Training and Doctrine Command, 1986.

Jung, Harald. "Class Struggles in El Salvador." *New Left Review* no. 122, (July/August 1980): 3–25.

Kincaid, A. Douglas. "Peasants into Rebels: Community and Class in Rural El Salvador." *Comparative Studies in Society and History* 29, no. 3, (1987): 466–494.

Kissinger Commission. See National Bipartisan Commission on Central America.

Klare, Michael, and Peter Kornbluh, eds. *Low-Intensity Warfare: Counterinsurgency, Proinsurgency and Antiterrorism in the Eighties.* New York: Random House, 1988.

Kolko, Gabriel. *Anatomy of a War: Vietnam, the United States, and the Modern Historical Experience.* New York: Pantheon Books, 1985.

LaFeber, Walter. *Inevitable Revolutions: The United States in Central America.* New York: W. W. Norton, 1983.

Lawyers Committee for Human Rights. *Update on Investigation of the Murder of Six Jesuit Priests in El Salvador.* New York: Lawyers Committee for Human Rights, 1991.

Lenin, V. I. "The State and Revolution." In *Selected Works.* New York: International Publishers, 1971.

Lindo-Fuentes, Héctor. *Weak Foundations: The Economy of El Salvador in the Nineteenth Century.* Berkeley: University of California Press, 1990.

LeoGrande, William. "After the Battle of El Salvador." *World Policy Journal* (Spring 1990): 331–356.

Lernoux, Penny. *Cry of the People: United States Involvement in the Rise of Fascism,*

Torture, and Murder and the Persecution of the Catholic Church in Latin America.
New York: Doubleday, 1980.

López Vallecillos, Italo. "Fuerzas sociales y cambio social en El Salvador."
Estudios Centroamericanos 369/370 (July/August 1979): 557–590.

———. "Rasgos sociales y tendencias políticas en El Salvador (1969–1979)."
Estudios Centroamericanos 372/373 (October/November 1979): 863–884.

Luttwak, Edward N. *Strategy: The Logic of War and Peace.* Cambridge, Mass.:
Belnap Press of Harvard University Press, 1987.

Manwaring, Max G., and Court Prisk, eds. *El Salvador at War: An Oral History of
the Conflict from the 1979 Insurrection to the Present.* Washington, D.C.:
National Defense University Press, 1988.

Mario Lungo, U. *La lucha de las masas en El Salvador.* San Salvador: UCA
Editores, 1987.

———. *El Salvador 1981–1984: la dimensión política de la guerra.* San Salvador:
UCA Editores, 1985.

Martín-Baró, Ignacio. "La guerra civil en El Salvador." *Estudios Centroamericanos*
387/388 (January/February 1981): 17–32.

———. "El Salvador 1987." *Estudios Centroamericanos* 471/472
(January/February 1988): 21–45.

Marx, Karl. *Surveys from Exile, Political Writings.* Volume II, ed. David Fernbach.
New York: Vintage Books, 1974.

Marx, Karl, and Frederick Engels. *Selected Works.* New York: International
Publishers, 1968.

McClintock, Michael. *The American Connection, Volume One: State Terror and
Popular Resistance in El Salvador.* London: Zed Books, 1985.

Mena Sandoval, Francisco Emilio. *Del ejército nacional al ejército guerrillero.*
Ediciones Arcoiris, n.d.

Menjívar, Rafael. *Acumulación originaria y desarrollo del capitalismo en El Salvador.*
San José, Costa Rica: Editorial Universitaria Centroamericana, 1977.

———. *Formación y lucha del proletariado salvadoreño.* San Salvador: UCA, 1979.

Miles, Sara. "The Real War: Low-Intensity Conflict in Central America."
NACLA Report on the Americas (April–May, 1986): 17–48.

Montes, Segundo. *El agro salvadoreño* (1973–1980). San Salvador: UCA, 1986.

Montgomery, Tommie Sue. *Revolution in El Salvador: From Civil Strife to Civil
Peace.* Boulder, Colo.: Westview Press, 1995.

Moore, Barrington, Jr. *Social Origins of Dictatorship and Democracy: Lord and
Peasant in the Making of the Modern World.* Boston: Beacon Press, 1966.

Nairn, Allan. "Behind the Death Squads." *The Progressive* 48, no. 5 (May 1984):
20–29.

National Bipartisan Commission on Central America. *Report of the President's
National Bipartisan Commission on Central America.* New York: Macmillan,
1984.

National Security Archive. *The Making of U.S. Policy: El Salvador 1977–1984.*
Previously classified documentation from the State Department and other
federal agencies. Published on microfiche with a two-volume printed
index. Alexandria, Va.: Chadwyck-Healey, 1989.

Paige, Jeffery M. *Agrarian Revolution: Social Movements and Export Agriculture in
the Underdeveloped World.* New York: Free Press, 1975.

Pearce, Jenny. *Promised Land: Peasant Rebellion in Chalatenango, El Salvador.* New
York: Monthly Review Press, 1986.

Pickering, Thomas (Ambassador). Interview by Max G. Manwaring, edited by
Wendy R. Christensen, 28 August 1987, for use in the Oral History of the

Conflict in El Salvador, prepared by the BDM Management Services Co. for the Small Wars Operational Requirements Division (SWORD), USSOUTHCOM, Republic of Panama.

Policy Alternatives for the Caribbean and Central America. *Changing Course: Blueprint for Peace in Central America and the Caribbean.* Washington, D.C.: Institute for Policy Studies, 1984.

Pomeroy, William J., ed. *Guerrilla Warfare and Marxism: A Collection of Writings from Karl Marx to the Present on Armed Struggles for Liberation and for Socialism.* New York: International Publishers, 1968.

Ponce, René Emilio (Colonel). Interview by Max G. Manwaring, translated by A. E. Letzer, 22 January 1987, for use in the Oral History of the Conflict in El Salvador, prepared by the BDM Management Services Co. for the Small Wars Operational Requirements Division (SWORD), USSOUTH-COM, Republic of Panama.

Popkin, Samuel, L. *The Rational Peasant.* Berkeley: University of California Press, 1979.

Prisk, Courtney E., ed. *The Comandante Speaks: Memoirs of an El Salvadoran Guerrilla Leader.* Boulder: Westview Press, 1991.

Regional Triangle Institute. *Impact Evaluation: Special Programs in Chalatenango and the Eastern Region.* North Carolina, 1990.

Samayoa, Salvador. "El movimiento obrero en El Salvador: Resurgimiento o agitación?" *Estudios Centroamericanos* 371 (September 1979): 793–800.

Sánchez, Fernando. "Crisis y política económica Demócrata Cristiana." *Estudios Centroamericanos* 453 (July 1986): 534–550.

Schwarz, Benjamin C. *American Counterinsurgency Doctrine and El Salvador: The Frustrations of Reform and the Illusions of Nation Building.* RAND Study R-4042-USDP prepared for the Under Secretary of Defense for Policy. Santa Monica, Calif.: RAND, 1991.

Scott, James C. *The Moral Economy of the Peasant: Rebellion and Subsistence in Southeast Asia.* New Haven, Conn.: Yale University Press, 1976.

Selbin, Eric. *Modern Latin American Revolutions.* Boulder, Colo.: Westview Press, 1993.

Sevilla, Manuel. *La concentración económica en El Salvador.* Instituto de Investigaciones Económicas y Sociales (INIES) y Coordinadora Regional de Investigaciones Económicas y Sociales (CRIES). Managua: INIES, 1985.

Sharpe, Kenneth E. "El Salvador Revisited: Why Duarte is in Trouble." *World Policy Journal* (Summer 1986): 473–494.

Shenk, Janet. "El Salvador: Central America's Forgotten War." *Mother Jones* (July/August 1986): 60.

———. "Can the Guerrillas Win?" *Mother Jones* (April 1988): 35.

Simon, Laurence R, and James C. Stephens, Jr. *El Salvador Land Reform 1981–1982: Impact Audit.* Oxfam America, 1982.

Skocpol, Theda. *States and Social Revolutions: A Comparative Analysis of France, Russia, and China.* Cambridge: Cambridge University Press, 1979.

Speaker's Task Force on El Salvador. "Interim Report." Washington, D.C., April 30, 1990. Photocopy.

Stanley, William. *The Protection Racket State: Elite Politics, Military Extortion, and the Origins of El Salvador's Civil War.* Philadelphia: Temple University Press. Forthcoming.

Summers, Harry G., Jr. *On Strategy: A Critical Analysis of the Vietnam War.* New York: Dell Publishing Co., 1982.

Tse-tung, Mao. *Selected Works.* New York: International Publishers, 1954.

United Nations, Economic Commission for Latin America. *Economic Survey of Latin America, 1978.* Santiago, Chile: United Nations, 1980. (See also ECLA annual reports for 1979–1991.)

———. *From Madness to Hope: The 12-Year War in El Salvador.* Report of the Commission on the Truth for El Salvador. New York: United Nations, 1993.

U.S. Agency for International Development, Office of Central American Affairs. *El Salvador: An Overview of Current Political, Social and Economic Conditions.* Washington, D.C., January 1989.

U.S. Department of State. Declassified documents. (See note on U.S. declassified documents.)

U.S. House of Representatives. Arms Control and Foreign Policy Caucus. *Bankrolling Failure: United States Policy in El Salvador and the Urgent Need for Reform.* Washington, D.C., 1987.

———. *Barriers to Reform: A Profile of El Salvador's Military Leaders.* Washington, D.C., 1990.

U.S. Library of Congress. Declassified documents. (See note on U.S. declassified documents.)

Vickers, George. "The Political Reality After Eleven Years of War." In *Is There a Transition to Democracy in El Salvador?* ed. Joseph S. Tulchin with Gary Bland. Woodrow Wilson Center Current Studies on Latin America. Boulder, Colo., and London: Lynne Rienner Publishers, 1992.

Vides Casanova, Carlos (General). Interview by Max G. Manwaring, translated by A. E. Letzer, both of BDM Management Services Co. for the Small Wars Operational Requirements Division (SWORD), J-5, USSOUTHCOM, Republic of Panama, 19 December 1987.

Vilas, Carlos M. *Between Earthquakes and Volcanoes: Market, State, and the Revolutions in Central America.* New York: Monthly Review Press, 1995.

Villalobos, Joaquín. *Acerca de la situación militar en El Salvador.* Comandancia General del FMLN. El Salvador, July 1981.

———. *Por qué lucha el FMLN?* Morazán: Ed. Sistema Radio Venceremos (September 1983).

———. *El Salvador: El estado actual de la guerra y sus perspectivas.* Madrid: Textos Breves, 1986.

———. *The War in El Salvador: Current Situation and Outlook for the Future.* San Francisco: Solidarity Publications, 1986.

Von Clausewitz, Carl. *On War.* Anatol Rapoport, ed. London: Penguin Books, 1968.

Waghelstein, John (Colonel). "Post-Vietnam Counterinsurgency Doctrine." *Military Review.* January 1985.

———. *El Salvador: Observations and Experiences in Counterinsurgency.* Carlisle Barracks, Penn.: U.S. Army War College, 1985.

———. Interview by Colonel Charles A. Carlton, Jr., U.S. Army Military History Institute. Senior Officers Oral History Program, Project 85-7, El Salvador, 1985.

Webre, Stephen. *José Napoleón Duarte and the Christian Democratic Party in Salvadoran Politics (1960–1972).* Baton Rouge: Louisiana State University Press, 1979.

White, Alistair. *El Salvador.* Nations of the Modern World. New York: Praeger Publishers, 1973.

Whitfield, Teresa. *Paying the Price: Ignacio Ellacuría and the Murdered Jesuits of El Salvador.* Philadelphia: Temple University Press, 1995.

Wickham-Crowley, Timothy. "Understanding Failed Revolutions in El Salvador: A Comparative Analysis of Regime Types and Social Structures." *Politics and Society* 17, no. 4 (1989): 511–537.

————. *Guerrillas and Revolution in Latin America: A Comparative Study of Insurgents and Regimes Since 1956*. Princeton, N.J.: Princeton University Press, 1992.

Woerner, Fred F. (Brigadier General). *Report of the El Salvador Military Strategy Assistance Team (Draft)*. Photocopy of classified report released with excisions under the Freedom of Information Act. San Salvador, 12 September–8 November 1981.

————. Interview by Max G. Manwaring, for use in the Oral History of the Conflict in El Salvador prepared by the BDM Management Services Co. for the Small Wars Operational Requirements Division (SWORD), USSOUTHCOM, Republic of Panama, November 1987.

Wolf, Eric. *Peasant Wars of the Twentieth Century*. New York: Harper and Row, 1969.

Zamora, Rubén. "In Salvador Time Waits for No One." *The Nation*, 27 February 1989: 1.

Copies of interviews with Cash, Einaudi, García, Herrick, Hinton, Pickering, Ponce, Vides Casanova, and Woerner and the Woerner Report were obtained from National Security Archive, Gelman Library, The George Washington University, 2130 H St., NW, Washington, D.C. 20037.

Index

About the Book

This in-depth study of the recent civil war in El Salvador supports the author's broader contention that the strategies adopted by incumbent regimes and insurgent movements are key to explaining why revolutions occur—and the conditions under which they succeed or fail.

Arguing that prevailing theories of revolution underemphasize the importance of choices and the dynamic interaction between conflicting parties, Byrne demonstrates that strategy played a critical role in the outcome of El Salvador's civil war. His analysis is based in large part on a close examination of more than 12,000 recently declassified U.S. documents, documents of the FMLN insurgents, and interviews with leading participants in the conflict.

Hugh Byrne is a consultant to NGOs concerned with U.S. policy in Latin America.